THE ARAB PUBLIC SPHERE IN ISRAEL

INDIANA SERIES IN MIDDLE EAST STUDIES

Mark Tessler, general editor

The Arab Public Sphere in Israel

Media Space and Cultural Resistance

AMAL JAMAL

INDIANA UNIVERSITY PRESS
Bloomington and Indianapolis

This book is a publication of

Indiana University Press
601 North Morton Street
Bloomington, IN 47404-3797 USA

www.iupress.indiana.edu

Telephone orders	800-842-6796
Fax orders	812-855-7931
Orders by e-mail	iuporder@indiana.edu

Manufactured in the United States of America

LIBRARY OF CONGRESS CATALOGING-IN-PUBLICATION DATA

Jamal, Amal.
The Arab public sphere in Israel : media space and cultural resistance / Amal Jamal.
p. cm. — (Indiana series in Middle East studies)
Includes bibliographical references and index.
ISBN 978-0-253-35386-3 (cloth : alk. paper)—ISBN 978-0-253-22141-4 (pbk. : alk. paper)
1. Mass media and minorities—Israel. 2. Palestinian Arabs—Israel—Communication.
3. Mass media—Political aspects—Israel. 4. Mass media policy—Israel. I. Title.
P94.5.M55217545 2009
302.2308992'7405694—dc22   2009017806

1 2 3 4 5 14 13 12 11 10 09

This book is dedicated to my father,

who through his forced silence

made me understand the meaning

and power of communication.

Do not look at yourself through what is written about you.

Do not look for the Canaanites to prove that you exist.

Just grasp this reality of yours and your name

and learn how to write your own evidence.

It is you, you, not your shadow, that is expelled this night.

MAHMOUD DARWISH

Contents

Preface

One of the most central dimensions of globalization is the fact that many aspects of human existence, no matter where, have become transparent as a result of technological evolution. The world has become open to observation and examination in ways that were not available in the past. This is especially true for people who did not have the ability to travel and who were locked within their specific environment. Technology has made it possible for the world to come to people, no matter where they are, instead of the dominant patterns of the past, where people had to go there and be on the spot in order to see something. This process has led to the shifting of the world, a phenomenon that followed upon an epoch in which the act of shifting had taken place mainly within the human subject. The world, as a physical place and as a cultural complex full of diversity, has become panoramic, exposed in a way that it never was before. Not only has technology made it possible to contract the relationship between place and time and to travel from one place to another within a very short time, but it has also drawn remote places and foreign cultures closer to us. It has placed them on our operating table, ready for any surgery we choose to perform in order to peruse whatever part of the global body we choose to examine.

This structural change entails many subshifts that are necessary for understanding our world today. One important one is the shifting meaning of physical locality and culture. For ages we were tightly limited by and to our physical location. Despite the fact that this locality could have been large enough to be a nation-state, we were grounded and physically limited, albeit transcended by the human imagination, which has always ventured into spaces that are far beyond the physicality of the mind. Political agents, such as the tribe, the village, the city-state, and the modern nation-state, have all endeavored to tighten the bonds between physical locality and cultural, moral, and political perceptions and loyalty. These agents sought to impose particularity and interruption, or at least to control the forms of communication and exchanges between their subjects and alien others. The collective body of these agents demanded loyalty as a precondition for freedom. Even with the rise of liberal forms of collectivities, these were constructed in close connection with the body politic and the homeland, as a romanticized form of a physical place. These forms of power and control began shifting with the expansion of globalization processes. The gaps between physical locality and loyalty to cultural and political constructs and perceptions of human existence began growing as a result of changes in the meaning in which we exist in the world. The space in which we exist expanded, and as a result, the meaning of existence changed.

Another central subshift resulting from technological globalization is the shift from that which is direct and immediate, observable to the eye, which could be assumed in the past, to the recognition that observation is mediated, not only when tools of observation are involved but also by other human subjects. Our view of remote places is mediated both by technology and by the subjective frames of other human beings that influence sight and perception. Our ability to view places that we have never visited, but which are currently being brought into our living rooms, is not firsthand observation. It is mediated by technological tools, such as the zoom of the camera and the hermeneutical perception of the mediating subject/agent. This shift is of great importance, since it entails the intervention of a combination of objective and subjective "agents" whose role is not always clearly defined. The division of labor between the camera, as a metaphor for modern communication, and the cameraman is far from being obvious. The "camera" is not simply a tool of the human subject. It is also an extension of her eye/perception, turning the observed object into an object of the "extended eye." The world exposed to us is far beyond our ability to conceive, which initiates an act of selection and filtering. We become readers of texts and of images that we choose from endless texts and images. We construct our own picture of the mediated world, without always being consciously aware of the mediation process.

The act of mediation is politically and culturally vital, since it is never neutral. Since the mediating object—the camera—is never separated from the mediating subject, the texts and images we receive are loaded with decisions regarding styles, genres, forms, and prisms. The mediating agents utilize their tools and manipulate their role in order to promote particular perceptions of the world. They veil their intentions and mask their goals with different means, among which are neutrality, plurality, beauty, and aspirations. The intentions and goals could be psychological, epistemological, cultural, and political. They come to construct the subject through a complex process of interpellation that aims at disciplining her and taming her views and actions to the confines of an accepted conformist repertoire. The mediating agent can be one person or a complex social structure, such as society or state. In the case of the latter, the mediation process is made into policy that aims at limiting the set of choices available for the subjects and framing their minds in such a way that enables surveillance and fosters discipline.

These changes resulting from globalization make it challenging to examine complex political and cultural processes, such as the one explicated in this book. The reading of state-minority relations through the media in the age of globalization becomes a phenomenon that obliges one to use complex theoretical modeling. The best way to analyze these complex processes and understand their dynamics is through dialectical methods that enable better observation of the impact of the contact between structural factors and subjective agents. Dialectics, and more accurately interpretive dialectics, enables some insight into the complexities of social and political control and resistance. It enables one to expose the mechanisms of symbolic surveillance and disciplining, while keeping the other eye focused on the countering communicative action that seeks resistance and opposition.

The manufacturing of consent and the disciplining of minority subjects sought by the state of Israel have been transformed in the age of global media. Globalization has made surveillance and control of perceptions more difficult for political structures and agents. This does not mean that such efforts are not possible or attempted. States have adapted the sophistication of surveillance and disciplining systems to the new modes of the open globalized world. Economic interests of social agents have become basic tools of state political power. Surveillance, control, and disciplining are conducted by social agents contracted with political agents of the state to promote consent.

Nonetheless, the efforts to control cultural space and images of the world have become more complex than ever before. The ability of the human subject to visit the world, albeit symbolically, beyond the confines wrought by direct manipulative state intervention has become almost limitless. The physical location of the modern subjects, including minority groups, has been transcended. The meaning of basic physical existence has been fundamentally impacted by the endless expansion of the symbolic imagination of the world. Human subjects are able to connect with cultural and physical spaces that lie far beyond their immediate locality. Although this ability does not replace the need for the physical touch of "homeness," it nevertheless enables the expansion of such a need and increases the impact of the political agents in control of the physical locality and their ability to control perceptions of homeness. Human agents can no longer be trapped in one physical or symbolic locality. Although not necessarily able to escape the complexities of the iron cage or the intricate composition of the modern "net," she is able to choose between different types or aspects of available cages or nets.

The following examination of state-minority relations through the prism of the media in the global age in Israel demonstrates the transformations that have taken place not only between the state of Israel and its Arab minority but also in the world in general. The specific case illustrates the complexity of a more general process of the information age or the postmodern world. Minority groups transcend their physical locality and escape the immediate surveillance and disciplining agents of the state and connect to other cultural spaces where they feel more at home. This is a particular dimension of the fusions of horizons that may have political impact in the future. The Arab minority, which fell under Israeli control and disciplining policies that continue until this very day, chose to redefine its location in the age of globalized media. It chose to resist modern state disciplining mechanisms with symbolic means. It chose consciously to locate itself in between cultural media spaces that establish new forms of double consciousness as a postmodern form of resistance to state power without renouncing its immediate political reality completely. This book is a practical translation of this complex process, which has had and will continue to have cultural meaning and political impact.

The Palestinian minority in Israel has become an important political player in the last decades. Whereas in the early years of the state this minority had to accommodate itself to Israeli policies as a tactic to guarantee its survival in its homeland, it has become apparent in the past three decades that the main characteristic of Arab politics in Israel is the contentious collective behavior in facing Israeli politics of exclusive ethnonational politics. This minority sought to assert its identity as an indigenous homeland minority, while demanding equal citizenship rights in the Israeli state. Collective Arab action was supported by growing cultural production, especially journalistic and poetic writings that contributed to the rise of critical national consciousness. This consciousness became manifested in various forms, especially in the rising number of Arab journalistic outlets. The political affiliation of newspapers and the rise of private ones have led to the rise of a local Arab public sphere in Israel that has its own characteristics, separate from the general Israeli public sphere. The globalization of media in the past decades has led to the transformation of this public sphere, which has transcended its local physical location and entered the Arab public sphere in the Arab world. The Arab elite in Israel not only consume media contents from the Arab world but also seek to engrave their place on the Arab public sphere. The number of Arab politicians, intellectuals, and journalists from Israel who are interviewed and presented on Arab satellite television programs is constantly growing. Poets and artists from the Arab Palestinian minority in Israel have become central cultural figures in the Arab world and are covered and represented by Arab television channels located in Arab countries.

These recent developments are crucial to the understanding of state-minority relations in Israel. They reflect the constitution of the Arab public sphere in Israel as an autonomous sphere, where debates and discussion of issues of collective concern take place. This rising public sphere has direct political impact on the location of the Arab minority in the broader Israeli-Palestinian relations. The Arab minority has carved out its own special place in between its conflictual groups of affiliation, seeking to influence by ways and methods that deserve attention. Therefore comes this book.

Acknowledgments

This book was written in stages and in several locations. Many people were involved in gathering the materials that form the essence of this book. My assistants, Umayma Diab, Suleiman Mahamed, Dana Yasur-Landau, David Yitzhak Haim, Yael Proaktor, Noga Parag, and Yathreb Zoabi have helped in various stages of this research. I owe them much for their loyalty and eagerness in gathering and analyzing the materials and organizing them in conceivable form. Special thanks go to Haneen Zoubi, Nabil Salah, Dr. Mustafa Kabha, and Dr. Yariv Tsfati for their comments on preliminary versions of parts of this book. I am very grateful to Yasmin Alkalay, who assisted in the statistical analyses and invested a great deal of time in making them comprehensible.

Special thanks go to my colleague and friend Professor Carolyn Landry, who read the text and invested much energy in editing and commenting on it. Without her help, this book would not have been publishable.

Nothing in these words of appreciation reduces any of my responsibility for the contents of the book.

This study was conducted with the help of various foundations. I wish to express my thanks to the European Union, the United States Institute of Peace, and the Palestinian-American Research Council for their financial support.

Last but not least, I wish to thank all the members of my family, especially my wife, Randa, who showed much understanding and support during the time I was struggling to finalize this book.

THE ARAB PUBLIC SPHERE IN ISRAEL

Introduction

This book examines the development and special characteristics of the Arab public sphere as a counterhegemonic space in Israel. Its significance stems from its seminal endeavor to shed light on recent changes in state-minority relations in Israel, focusing on the rise of the Arab public sphere and new patterns of communicative behavior among the Arab minority that have not yet been thoroughly examined in the literature. Although studies in political communication in Israel have mostly focused on the public sphere as a general and universal space in which ideas and opinions are exchanged, and although these studies contributed very much to the understanding of Israeli political culture, they do not fully mirror the entire Israeli reality. These studies ignore the locus of the Arab minority in the Israeli public sphere and do not adequately value its special characteristic as a "minority public sphere as counterhegemonic space" and its indispensable role in manifesting alternative voices and different patterns of audience behavior.[1] The Israeli public sphere cannot be fully understood if we do not attend to one of the most central developments within it, namely, the growing alienation of the Arab audience from Israeli media and their development of media institutions in their own minority language and adapted to their own media consumption patterns.

The book demonstrates that excluding homeland minorities from the dominant public sphere means excluding minority leaders from processes of opinion making and representation as well as excluding minority entrepreneurs from the economic benefits associated with modern mass media. Such patterns of exclusion lead social leaders and economic entrepreneurs to search for public spheres that counteract state hegemony, enabling them to influence the process of opinion making and cultural production in their society as well as to benefit from the economic gains associated with mass media. This behavior is evident in the rise in the number of private Arab media institutions since the early 1980s. It is also manifested in audience behavior in Arab society, which utilizes media outlets available from the Arab world to overcome the constraints on their political, cultural, and economic needs and interests.

The book also demonstrates that local, regional, and global medias are viewed by the Arab minority audience as a structural opportunity that can be utilized to overcome both structural and symbolic limitations set by the hegemonic majority and the dominant state. The media consumption patterns and communicative behavior of the Arab minority reflect collective endeavors to overcome the physical location of the Arab minority in the Israeli state, seeking to become part of the cultural space of what they view as their kin nation. This behavior demonstrates that the Arab minority in Israel, which was viewed in the past as a "captive minority," contained within local media space allotted to it by the state, has become an active player in the media landscape by availing itself of modern technology.

The globalization of the mass media is seen as a major factor influencing Arab minority audience behavior, leading to the rise of a "double consciousness," reflecting the gap between the physical location of the Arab audience and its cultural and national aspirations. In general terms, the book utilizes the examination of communicative behavior and media consumption patterns in Israel in order to make a general claim, namely, that the globalization of mass media offers minorities opportunities to overcome state control and surveillance policies and develop counterhegemonic public spheres that meet the needs, interests, and aspirations of the minority. Although this claim does not mean that minorities are able to overcome all limitations imposed on them by their structural location, especially in cases where the state is suppressive, still they are able through media outlets to establish their own spheres where they connect with social, cultural, and political trends taking place beyond their immediate environment.

The book will demonstrate how the alienation from Israeli public culture, represented by the media, leads to the rise of cultural patterns, manifested in the consumption of cultural programs exclusively from the Arab world by the Arab minority in Israel. This trend mirrors the strengthening Palestinian and Arab identity among the Arab population in Israel. On the other hand, this trend does not mean that the Arab audience escapes the Israeli media completely. The Arab public remains connected to its Israeli environment politically and economically. Therefore, it remains attentive to Israeli media contents that serve its daily survival. The patterns of media consumption reiterate the differentiation made in the literature between sentimental and instrumental identities, demonstrating that Arab society in Israel is Israeli and thereby different from the rest of the Palestinian communities, but its Israeliness is only instrumental.[2] Hence the claim of double consciousness does not mean and should not mean equal traits of the various components of affiliation. It means that these components coexist and become a source of strength, manifested in the ability of Arab citizens of Israel to tune into both Israeli and Arab media outlets simultaneously and to utilize this ability to promote the influence on their social and political environment.

Since the end of World War II, minorities have become increasingly significant segments of various nation-states.[3] The phenomenon of national minorities demanding special rights in their countries of birth has become a familiar phenomenon. Although the strategies adopted in their struggle for equality differ from country to country and from one minority to another, a major theme in this struggle has been communicative behavior and media consumption and their role in constituting a counterhegemonic public sphere in which the dominant majority is challenged.[4] The rise of minority media institutions and of advocacy for better media representation of minority groups can be viewed as one strategy adopted by minorities to cope with their minority status.[5] Such strategies become more pronounced as the relationship between the minority and the majority deteriorates.[6] Many minority groups have adopted this approach, such as the Hungarian minority in Rumania, the Kurds in Turkey, the Maori in New Zealand, the Russian minority in the Baltic States, and the Turkish minority in Holland.[7]

In light of the scope of this phenomenon, communicative behavior and media consumption patterns exhibited by minorities become an important focus for research.[8] They constitute an avenue that is essential for a deepening of our understanding of minority mobilization strategies and of their future relationship with their state and its dominant majority. Shedding light on the role of minority media in the public sphere, especially on the institutionalization of minority media organizations and on the patterns of media consumption among minority audiences, can contribute to our understanding of the impact that modern media have on the forms of deliberation that are enacted between majorities and minorities in particular political contexts. It can contribute to our understanding of the complexity and the contradictory characteristics of the public sphere in multiethnic political realities. The study of Arab minority communicative behavior falls within this theoretical framework and will contribute to the growing literature on minority media and patterns of minority communicative behavior.

The examination of Arab communicative activity in Israel is located within the genre of literature on the centrality of the public sphere as a realm of social, cultural, and political negotiations and deliberations. However, initial examinations of the public sphere have not paid sufficient attention to its multiple and even contradictory characteristics.[9] This has been especially true with regard to the unique characteristics of the public sphere within the context of state-minority relations and ethnic conflict. These studies have not explored the dynamics of counterhegemonic public spheres in conflictual contexts. This absence of attention to minority counterhegemonic public spheres has also characterized the Israeli academic scene.[10] The hegemonic Jewish Hebrew-speaking public sphere has generally been equated with the Israeli public sphere per se, ignoring the fact that 20 percent of the Israeli public speaks and communicates in a different language. This lack of attention is manifested in all kinds of studies that examine the media as the main mechanism of debating in the modern public sphere. Only a very few studies, only recently and only reluctantly, have paid a little attention to the place of Arab media in shaping the Israeli public sphere.

Although increasing attention is being paid to the role of the media in conflict, this literature focuses on international conflict and pays little attention to majority-minority relations internal to ethnic states.[11] An exception to this rule of ignoring minorities and their role in conflict has been immigrant minorities, which do attract media attention.[12] But examining the development and special characteristics of the minority public sphere in the context of ethnic conflict can add to our understanding of the theory of the public sphere as a whole and of its multiple and various characteristics and can shed light on one of the most important but least addressed dimensions of majority-minority relations in Israel that has major political implications.

This book describes the public sphere that the Arab minority in Israel has developed, as manifested in the rising number of local Arab media institutions that produce contents in Arabic for the Arab audience and in the emergence of particular patterns of audience behavior vis-à-vis political and cultural media contents received through Arabic satellite television broadcasting from the Arab world. The special characteristics of this Arab public sphere in Israel are rooted in the efforts made to counter state policies of control and identity formation in Arab society. This involves efforts both to balance the marginalization of the Arab public in the Israeli public sphere and to fight the negative portrayal of Arabs in Israeli media.

The emerging Arab public sphere is physically located in Israel, but it is separate from the Jewish public sphere in terms of language, cultural contents, and political orientation. Although it has selective affinity with the Israeli public sphere, it is more related to Arab public spheres in the Arab world and is influenced by the debates taking place there concerning social, cultural, and religious affairs. The Arab public in Israel began withdrawing from the Israeli public sphere because the Israeli Jewish public did not give Arab affairs genuine and positive attention. Moreover, it began withdrawing when the Arab public discovered the alternative spheres where one could express opinions and ideas without having to gain access through the hegemonic Jewish gatekeepers and when this public found alternative cultural media content that met its needs. This cultural disengagement marks a new orientation in the struggle of the Arab community with its exclusion from the Israeli public sphere. The Arab minority does not ignore its Israeli affiliation but has simultaneously developed its own public sphere that is rich with deliberations on internal Arab affairs and with media contents that originate in Arab countries in the region.

The special characteristics of the Arab public sphere in Israel, which has developed in the last few decades, demonstrate that mainstream understanding of the public sphere is not sufficient to capture the complexities of public opinion formation and communicative behavior in a multinational conflictual context. Indeed, the currently dominant theories of the public sphere are still biased toward the majoritarian procedural dimension of opinion making. Even deliberative models of democratic theory that are based on the theoretical foundations of the public sphere are still procedurally and liberally biased and focus on the national level of opinion making.[13] Most theories of the public sphere and deliberative democracy take the liberal democratic states, especially the United States and the United Kingdom, as their sociopolitical model. Although debates on the meaning and characteristics of the public sphere sometimes take social diversity into consideration and point out the possibility of contradictions and tensions between various social groups, most treatments of the public sphere do not concern themselves with the development of the public sphere(s) in the context of ethnic conflict where the state and the dominant majority in it, on the one hand, and the minority, on the other, lead two separate national and cultural debates concerning fundamental social, cultural, and political matters.

Moreover, the prevailing debate on the Israeli public sphere lacks a thorough treatment of the state as a dominant agency in shaping public consciousness, despite the fact that most of the media is privately owned. Even critical treatments of the Israeli public sphere have focused on debates within Jewish society, equating them with Israeli space.[14] Such studies have ignored the inherent relationship between the economic role of the state and its cultural role as an ideological agency aiming to control its social scene, especially pronounced when we are talking about an ethnic state seeking to dominate an indigenous homeland national minority within it. As a result of the traditional theoretical split between political economy and cultural studies, the dominant examinations of the Israeli public sphere and the place of the Arab minority in it do not focus enough attention on the inherent relationship between state identity, economic interests, ideological hegemony, and social control. These studies do not pay attention to the ethnic nature of the state and the dominant exclusive ethnic ideology among the hegemonic Jewish majority and their implications for the Arab minority's search for a space in which its voices can be legitimately manifested in the Israeli public sphere.

Recent developments in the theoretical literature on the public sphere demonstrate the centrality of the media and audience behavior in shaping public opinion.[15] The study of communicative behavior and media consumption has become a well-established field in academia. Hence we find an increasing number of publications dealing with audience analysis, but not much research has addressed the communicative behavior and media consumption of national minorities.[16] Furthermore, the increase in attention paid to audience analysis does not include attention to audience behavior in the context of ethnic conflict.

In Israel, many studies have been carried out on communicative behavior and the culture of media consumption, particularly within Jewish society.[17] These studies indicate trends that support the above stated observations. Several studies have dealt in depth with factors such as cultural diversity among Israel's Jewish population and its relationship to media consumption patterns, and yet no such study has been carried out among the Arab population in Israel, which numbers over a million people. This society differs from Israel's Jewish residents in terms of culture, language, and nationality. In terms of citizenship, Arab society in Israel is part of the Israeli political space. In terms of culture and language, however, this population belongs to the Arab national and cultural space that lies primarily beyond Israel's borders even though no direct contact was maintained with that space for many years. The way Arab society copes with this national and cultural reality and the extent to which the media is a factor or sphere enabling Arab society to cope with the Israeli reality constitutes an issue vital to our understanding of the communicative behavior and media culture characterizing both this population and its relationship to the dominant culture in Israel. The role of the Israeli media as a public sphere for expressing the needs, interests, and desires of the Arab minority is an important question deserving of an adequate answer. Moreover, the role that minority media plays as well as the salient audience behavior in Arab society are important avenues to explore.

The book does not attempt to delve into the theoretical debates and the complexities of public opinion and the public sphere. Nor does it aim to be a pure empirical study on audience behavior. In the following chapters, I bring together several theoretical and empirical threads in order to draw attention to the complexities of the public sphere and the factors that shape public opinion making in a multinational conflictual context. Light is shed on the communicative behavior of the Arab homeland national minority in a state that has long sought to control its ideological space and shape its public opinion. Since this study was conducted in the age of globalization, it concentrates on the impact of media globalization on the public sphere and patterns of public opinion making. It focuses on the communicative strategy chosen by the Arab audience to cope with the hegemonic public sphere in Israel and the communication policies of the state aimed at controlling Arab public opinion.

In order to demonstrate what has been claimed so far, this book utilizes several methodological tools. It follows common patterns of research that combine qualitative ethnographic sociohistorical methods with quantitative examinations of behavior and attitudes.[18] It begins with three sociohistorical chapters that critically reflect on the Israeli media policies toward the Arab minority and the counter communicative behavior of the latter. This qualitative account of historical developments of media policies provides the background for the quantitative analysis conducted based on a comprehensive public opinion survey. Public opinion surveys have been conducted since the early nineteenth century. For approximately 100 years, these surveys queried the dominant elite under the assumption that this group had the greatest impact on public opinion and directly reflected the general public's attitudes. Since the end of the nineteenth century, however, with the increasing importance of "public opinion" as a factor in political decision making, surveys addressing ever-widening population segments gradually became more acceptable as instruments of scientific study. With the behavioral revolution of the 1950s and 1960s, the survey became the principal tool in assessing public attitudes and opinions on a broad range of issues and spanning increasingly large populations.[19]

This trend was reflected in media producers' behavior, with surveys employed primarily by newspapers to ascertain public opinion, chiefly during elections. Eventually, the number of surveys increased as the aims altered. In addition to their traditional objectives, surveys were now used to reinforce the credibility of the information transmitted by the media.[20] This trend had widespread ramifications. One positive result was that surveys became more transparent.[21] Yet, as the perception of them as credible instruments for measuring public opinion improved, their influence on the opinions they were intended to measure grew. In the end, the frequency of surveys reduced their credibility, particularly given growing public awareness of the manipulation of survey results by politicians and the media itself.[22] The revelation of bias in survey methodologies in the area of consumption for the benefit of business and economic interests has also damaged their credibility as scientific tools.[23] Despite the convergence of these negative impacts along with the objective limitations of the method—evidenced by sampling error, scheduling defects, and limited reliability—no alternative to public opinion surveys has been found for gathering the given information on such a large scale.[24]

The findings presented from chapter 4 onwards are based on two surveys: one is random sample, and one is selective. The first sample included 594 participants, representing all components of the Arab population in Israel. A proportional stratified model was used to ensure representation. Staggered sampling increases the accuracy of the parameter measure when the main characteristics of the researched population are known. The researched population is thus divided into homogeneous groups according to their proportion in the general population, with specific participants randomly selected by area of residence. Because 95 percent of Israeli families have a telephone, households were chosen according to telephone number. Interviewees were randomly selected among household members according to age: 18 and older. Each interview lasted 60–90 minutes and was conducted in December 2004 or January 2005. The estimated standard deviation for the sample is 2 percent, with a refusal rate of 31 percent, a level acceptable in research of this type. We should clarify that the model deliberately refrained from sampling Palestinian residents of East Jerusalem or Syrian residents of the Golan Heights because these areas are occupied territories. Hence the research population consisted of Arab citizens of Israel exclusively.

The second sample was more selective and focused on sampling the elite of the Arab community in Israel. Personal interviews were conducted with 229 politicians, artists, authors, bankers, educators, civil activists, and university professors. The representation of each of these groups of leaders was almost proportional to their percentage in the wider population. The personal interviews with the leaders were conducted between 10 June 2007 and 7 January 2008, and each lasted 60–90 minutes. The data of this sample will not be introduced fully. It will be used only to demonstrate the similarities between the general public and the elite in relation to media consumption patterns, which provides further evidence for the main thesis of the book, namely, that Arab society in Israel has developed its own particular consumption culture that negotiates the divide between the practical requirements of the average Arab person in Israel and the search for a congenial cultural and political environment. In other words, the Arab elite, similar to the general Arab public, has developed its own public sphere characterized by a differentiation between the practical and the affective, between the instrumental and the cultural, that do not necessarily contradict each other but rather coexist, creating what has been called double consciousness.

The book is divided into seven chapters. The first chapter elaborates some of the theoretical and methodological points made so far and frames the study in a more comprehensive context. It presents a brief review of the literature on minority media and its audience, and it goes on to elaborate the theoretical and methodological context of the study. The second chapter provides a brief history of the emergence and special characteristics of the Arab minority in Israel. This chapter sheds light on the fact that the Arab minority is a homeland indigenous minority that belongs to a broader nation. The affiliation of the Arab minority in Israel with the Palestinian people and the Arab nation condition its behavior in general and its communicative behavior in particular. The chapter demonstrates how the treatment of the Arab minority by the Israeli state forms a major factor in its attitudes and behavior. The third chapter focuses attention on Israeli media policies as a means of control and surveillance. It demonstrates how the state established its own media institutions that aimed at penetrating Arab society and framing its collective imagination and public opinion. The fourth chapter is historical. It is devoted to the rise of media institutions in Arabic originating in the attempts made by political parties and movements on the one hand and economic entrepreneurs on the other to counter state policies and share the benefits of media business. This chapter follows the rise of party-affiliated newspapers and the emergence of privately owned newspapers that turn political and cultural representation into an economic enterprise. The fifth chapter delves into the empirical findings of the survey conducted for the purposes of this study. It is the first of three chapters that focus on audience behavior. It sheds light on patterns of newspaper reading among the Arab public, demonstrating the differences between party-affiliated and privately owned newspapers, as well as the centrality of trust in explaining media consumption patterns. The sixth chapter reflects the mistrust of the Arab audience toward the Hebrew mass media, which misrepresents Arabs and marginalizes their place in the Israeli public sphere. This chapter reiterates the importance of trust in explaining media audience without ignoring the centrality of language and culture in its communicative behavior. The seventh chapter is devoted to the electronic media, especially to the patterns of consumption among the Arab population. This chapter demonstrates that consumption patterns are based on the combination of cultural routines, rational choice, and structural opportunities. It describes the consumption of selective Israeli media contents and deliberative choice in consuming Arab media contents originating in the Arab world, demonstrating the meaning of "double consciousness" as reflected in patterns of collective communicative behavior. The chapter reflects on the impact that media consumption could have on political attitudes and behavior. It attempts to establish a link between the consumption of Arabic television content from Arab satellite television channels from the Arab world and potential change in the political attitudes and behavior of the Arab community in Israel. Although this chapter provides only initial data on this topic, it contributes to our understanding of minority strategies for coping with their inferior status within their own states. The final chapter tries to link the historical, sociological, and empirical chapters.

ONE

Media Space, Political Control, and Cultural Resistance

Minority (Mis)Representation and the Rise of Minority Media

When looking at the literature on media and minorities, one notices a clear trend in the attention paid to this relationship that may be helpful for understanding the communicative behavior of the Arab community in Israel. At the initial stage, most studies that analyzed the social, political, and cultural roles of the media focused on its function in social change, mobilization, and control. Neither the liberal-pluralist nor the critical-Marxist, the analytic strategies dominating the scene, paid sufficient attention to social diversity, disparities, and conflicts between social groups as they played out in the media.[1]

Since the 1960s, especially with the rise of the civil rights movement in the United States, more attention has been given to the representation of various social groups in news outlets.[2] Under the influence of constructivist theories of identity formation, theorists realize that the media plays a central role in the construction of social identities and feeds into social conflict.[3] As a consequence, the representation of various social groups in the media occupies a rising number of scholars.[4] Furthermore, the role of the media in shaping the ways in which people look at their social reality is the focus of many studies.[5] As a result, the lack of representation of minority groups or the stereotyping of these groups in mainstream media has been targeted as a major source of inequality and an important factor in maintaining social disparity.[6] A growing number of scholars seek to demonstrate the relationship between minority representation in the media and racism, discrimination, and marginalization.[7] Lack of equal representation and stereotyping of minorities has been a central strand in media studies, something that has only recently been taken up by the Israeli academic community.

Only in the 1990s were questions finally raised regarding the role that the media plays in constructing social identities and shaping ethnic relations in Israel. Ella Shohat was a pioneer in pointing out the role that cinema plays both in suppressing Oriental Jewish identity and in colonizing the minds of Oriental Jews with an Ashkenazi Zionist worldview.[8] This trend was later expanded to include the role of the media in establishing social hierarchies and in symbolically eliminating the Israeli social and geographic periphery, emphasizing instead the metropolitan centers.[9] Despite the fact that the marginality of the Arab minority and its stereotyping in the Israeli Hebrew media have begun to draw some attention, this attention is still insubstantial and lacking in rigorous theoretical grounding. The marginality of Arabs in mainstream Israeli media is being described rather than explained. Little attention has been paid to the major reasons behind such marginality, something that requires more historical and empirical attention. The history of the Israeli media and the role played by the state in shaping the placement of the Arab minority in Israeli society and polity needs to be considered in order to provide a convincing explanation for the communicative behavior of the Arab community. The following study is located within the context of state-minority relations in order to shed light on the historical and political factors that explain Arab communicative behavior, especially the strategies chosen to deal with the marginal and negative representation of Arabs in Israeli media.

In recent decades, the study of patterns of media consumption and of consumer satisfaction with media content has become a highly developed field of research.[10] The increasing power of the media to shape public and political agendas, coupled with a massive increase in the avenues of transmission, has raised questions concerning media consumption, particularly its significance in societies composed of culturally, ethnically, and nationally diverse groups. The relationship between media culture and sociocultural diversity is one key to understanding political dynamics in multicultural societies.[11] The influence of the newspapers people read, the radio stations they listen to, and the television networks they watch has become immense. The factors affecting media consumption patterns in general and the impact of media consumption in particular have thus attracted the analytic gaze of media researchers, sociologists, and political scientists.[12]

An important assumption in this field of research is that patterns of media consumption correlate with individual or group worldviews, cultural considerations, and political interests. Abundant research has established the salience of media consumption as an indicator of behavioral, cultural, political, and economic trends. Patterns of consumption, the contents consumed, the times of consumption, and the degree of satisfaction and reliance on the media as a source of information and entertainment constitute gauges of consumers' identities.[13] Communicative behavior and media consumption thus serve as important indicators of consumers' organization and exploitation of time while simultaneously revealing sociocultural affiliations and illuminating significant sociopolitical processes. Many researchers maintain that the technological developments that have contributed to the growth of the media as a dominant social institution have diminished the influence of traditional social agents, such as the family, or other modern agents, such as political parties. Simultaneously, these trends have contributed to the evolution of political and social identities that transcend the immediate boundaries of sociocultural space.[14] The mediation performed by the mass media has thus altered social relationships, empowering those social groups that control media content at the expense of other groups.[15] These events explain why the issues of who controls the media and what contents various social groups consume are so important.

Therefore, the analysis and understanding of consumption patterns can reveal how different social groups construct their relationships with their environment. It follows that media consumption and satisfaction also provide indicators of how consumers relate to the social, political, and cultural actors in their environment. This is particularly true in multiethnic and multicultural societies where each social group develops its own consumption pattern on the basis of existing constraints and opportunities. One of the main assumptions guiding this book is that media consumption patterns influence the individual's cultural and personal space while also reflecting rationally calculated preferences; hence the description and comprehension of these patterns have become important features of sociological and political research in all societies.

Communicative behavior and media consumption patterns are not solely affected by rational considerations. Research in this field has long since demonstrated the influence of custom and structural constraints, such as language limitations. Not only are communicative behavior and media consumption often uncalculated; they may not even be homogeneously conscious. Consumers do not perceive the media exclusively as a source of news; for them, it is primarily a medium for home entertainment, universally available. It follows that the entertainment aspects are important and must be factored into an analysis of communicative behavior and media policies. Yet perceiving these as important dimensions of a cultural and political habitus, characterized by entertainment preferences, allows access to another source of information regarding the role of dominance in a society's sociocultural structure and of the transmission of dominant characteristics.[16] As demonstrated by research conducted at the Media Studies Unit at the Centre for Contemporary Cultural Research, the University of Birmingham, consumption patterns occupy a central place in the creation of sociocultural hegemony primarily due to the ideological encoding inherent in media content.[17]

Communicative behavior and media consumption are important avenues of political behavior, especially when other means are rather limited. They are part of a broader strategy of contentious politics that seeks to overcome the structural limitations set by the dominant matrix of power. This claim is especially true in the case of minorities that are dominated by a control system in which political, legal, economic, and cultural means are utilized in order to ensure the subjugation of the minority.

The media consumption patterns exhibited by Arab society in Israel therefore constitute an important subject for research. Their study enables us to gain insight into how Arabs, as a homeland national minority living in a nationalizing state, have responded to the complex factors that structure their existence. Many questions thereby arise concerning the most popular radio stations and television channels and the implications that such patterns of collective behavior could have on the perceptions and conduct of homeland national minorities.

Communicative behavior and media consumption have economic dimensions, particularly in societies where the media is privately rather than publicly owned. Whenever all or most of the media is a private sector endeavor, economic variables become salient. In the past few decades, the media has become a major industry and source for the accumulation of wealth in addition to being a cultural domain.[18] Production of media content has therefore become a culturally grounded tool for accumulating wealth, as demonstrated by Time Warner, ARTE, CNN, Al-Jazeera, MBC, LBC, and Israel's Channel 2.

Ownership of the media and the economic logic directing its operation have crucial implications for its sociocultural role, on the one hand, and our understanding of its political role, on the other.[19] The way in which the media shapes public opinion varies, in fact, by type of ownership.[20] When publicly owned, the media operates in the name of the public good and common interest, and therefore it is publicly monitored.[21] Although the privately owned media ought to operate under the same banner of public interest, guaranteeing this goal is a more complex and arduous task. The privately owned media is mostly motivated by the search for increasing consumer ratings, which is automatically translated into increased profit. Communicative behavior and media consumption patterns thus accrue economic relevance and, in addition to their political and cultural significance, constitute an integral part of society's mechanisms for amassing wealth.[22]

Moreover, communicative behavior and media consumption patterns could turn cultural factors into central political means to achieve collective goals. This is especially true in the case of national minorities, when entrepreneurs from the minority establish their own private media institutions for economic profit. As experience has taught us, economic ventures can become a central factor in the cultural and political fields by which the mobilization of minority members is ensured.[23] In other words, minority groups could establish their own media space in order to protect their cultural and political interests and express their national identity.

A thorough treatment of Arab communicative behavior can benefit from recent developments in scholarship. As a result of new perceptions regarding the role of the media in social reality and the controversies regarding its impact on shaping attitudes and identities, a new trend began emerging concerning media and minorities that drew attention to ownership as a major factor in determining the nature of the contents produced in the media.[24] Other scholarship reiterated the centrality of ownership and its impact on the chances that minorities would win attention in the media. The financial control of media institutions frees the minority from external control of cultural and political content and provides maneuvering spaces that would not otherwise exist.

New research demonstrated that minority media provides minorities with opportunities that did not exist before. These opportunities strengthen their citizenship and provide them with networks of communication that enhance their internal solidarity and, as a result, their ability to face policies of discrimination in the mainstream media as well as in state policies.[25]

The growing attention paid to minority media was reinforced by major developments in Europe concerning the language rights of minorities and the role the media plays in maintaining these languages.[26] In this regard, many scholars pointed out the importance not only of ownership but also of the language in which the media is produced as a factor that impacts the chances that minorities are fairly represented and their voices are brought into the public sphere.

The chances that a minority language media develops depend on various factors that have been partially debated in the literature. Ned Thomas points out cultural and linguistic survival as a major factor in obtaining of minority language media outlets.[27] Mike Cormack adds several factors, including the size of the minority, the existence of popular campaigns supporting the minority media, the role of leadership and organization in the minority group, the political culture of the state, the strength/weakness of the central government, the symbolic status of the minority language, and international trends.[28] In Cormack's view, all these factors are political and have to be taken in accumulation rather than individually.

Cormack's presentation of the factors that explain the chances of the rise of minority language media does not address economic factors and the existence of alternative media outlets that influence considerations of costs and gains among minority entrepreneurs. Although Cormack mentions briefly the existence of alternative media institutions in the minority language, he does not give enough weight to the communicative behavior of minorities. The following study demonstrates that economic opportunities of minority entrepreneurs and the availability of alternative media outlets from neighboring kin states are major factors in developing an Arab public sphere in Israel and in explaining the broader communicative behavior of its Arab minority. Studies of national minorities have demonstrated that they are major consumers of media outlets from their kin states in their own mother tongue.[29] This communicative behavior may impact both the socialization of such minorities, especially their perception of their identity, and their political behavior, an impact that an in-depth examination of audience attitudes in the minority community could verify. The balance that minorities establish between their consumption of mainstream media within their own state and of media that is rooted in their kin states becomes crucial. Hence examining the communicative behavior of the Arab minority in Israel may shed light on new dimensions of audience behavior that have yet to win sufficient attention in scholarly literature.

Another important aspect of the communicative behavior of the Arab minority in Israel is the growth in the number of newspapers in Arabic in the Israeli public sphere since the mid-1980s. The role and impact of these newspapers on the communicative behavior of the Arab community opens an avenue of research that has still not been seriously broached. It is puzzling to see the effervescent and vibrant newspaper scene in the Arab society, where the number of newspapers is constantly on the rise, in contrast to the absence of local Arabic television broadcasts. The indifference of the Arab leadership to a strategy of establishing a public television channel in Arabic requires explanation. Resolving this puzzle may enrich the literature on the communicative behavior of minorities and on the factors that influence the establishing of minority language media. The fact that the cost of audiovisual media is relatively high and that there is no governmental financial support for such an initiative, especially in a case in which the size of the minority is marginal with respect to the chances of the economic success of such media, may be part of the explanation for the position taken by Arab leadership in Israel.

The following study will provide a more comprehensive answer to these questions, demonstrating that Arab leadership as well as Arab society in general are satisfied, at least passively, with the Arabic media product provided by institutions from the Arab world, especially when compared with the poor and state-controlled programming that can be obtained from a local public television channel. The data provided in the forthcoming chapters demonstrates that the Arab audience has made a clear decision with regard to media consumption that benefits from the institutional structure and the globalization of outlets. This communicative behavior is reinforced by the fact that the state has been following a clear policy that seeks to control the agenda of the Arab minority and opposes the extension of financial support to establish minority media that would protect the cultural and linguistic needs and rights of this minority.

Media Consumption in the Global Age

Research on media consumption is a complex task due to the difficulties of defining the research population (specific consumers), the research goals, and the methodology employed. Prior to recognition of the consumer public as the primary target of communication research, attention had been focused on the study of media contents and media effectiveness in relation to the formation of public opinion. In recent years, however, new approaches to the study of the media consuming population have been devised.[30] Development of these approaches was stimulated by the technological advances that enable consumers to individually select contents, an option that eliminates consumer dependence on a rigid infrastructure as well as on producers and their agendas.

This empowerment transformed research of the media consuming public into a highly complicated undertaking as the range of consumption decisions expanded. Moreover, the increasing sophistication of communication theories, effectively establishing the powerful influence of the media on public opinion and the public agenda, promoted this research domain into a primary focus for those wishing to understand the media's effect on culture, social structure, and individual behavior.[31] From the vantage point of producers, the economic implications inherent in the massive increase in the size of the consumer public induced many profit-oriented firms to invest in public opinion surveys and research on consumption patterns. These developments were, of course, based on the traditional acceptance of the public as the focal actor in a democratic process imbued with pluralist ideas.

The increasing salience of the media consuming public engendered new research challenges. The core issue of population definition has thus been problematized. Should consumers be treated as a unified group or as a collection of individuals who, other than consuming a specific product, lack common characteristics? In other words, are consumers an a priori recognizable "public" prior to their participation in media consumption, or does media consumption produce a public by influencing preferences and constructing common identities? Responses to these questions vary. In order for media consumers to be considered a "public" in sociological research terms, they must meet certain criteria: for instance, the existence of social boundaries differentiating one group from another, self-awareness, a high level of face-to-face interaction, and common norms and values. The weaker the compliance with these criteria, the stronger becomes the tendency to consider consumers as a mass rather than a public. Alternatively, the stronger the compliance, the more appropriate it becomes to designate this group as a "public." Thus, in the context of communication research, relating to a group of people as a mass rather than a public depends on the characteristics of their media consumption.[32] The greater the similarity of type and level of media consumed, the more one can relate to a group as a public. Alternatively, the fewer the shared consumption characteristics, the more one should relate to consumers as a mass.

Research on media consumption among minority groups—including national minorities—throughout the world has plainly shown that these groups develop distinctive consumption patterns that differentiate them from the surrounding majority culture.[33] This finding tends to hold true especially in cases marked by open conflict between the majority and minority groups.[34]

The literature can be divided into two streams determined by the goals motivating two broad types of public opinion surveys. One group of studies focuses on the goals of the media industry, primarily in the private sector, which tends to conduct surveys to further its control of consumers and management of consumption. These surveys examine existing and potential consumption patterns and preferences that are considered as input for product development and advertising campaigns. In addition, these surveys are designed to identify new consumer markets, test acceptance of new media products, and assess media efficacy in promoting these products.

The goals of the other group of studies center on the needs, interests, and preferences of consumers themselves. Studies conducted for this purpose are usually initiated to empower consumers. These studies tend to test the media's acceptance of responsibility vis-à-vis consumers. In addition, these studies tend to focus on the expression of consumers' needs in media content, consumer satisfaction with such content, and consumer trust in the media.

Many scholars, particularly those associated with the school of cultural criticism, tend to view the public as a primarily passive recipient of media messages. This public is perceived as prey to media industry manipulation. A related assumption is that, despite their oppositional consumption, consumers internalize communicated messages. These assumptions have motivated theorizing regarding the formation of consciousness by members of the Frankfurt School and other researchers belonging to the critical tradition, such as Herbert Marcuse, Raymond Williams, Todd Gitlin, and Noam

Chomsky.[35] Based on this perspective, the respective theories stress the ideological, cultural, and political manipulation that media firms employ to maintain their hegemony. The research conducted by proponents of this approach therefore focuses on media production and the ideologies served. Consumers' autonomy is consequently marginalized. The audience is characterized as having "popular" taste (preferences) and consuming low (as opposed to high) culture.

In contrast to this view, one should seriously consider the position that consumers are at least partially active. The consumer's activity is exhibited in the free choice of contents, varying levels of attention paid, differing reactions to contents, and numerous patterns of decoding (interpreting) messages.[36] This study demonstrates that active media consuming publics, such as the Arab public in Israel, are capable of resisting—again, at least partially—the techniques of persuasion and manipulation that the media employs, especially outlets from a dominant majority that is suspected of seeking hegemony. This assumption leans in part on theories addressing the role of the spectator that date as far back as the era of classical Greek and Roman theater.[37] Technological developments, primarily digital technologies, reinforce the public's ability to control their selection of the contents offered, although not necessarily the contents themselves (we currently leave aside blogs, iPods, ham radio transmissions, Indymedia, etc.). Technology is thus perceived as a factor empowering media consumers in some ways, in a market characterized by strong ratings competition.[38] This conjunction between attitudes and technology has generated theories and research approaches that try to place the average media consumer at the center.[39]

Much of the research conducted in multiethnic societies has adopted this point of departure when testing the media's contribution to minority group integration into the majority society.[40] Other research has explored media practices aimed at maintaining the minority group's unique national, cultural, and linguistic identity. The present study belongs to this general trend dealing with how minorities cope with the communication-related, structural, and cultural conditions of their environment. With respect to these aims, the questions address the patterns of media consumption, the reasons for choosing the media consumed, the reasons for choosing the contents consumed, and the public's satisfaction with, and trust of, the contents it consumes.

Following common knowledge from the literature, the point of departure of this book is that, in cases of minority groups in states dominated by other ethnic majorities, the communicative behavior and media consumption patterns of minority groups reflect their protest against hegemonial efforts and their resistance to framing their minds according to the interests of a dominant majority. Hence minorities may turn the media structure available to them into an opportunity, instead of viewing it as a trap.[41] Minorities develop their own media consuming patterns that meet their needs, aspirations, and interests.

Media consumption may rest on various motivations. Before reviewing existing explanatory models, we should note Denis McQuail's comment that the complexity and multiplicity—the existence of overlapping media consuming publics—of consumption patterns preclude the possibility of constructing a simple or single explanatory theory or model.[42] One can speak of two traditionally accepted approaches, dominant in explaining media consumption patterns and the creation of a consumer public. The first, the structural approach, focuses on the effect of various factors and media institutions on consumption patterns. A major stream belonging to this approach stresses the components of communication: the media available, the options available, and the accessibility of message contents. The interaction between these components gives rise to what Lennart Weibull terms "media orientation."[43] This stance, constructed on the joint foundations of social background and previous media experience, is reflected in the consumer's loyalty to particular media or contents, preferences and interests, consumption routines, and expectations of media quality, among other factors. Media orientation is further influenced by the media's structure, which can be broken down into the contents offered at the time of consumption, consumption features (e.g., quantity of time devoted to consumption), and the social context of media choice, manifested by the influence of family or social environment on consumer behavior.

In contrast to structural models, behavioral models focus primarily on individuals: their preferences, needs, expectations, and drives. Behavioral research was born in the 1940s. Members of this school have identified the principal motivations for media consumption as entertainment and gratification of emotional needs, acquisition of information to fulfill cognitive needs, social needs (primarily identity), and mood management, the total of which supports programming geared to escapism and similar contents.[44] Although the present research does not examine the individual's motivations for media consumption, it does investigate some of the motivations directing the Arab public's choice of media contents in Israel.

One of the behavioral models exerting the greatest influence in the field of propaganda and media consumption research is that constructed by Elihu Katz, Jay Blumler, and Michael Gurevitch.[45] They argue that media choice is determined by the viewer's sociopsychological background, which arouses expectations. These expectations motivate individuals to expose themselves to specific media that, in turn, gratify individual needs. Although this model belongs to the individualistic stream, it admits that consumers display collective characteristics, primarily common expectations and needs derived from a shared social background. It is these factors that help to transform individual consumers into a public or an audience.[46]

In his 1997 study of media consumers, *Audience Analysis,* McQuail proposed an integrated model to explain the motivation to consume media. He associated media consumption with specific social situations rather than solely with structural or behavioral factors. He presents a pragmatic model, similar to that of Weibull, but according to McQuail, the integration of factors characterizing the consuming public and media structure is the key to understanding consumption patterns. He therefore stresses the consumer's social and cultural background, as well as demographic characteristics such as age, level of education, and media-related needs, including knowledge accumulation, compliance with personal preferences, entertainment and leisure time routines, and level of self-awareness. As regards the media itself, McQuail argues for the significance of the operative infrastructure, observed in features such as number of channels, technological integration capabilities, the structure of need satisfaction, types of message content, the media's popularity, programming, and the extent to which programs fit the consumer's schedule. The interaction between these two dimensions— consumers and the media—creates consumption patterns that spur the development of distinctive media consuming publics. Although this study cannot examine all factors presented in McQuail's model, some of the factors that he proposes can be identified as influencing consumption patterns among the Arabs in Israel.

Turning to the particularities of the population of interest to us here, other factors enter the picture, beyond those cited in the above models. Arab society in Israel represents a minority residing in a country defining itself in national and cultural terms that are foreign, or even hostile, to the Arab identity and culture.[47] This requires the introduction of two additional sets of variables. The first relates to the minority's national affiliation, cultural identity, and history. Based on findings from studies conducted elsewhere, it is well known that national affiliation affects media consumption patterns, creating a distinctive public, separate from the media consuming public of the dominant majority.[48]

It goes without saying that the national and cultural affiliations of the Arab population may be manifested in a shared interpretive repertoire that promotes the development of common attitudes toward media contents. Such repertoires have been identified by media consumption research conducted among other minorities.[49] Hence it is hypothesized that communicative behavior and media consumption play an important role in expressing and maintaining social, national, and cultural identity.[50] Minorities tend to develop unique communicative behavior and media consumption patterns that help them to protect their identities and shape it in accordance with their interests. Minority consumers perceive the media as a repository of their identity and culture so that it functions as a symbolic milieu, even if consumers are often critical and dissatisfied with some contents.[51]

The second unique factor to be considered in this context is Arab society's exposure to two separate and even opposing media systems: one Israeli, the other Arab. Differences between these two systems begin with language and expand to envelop other aspects of culture and politics. This factor brought up several questions concerning the size of media consumption from each of the respective systems by the Arab public and the sort of contents consumed from each of these systems. Answering these questions facilitates a better understanding of the ways the Arab minority in Israel utilizes the split media structure in order to transform its split between its physical and cultural location into an opportunity rather than a trap.

Understanding Minority Strategies of Countering State Hegemony

Scholarship on the relationship between Israel and the Arab-Palestinian minority has been growing rapidly. This relationship is complex, and it has undergone many changes over time. One of the recent markers of this relationship has been the growing tension between the two, especially after the events of October 2000, when thousands of Arab youth interrupted the public order in Israel with demonstrations triggered by the outbreak of the second Palestinian intifada. This led to the deaths of many Palestinians in the first two days as a result of the excessive force used by the Israeli army.[52] The massive mobilization of Arab citizens in the streets, and the belligerent reaction of the Israeli police to this mobilization, resulted in the killing of thirteen young Arab men, twelve of them Israeli citizens, within a period of ten days.[53]

The scope and power of these events raised many questions concerning the relationship between the Israeli state and its Arab minority. The Jewish majority boycotted Arab towns and villages for a long time in retaliation. Arabs, on the other hand, lost faith in state authorities and showed much alienation from it. Despite the fact that several years have passed and the tension has eased, the October 2000 riots are still considered a turning point in the relationship between Israel and its Palestinian minority.

When examining the events and the reactions to them from some distance, one sees that some analysts showed understanding of the events based on their deep knowledge of Arab alienation from state policies over the years. They claimed that despite some use of violence, the Arab protest remained within the realm of contentious politics and was triggered by the long-standing discrimination and deprivation policy of the Israeli government against the Arab minority.[54] They added, in the given circumstances, when the second Palestinian intifada broke out, one could not have expected this alienated population to stand still and watch the Israeli army crushing their relatives in the occupied territories. In contrast, other observers viewed the events as reflecting a radicalization of the Arab community.[55] Many claimed that the resort to violence in early October 2000 by thousands of Arab citizens is indicative of their dangerousness. These analysts used the events to establish a common claim that there is a potential threat inherent in the mere existence of a big Arab community in Israel.[56] Based on such an understanding, many have recommended adopting an aggressive policy to contain this community.

This view of the Arab population as a security threat, albeit not new, was reiterated by the head of the Israeli General Security Service (GSS), Yuval Disken, in May 2007. After the publication of the "Future Vision" documents,[57] formulated by Arab intellectuals and politicians challenging the official ideology of the state, Disken claimed in a governmental meeting that the Arabs form a strategic threat to the state and that the GSS will confront attempts to change the nature of the state from being Jewish and democratic into a state of all its citizens even when the methods used are democratic.[58] The Future Vision documents were viewed as a major change in Arab politics, despite the fact that they did not contain any political claim that was not expressed earlier by Arab politicians and intellectuals.[59]

The rising mobilization in Arab society, especially the rise of new social movements and the establishing of an extensive network of civil organizations, falls within what scholars have called the phenomenon of national revival.[60] National revival marks the growing emphasis that social groups put on their national identity and affiliation, which has led to growing tensions and major predicaments in different countries of the world.[61] The national revival is related to many factors that we cannot delve into in this context. Nonetheless, it is important to note that one of the major factors is globalization, which caused many social groups to fear losing their identity.[62] In many globalizing countries in which minorities live, their national revival was manifested in their communicative action, where they sought to establish their own media institutions as a cultural sphere countering globalization.[63]

Nation-states have always been central agents of national identity formation. This is especially true in the case of nationalizing states, which seek to cope with the continuous sense of dissatisfaction with their identity as a result of the hegemonic role of "nationalizing nationalism." As Rogers Brubaker claims, nationalizing nationalism "involve(s) claims made in the name of a 'core nation' or nationality, defined in ethnocultural terms, and sharply distinguished from the citizenry as a whole. The core nation is understood as the legitimate 'owner' of the state, which is conceived as the state *of* and *for* the core nation."[64] Nationalizing states are usually busy with expanding the control and hegemony of the core nation by eradicating the presence of any alternative or competing ethnocultural nation.

Examining the Israeli case will demonstrate that nationalizing states do not accommodate the identity of cultural and national minorities within them. In contrast to multicultural states, such as Canada, or pluralistic states, such as the United Kingdom, nationalizing states are characterized by the exclusive identification of the state with the dominant ethnic nation, ignoring or even suppressing the presence of other nations in their hegemonic surroundings. As a result, the symbols, institutions, and resources of the state are dominated by the hegemonic nation, the actual import of which is the suppression and marginalization of minorities.

This policy has characterized many of the current pluralistic or multicultural states in the past. Various historical, political, economic, and cultural changes have led nation-states to change their policies toward their minorities, accommodating their identity and rights.[65] Integrationist as well as accommodative strategies of diversity regulation were introduced in order to ease social and political conflicts.[66] Whereas the integration of minority members characterized the strategies chosen for immigrant minorities, the accommodation of the minority's collective rights have been applied in the case of indigenous people. In some cases, hybrid models were utilized, such as in cases of homeland minorities.

Minorities, for their part, developed their own strategies to improve their status vis-à-vis their state.[67] This is particularly the case when we speak of homeland minorities living in nationalizing states, such as the case we are treating in the context of this book. Homeland minorities living in nationalizing states face continuous attempts of the state to hollow out their citizenship of any substantial dimension. This pattern of state behavior is especially sophisticated when we speak about nationalizing states with an ethno-democratic political system.[68] In this context, we witness attempts made by targeted minorities to develop their own alternative socialization mechanisms, starting with utilizing local familial habits and social practices and continuing into developing more modern mechanisms such as alternative educational institutions and media organizations in their own language.[69] Such mechanisms form counterhegemonic spaces that fight state socialization policies and attempts to penetrate minority culture. In the information age, especially based on the common notion that the media plays a major role as socialization force, minorities endeavor to counter the mainstream media by establishing their own institutions and seeking out available contents that meet their unique needs and respond to their cultural aspirations.

In contrast to accepted notions in the literature concerning national revival, which identifies minority mobilization with eroding governability and destabilization of the state, this book purports that minorities seek sophisticated forms of mobilization that will counter state policies without endangering their status. Building on such presumptions, this book demonstrates that the use of violence by the Arab minority in Israel in October 2000 was occasional and does not reflect the strategy chosen by the minority to face state policies and overcome its inferior civic status. This book demonstrates that the Arab minority has adopted civil and cultural means as its main strategy to resist state's discriminatory policies, protect its Palestinian national identity, and promote its civic status. The establishment of a separate Arab public sphere and the communicative behavior of Arab society reflect the most optimal strategy that the minority could have chosen, given the circumstances, in order to cope with Israeli policies of control and surveillance.

For the purpose of making this point clear, it is necessary to differentiate between "politics of radicalization" and "politics of contention." Politics of radicalization is countersystemic, in that national minorities mobilize resources to abolish citizenship and confront the state up to the point of secession. Politics of contention entails attempts to reframe the relationship of the minority with the state by introducing alternative models of common life, in which the minority has control over some of its collective spheres, even when the proposed models of life are not viewed positively by the dominant majority. Both forms of politics may begin by utilizing the rules of the game available in the political system. But, whereas the politics of radicalization aims at countering and even breaking the system, the politics of contention aims at transforming the system by reframing the interpretation of its own rules of the game. The two forms of politics are not mutually exclusive. There can be a shift from politics of contention to politics of radicalization, but this shift is not as predetermined as some people would like us to think.[70]

The literature on social movements can be helpful in this context. It is presumed that national or ethnic minorities adopt strategies similar to those of social movements to cope with their minority status. These strategies are not violent as long as alternative means are continuously available.[71] When minorities do shift from contentious to radical strategies, it is generally only after being convinced that all other possible options available to them as citizens have been exhausted.[72]

Minorities respond to state injustice and utilize all possible options available to them within the repertoire of citizenship before turning to more radical confrontations with the state.[73] Such a claim challenges existing theories of radicalization and secession that are presented as "natural" tendencies of minority nationalism.[74] The following study demonstrates that minority radicalization is a strategy of last resort, especially when the maneuvering space present within citizenship enables the development of cultural patterns of behavior that promote an effective struggle for better status. The following study demonstrates that the communicative behavior of the Arab minority in Israel strikes a balance between its attempts to protect its cultural needs and national rights, on the one hand, and its citizenship in Israel, on the other. In other words, the communicative behavior of the Arab minority in Israel demonstrates the need for complex models in order to understand the communicative behavior of homeland national minorities. The examination of the interrelationship between ethnic revivalism, politics of contention, and communicative action as an avenue of political contention can add to the understanding of the politics of the Arab minority in Israel and at the same time contribute to the theoretical literature on the special connection between media politics and ethnicity. The combination of the two fields of communication and ethnicity, which are usually treated separately in the literature, may help to shed light on dark spots of ethnic revivalism and minority-majority relations in ethnic states.[75]

Media Marginality and Cultural Structures of Opportunity

The treatment of the communicative behavior of the Arab minority in Israel challenges conceptual frameworks that were set by scholars of minority politics, especially scholars of the Arab minority in Israel. In the last few years we have witnessed the rise of conceptual frameworks that sought to describe state-minority relations and characterize the special situation of the Arab minority in Israel. One prominent conceptual framework is the "double periphery" model introduced first by Majid Al-Haj and developed later into "double marginality" by Ramzi Suleiman.[76] Al-Haj claimed that the Arab minority in Israel is located on the margins of two clashing societies: the Israeli and the Palestinian. The Arab community in Israel is Israeli in its citizenship but Palestinian in its nationality. It did not acquire influence reflective of its size in either society. Accordingly, the clash between Israelis and Palestinians has turned the Palestinian citizen of Israel into a marginal player, whose fate is determined by forces beyond his will. A second prominent conceptual framework used to describe the situation of the Arab minority in Israel is "trapped minority," presented by Dan Rabinowitz.[77] It claims that the Arab community in Israel is trapped within the Israeli state, which is bound in a constant state of war with the Palestinian people to which this minority belongs. This situation limits the maneuvering space of the Arab community and creates a clash of loyalties that is impossible to resolve.

There is no doubt that the basic description presented by these scholars is accurate. They have succeeded in summarizing one of the most central dimensions of Arab existence in Israel. However, both conceptual frameworks depict the Arab minority as a passive entity within its objective reality. While both frameworks are structurally true, they do not reflect the dynamic nature of the political reality of the Arab minority. Arab citizens of Israel have developed different means to cope with their structural constraints. These attempts cannot be grasped by the frameworks presented by these scholars. They view the structural reality of the Arab community as a constraint. However, the dynamic nature of Arab reality in Israel is such that this community has developed means to overcome some of its structural constraints and even turn them into an opportunity and a resource. The fact that the Arab community speaks both languages, Hebrew and Arabic, enables it to be party to both sides and hence to be involved in the political and cultural reality of both sides. These efforts are facilitated by globalization processes, especially in the media and communication fields. Furthermore, the Arab community has been very active in becoming a vibrant political subject that has a say in the complex environment in which it finds itself.[78]

As indicated earlier, this book focuses on one of the most challenging cultural practices in recent decades: communicative behavior and media consumption as a strategy of national minorities to deal with their minority status. Theorists such as Karl Deutsch and Jürgen Habermas have highlighted the importance of communicative interactions and behavior as indicators of collective (national and cultural) consciousness.[79] Communicative action is a very central and significant social action.[80] It reflects attempts and strategies followed by social groups to cope with surrounding political circumstances. Communicative action in Habermas's thinking is an abstract concept.[81] It is a communication that is "oriented to achieving, sustaining, and reviewing consensus—and indeed a consensus that rests on the inter-subjective recognition of criticisable validity claims."[82] According to Habermas, the concept of communicative action "presupposes the use of language as a medium for a kind of reaching understanding, in the course of which participants, through relating to a world, reciprocally raise validity claims that can be accepted or contested."[83] Here we will focus on one dimension of the Habermasian concept, namely, the attempt of human groups, especially minorities, to choose whatever they want to "hear" or express in order to promote their position in a given political context. Several chapters of the book examine different dimensions of the "media orientation" of the Arab minority in Israel.

One of the most important analytical concepts that can encompass the communicative behavior of national or cultural minorities in the age of mass media was presented early in the twentieth century by the African American scholar W. E. B. Du Bois. Du Bois presented the concept of "double consciousness" in order to explain the complexity of the situation in which the African

American community lives in the United States. In his contemplations on the reality facing "Negro Americans," Du Bois describes double consciousness as "the sense of always looking at one's soul by the tape of a world that looks on in amused contempt and pity. One ever feels his twoness,—an American, a Negro; two warring souls, two thoughts, two unreconciled strivings; two warring ideals in one dark body, whose dogged strength alone keeps it from being torn asunder."[84] This sense of twoness or double consciousness is characterized by Du Bois as the attraction to one's national group and the inability to escape the temptation of integration into the larger social and political reality. This paradoxical position is not necessarily negative. As might be understood from Du Bois, it can constitute a strategic positioning in which one is connected to two different cultural worlds simultaneously and is able to seize the opportunities available in both. Although this positioning is not necessarily undertaken by choice, it can still be possible to choose from among whatever one sees fit from both worlds. Homi Bhabha echoes this duality through his concept of in-betweenness, which, while often serving as a source of frustration, can also be a source of power.[85]

The media culture of the Arab community in Israel can be better understood when approached using these conceptual tools provided by Du Bois and Bhabha. Thrown into the status of a defeated minority in a new and alien state established on its national soil, the Arab minority had to develop strategies of struggle that enable it to deal with the new dual reality of its Palestinian and Israeli affiliation. Analysis of the communicative action and audience behavior in this community can contribute to our understanding of developments in the strategies of struggle adopted by the Arab indigenous minority in Israel. Like other social groups that exercise no real control over official socialization mechanisms in their own state, the Arab community has searched for strategies to overcome attempts made by the state to narrate and control its public agenda and collective memory and to simultaneously communicate with its kin nation. The media has served as a key mechanism in reaching this goal—a process that was intensified with the globalization of media and the rise of satellite TV networks in the Middle East region.[86]

Media globalization enables minorities to develop their own special media consumption patterns that assist them in overcoming limits set by their physical location in a state foreign to their culture. The media culture of national minorities demonstrates how state sovereignty has been transformed in the global age. Although we cannot speak of total erosion of state power, today people living in one state physically can nonetheless experience an entirely different place culturally. The media culture of the Arab minority in Israel demonstrates how social groups can be located in two separate media spaces simultaneously—illustrated by and illustrating the meaning of the two related concepts, "double consciousness" and "in-betweenness."

TWO

The Indigenous Arab Minority in the Israeli State

The Palestinian national movement was defeated in 1948–49. The roots of the defeat and the Israeli policy that resulted are heavily debated among scholars of the period. Whereas some scholars accuse Israel of ethnic cleansing,[1] others claim that despite the expulsion that occurred there was no clear and preplanned policy that led to hundreds of thousands of Palestinians fleeing.[2] Several Israeli scholars claim that there was a mixture of policy orders, some of which were to encourage the population to leave some areas. They claim that some Palestinians left by choice and others out of fear of being in a war zone. The growing historical evidence supports the ethnic cleansing thesis, something that has direct impact on the collective consciousness of all Palestinians, including the Palestinian population in Israel, which is the subject of this book. Growing evidence of the 1948 war and of the repressive political and cultural regime that followed that war has been a strong factor nourishing the endeavor of the Palestinian population in Israel to reconnect with its cultural and national environment.

The debate among the historians does not come to terms with the fact that the 150,000–175,000 Palestinian Arabs who became part of the state of Israel after the war were subject to a fierce military regime that violated all their basic human rights and their rights of citizenship. The war and its immediate consequences have led to the tragic situation of the Palestinian minority. This minority became part of a defeated people that lost its homeland and turned into groups of refugees scattered in different states in the Middle East. Within Israel it was immediately cut off from the rest of the Arab world and sealed in its own segregated poor areas. This minority was left without its political, intellectual, economic, and cultural leadership. It was scattered in three areas: Galilee, the Triangle, and the Negev. The structure was mostly agrarian, small villages that lacked basic infrastructural facilities, such as roads, schools, electricity, and running water.

A small minority of Arabs remained in the big Palestinian cities inside Israel, such as Jaffa, Haifa, Akka, Ramleh, and Lid. These cities became predominantly Jewish as a result of settlement policies adopted by Zionist institutions before 1948 and by the state after 1948.[3] The remaining original Arab inhabitants soon found themselves living in the poorest neighborhoods.[4] These became ghettos as a result of the demographic segregation policies and the lack of governmental investment in basic infrastructures.[5]

The policies of the Israeli government toward the Arabs who remained in its territory after the 1948 war can hardly be summed up briefly. Beginning in May 1948, the Israeli government began to "normalize" the lives of its Jewish citizens by investing resources in new settlements and in employment. Any barrier hindering these goals was viewed as illegitimate. The Palestinian Arabs were viewed as a major hindrance to maximizing state control over land resources. As a result, Arab citizens were framed in militaristic terms that justified illegal policies under the cover of security reasoning.[6] State institutions—executive, legislative, and legal—introduced policies, laws, and rulings that formed a sophisticated system of dispossession, subjugation, and control.[7]

Despite the existential crisis that the remaining Palestinian population experienced, the Israeli authorities perceived them as a direct security threat to the existence of the newly founded state.[8] All state organs adopted their policies toward the Arab population based on the official perception that state-minority relations were a security matter that should not be carried out without the direct involvement of the Israeli army and other security forces.[9]

The authorities articulated this policy outline through the establishment of the military government, which sought to control every aspect of Arab daily life.[10] The military government utilized the emergency laws of the mandate government from 1945 to promote its penetration of Arab society, something that exposed their lives to the strategic and tactical calculations of the military. The three Arab zones were put under heavy military scrutiny and ruled over by a governor who was invested with almost unlimited authority. He was entitled to detain people, to exile them, to announce curfews, to confiscate tracts of land of unlimited size, to extend movement permits, especially to those who were cooperating with the security services, etc.[11]

Framing the Arab-Palestinians who remained inside the borders of the state in security terms turned them into a constant military "threat."[12] This policy justified their treatment as dangerous aliens and a potential fifth column. This framing enabled the government to persuade the Jewish public to ignore the human conditions of their Arab neighbors and to justify any policy toward them, something that has continued to this day.

One of the most important aspects of the Israeli policies toward the Arab population is demography.[13] Reducing the number of Arabs that would remain inside Israel has been a very important goal of the Israeli government.[14] Most studies of the 1948 war, whether Zionist or post-Zionist, demonstrate that hundreds of villages were demolished and hundreds of thousands of Palestinians were expelled and not allowed to return to their homes after the war. The announced policy of the government at the time was that the refugees posed a threat to the security of the new state. As a result, not only were refugees from outside the armistice line prohibited from returning to their homes, but so were Palestinians who remained within the borders of the state of Israel.[15] This has led to the creation of what is called the Present Absentees or what in international law is called "Internally Displaced People," a new social category that exists in Israeli society to this very day.[16]

The exact number of Palestinian IDPs is hard to determine.[17] According to Majid Al-Haj, most were villagers from about 370 villages destroyed during and after the 1948 war.[18] Estimates from the early 1950s ranged from 31,000 to 50,000.[19] The National Committee for the Rights of the Internally Displaced in Israel claims that UN Relief and Works Agency's late 1940s registry report of 46,000 people is correct, stating that this number was verified by Israeli sociologist Sammy Smooha, who concluded that 23.1% of the Arabs in Israel were either IDPs or descendants of one.[20] Thus 250,000 Palestinian citizens of Israel would be IDPs. However, Israeli historian Hillel Cohen, who conducted extensive historical research on the IDPs, claims that these numbers are exaggerated.[21] He estimates the IDPs at around 15% of the Arab population, or 150,000 people today. But Cohen does not include IDPs who descend from families in which only one parent is an IDP. If we follow the Israeli legal definition, which includes all those who were not in their homes according to the Absent Property Law and as a result lost their homes and/or their lands, IDPs exceed 250,000 today.[22]

Israeli policies of evacuation and deportation did not stop with the end of the 1948 war.[23] The number of Palestinians who were deported from their villages increased as a result of the Israeli army's efforts to establish its control over the areas occupied during the war that the UN partition plan did not assign to the Jewish state. This led to evacuating several villages that were located in "security zones" (e.g., Ikrit, Kafar Bir'am) or in areas of Jewish settlement (e.g., El-Ghabsiya, Al-Majdal).[24]

The number of IDPs further increased in 1948–51 as a result of Israeli land policies in the Triangle area. In the Rhodes talks between Israel and Jordan, the two states agreed to exchange territories for security reasons.

The land that Israel received from Jordan—the Triangle area—was populated with 25,000 Palestinians and included 4,000–8,500 refugees.[25] Israel absorbed the original Palestinian inhabitants of these areas into the state while deporting most of the refugees. It did not allow the small number of refugees who remained to return to their original villages, and it prevented local inhabitants from regaining their private lands, which the Israeli army had captured prior to the cease-fire agreement with Jordan. All the lands located west of the cease-fire line that were captured by the Israeli army before the Rhodes talks were considered absentee property and transferred to the custodian of absentee property. Palestinians thereby lost thousands of acres of private land even though they became Israeli citizens.

Demographic fear remains one of the driving forces behind Israeli policies toward the Arab minority, despite the fact that over 95% of the lands in Israel are in Jewish public and private hands.[26] The Arab minority is purported to be a demographic threat that should be cured by various means.[27] Governmental as well as nongovernmental institutions are busy providing plans to deal with the Arab "threat." Judaizing was often carried out, but not always clearly declared as such, for various reasons, and has become a driving force behind other planning policies, such as land zoning and road infrastructures.[28] The settling of Jews on lands confiscated from Arabs, especially where Arabs still form the majority population, such as in the Galilee and the Triangle regions, draws massive governmental investments.[29] This settlement policy, which maintained the de facto segregation, aimed at turning the Arab towns into closed zones within Jewish regions without any space for future development. As one part of the Jewish solution to the Arab demographic growth, it leads to a major housing crisis and impossible demographic density in Arab towns. The flow of young Arab couples into Jewish cities, such as Carmiel, Upper Nazareth, and Haifa, as well as the attempts of Arab families to buy houses in Jewish settlements is a clear consequence of Israeli planning and settlement policies, something that is expected to intensify in the future.

The demographic policy is closely tied to the second policy outline that remains part and parcel of Israeli policy toward its Arab citizens, namely, land confiscation. This policy attempted to dissolve the physical and cultural bond between the remaining Arab population and its homeland.[30] For the purpose of controlling its geopolitical space, the state confiscated the greater part of Arab private land, establishing a new "land regime" that left it in control of 93% of its space.[31] The state created diverse legislative and administrative mechanisms to enable it to transfer Arab land to Jewish control.[32] Considering the fact that the land was the only property in Arab ownership that could produce income, expropriating the land had a direct socioeconomic effect on most Arab citizens that goes beyond the institutional and political influence it had on the national level. The average Arab citizen has to invest several years of labor in order to recoup, if possible, the value of one acre of their confiscated land. Furthermore, the transfer of land from Arab to Jewish hands, which continues by various means to the present day, has also deprived it of its Palestinian identity and characteristics, renaming the whole "new" space in accordance with Jewish history and national collective imagination.

According to Yiftachel, the policy of spatial planning in Israel has several dimensions, the central ones being the territorial, procedural, socioeconomic, and cultural.[33] There is an essential connection between these four dimensions that are united by the aim of reinforcing Jewish existence at the expense of the Arab population living in this territory. This connection becomes evident when one considers how planning policy determined the regions of development, on the grounds of ethnic affiliation, and how construction policy limits the opportunities for natural development of the Arab population.[34]

Even now, planning and construction regulations in Israel are institutionally and ideologically alien to Arab housing culture, something that explains the phenomenon of "illegal house building" in Arab towns and villages that leads to an intense policy of house demolition by the state.[35] The state utilizes all bureaucratic means possible to restrict Arab development plans. The road planning maps of Israel as well as the location of industrial and commercial areas in the development plans of the Galilee and the Negev promoted by all Israeli governments demonstrate the patterns by which Arab citizens are excluded from the development maps. Most of the governmental investment appropriated for the Negev by the Olmert government on November 27, 2006, was allocated to Jewish towns and infrastructures, despite the fact that the Bedouin population in that region is the most unfortunate population in all Israel.[36] This policy continues a long established discrimination against the Bedouin inhabitants of the Negev area. Since 1948, thousands of these Palestinian citizens have been expelled from their original places of habitation.

In the Negev, the state established seven permanent residential areas into which it sought to concentrate all the Bedouins, thereby impinging on their historical bond to their ancestral land and warping their lifestyle.[37] This process of land transfer from Arab to Jewish hands increased the number of IDPs and led to the categorization of fifty-eight villages as "unrecognized" because they were not legalized by the state planning authorities in the 1960s.[38] This situation with minor adjustments remains in force to the present day.

The planning of a new Jewish city in the Triangle area, which was recently made public, as well as the expansion of neighborhoods of Jewish cities, such as Upper Nazareth and Carmiel, toward Arab towns, both clearly set geodemographic limits on the ability of the Arab population to develop and expand. Furthermore, new environmental parameters introduced in the 2005 Master Plan for Development (Tama 35) are being translated into a policy narrowing the development possibilities of Arab towns by declaring surrounding lands as "Green Areas."[39] Notwithstanding the importance of maintaining natural green zones and protecting natural parks, the fact that such policies do not prevent the development of new neighborhoods in newly established Jewish settlements in the Galilee and do so in Arab villages reflects ethnicization of nature in Israeli land and settlement planning. Such ethnicization leads to intense resentment in the Arab community and feeds the growing tension between the state and its Arab minority.

A third policy outline of the Israeli government toward the Arab population involves the mistreatment of their leadership. Israel has employed a range of tactics to weaken and undermine an Arab leadership increasingly concerned with national issues and collective rights and increasingly willing to challenge the state's Jewish identity and the exclusive hegemony of the Jewish majority over state institutions. Besides co-optation and the nurturing of subservient Arab leaders content to limit their activities to demands for services and resources (practiced most successfully in the early years), the state's tactics include intimidation, arrest, detention of individual leaders, and legal measures such as banning or attempting to ban political parties or preventing them from running in elections.[40] The legal efforts have been less successful in recent years.[41] But the intimidation continues, as can be seen from the detentions in 2003 of several leaders of the Islamic movement and the trial of MK Azmi Bishara for declarations supporting the Palestinian right to resist Israeli occupation.[42]

More common today are the constant accusations and criticisms by Israeli official and unofficial sources—including many academics—aimed at delegitimizing Arab leadership internationally, among the Jewish majority, and even within Arab society itself. Arab leaders are accused of abusing "Israeli democracy" and Israeli "tolerance" in order to promote goals considered beyond their mandate, if not actually illegal. In this spirit Dan Shiftan of Haifa University has claimed that the "challenge that the Arab members of Knesset pose to the basic assumptions of a Jewish majority goes beyond the realm of a civic society discussion, which relies on common understandings as part of the democratic process."[43] Another common charge is that the Arab leaders devote their energies to the broader Palestinian problem at the expense of their "authentic duties" of serving the needs of their constituency.

Needless to say, the weaknesses of the leadership are encouraged and exploited by the state to facilitate its penetration of Arab society. In short,

Arab leadership in Israel is caught between the procedural democratic patterns of political behavior in the Israeli political system, on the one hand, and total institutional, discursive, and rhetorical hegemony of the Jewish majority, on the other. The Israeli authorities encourage the Jewish public to ignore Arab leaders, especially when it comes to leaders with authentic bonds with the Arab community. These leaders are usually not given enough space in the Israeli public sphere, especially in the Israeli media, and when they are addressed, they are usually presented in a very negative fashion.[44]

A fourth policy outline that is important in this context is the economic policy of the state of Israel toward the Arab population. It is impossible to address all aspects of this policy. Therefore, I will concentrate on one aspect, namely, the impact of the land expropriation policy on the situation of Arabs in the Israeli job market. The policy of land expropriation led to an intense proletarization process of the Arab labor force.[45] When we consider the fact that Palestinian society was mostly agrarian before 1948, the confiscation of land deprived most Palestinians of their main source of income. By 1970 most of the Arab labor force (71.5%) consisted of wage earners.[46] Twenty years later, the ratio had reached 83%. This process increased Arab dependence on the Jewish economy, a goal that had been sought by the Israeli government since 1948. The military government of 1948–66 was a major means of achieving this goal.[47] It allowed the governors of the different areas not only to facilitate the process of land confiscation but also to allot working and traveling permits to those "good Arabs" who submitted to the new political and economic order and sought to promote it among the rest of the Arab population.[48] Simultaneously, the military governors limited the freedom of movement of most Arabs, especially men.

After 1967 the integration of Arabs in Jewish economy was fraught with social and economic disadvantages. Arab workers were generally hired for the lowest-paying jobs.[49] The lack of an employment infrastructure in Arab towns, and the evident preference of Jewish employers for Jewish workers over Arab, caused gaps in income, inequality, and clear differences in the standard of living. Since 1948 we have witnessed a growing gap between the average incomes of Arab and Jewish families.[50]

The alterations in the job market during the 1980s and 1990s heightened the effect of the structural inferiority of the Arab labor force in Israel. These years had seen an expansion of the labor force in the categories of the scientific, academic, and professional occupations and in the service sector and a reduction in the number of people employed in manual work, including the agricultural sector. If we examine this process more closely, the discrimination against qualified and professional members of the Arab labor force becomes even more conspicuous. In 1999, 50.5% of the Ashkenazi

Jews (descendants of parents from European-American origins), and 23.7% of Mizrahi Jews (descendants of parents from Asian-African origins) were engaged in academic, professional, or administrative professions. Only 14.7% of the Arabs were occupied in the same fields in that year.[51] This same pattern of employment distribution is still valid, with growing gaps in favor of Jews.[52]

Most Arabs with an academic education are employed as teachers and headmasters. In 2002, 65% and in 2007, 58% of the Arab labor force was still defined as skilled and unskilled workers in the fields of agriculture, construction, light industry, and services.[53] The absence of Arab workers in many of the higher economic fields, like high-tech, informatics, aviation, and communication exemplifies the structural inequality that the Arab labor force is facing. Additionally, we should consider the marginal number or complete absence of Arab workers in most governmental offices and state companies, like the electric company, Mekorot (administration of the water economy in Israel), Bezeq (the national telephone association, although it was privatized in 2005), Solel Bone (a construction corporation), and Amidar (a public housing company). Of the 59,938 workers in the state's services in January 2000, only 2,835 (5%) were Arabs, most of whom worked in either the Ministry of Health or the Ministry of Education.[54]

The discrimination against Arab citizens includes a serious gap in wages. The data regarding the average wages, according to the National Insurance Institute, of Arab and Jewish settlements indicates that Arab income amounts to 60% of that in Jewish society.[55] According to recent information about the equality index presented by the Adva Center in December 2006, the average income of an Arab employee is 75% of that of the average urban employee in Israel.[56] It is important to note that the average income of a Jewish employee of Asian origin is 100% and the average income of a Jewish employee of Ashkenazi origin is 139%. This data mirrors the huge income gaps between Jews and Arabs in the field of income acquired through wages, without considering the differences that may become even greater when we evaluate income from capital investment or intergenerational transfer of wealth.

A troublesome phenomenon that resulted from the ethnic stratification in the Israeli job market is the exit of Arab men ages 45–65 from the job market. The social and cultural consequence has been an extremely high rate of unemployment among men who, in other societies, are considered to be at the peak of their productivity. Since Arab society is characterized by large families dependent on a single wage earner, the significance of men of that age dropping out of the job market is an increase in both poverty and dependence on welfare and social services.

This reality also has serious cultural implications. The father, who is considered the main authority in Arab families, loses one of his central sources of power. Beyond the psychological impact of such a process on the personal level, it has a major cultural impact on his role as a model for the younger generation. To that one must add the fact that, since most Arab workers have to find jobs outside their place of residence, people have to commute considerable distances in search of employment. As a consequence, most Arab men return late to their village, only sleep there, and leave again for work early the next morning. This process has intensified the deflation of the status of men without supplying mechanisms and tools to replace this authority with a constructive alternative, a central factor that may go a long way toward explaining the rise of criminality and social deviations in Arab society, such as alcoholism, drug use, violence, and vandalism.

The education system is one of the major tools of interpellation and socialization of the modern state.[57] The Arab education system is separate from the secular Jewish system. Some Israeli scholars view this fact as representing a collective right granted by the state to its Arab citizens.[58] However, a deeper look and realistic examination of the Arab educational system in Israel demonstrates that it is utilized as a control mechanism and an ideological apparatus, tightly supervised by the Israel General Security Service, the Shabak.[59] Jews hold the senior functions in the Ministry of Education, particularly those that have to do with determining the contents and dictating the didactic and pedagogic concepts of the instruction policy.[60] Only in recent years have a few Arabs been assigned major roles in the Arab education system, but they can only conduct policies that are determined from above. The Arab school system also suffers from severe shortages. Despite the modifications made in recent years and the attempts to reduce the gaps, there are still large shortages in basic educational infrastructures, such as schools, teachers, and instruction hours.[61] At the beginning of the school years 2005–2006 and 2006–2007, major shortages in school buildings and classrooms were reported in the news.[62] The gaps between the Jewish and Arab systems are largely responsible for the relatively low scores of Arab students in Israel, something that has economic as well as cultural implications.

Scholars of the Arab education system have documented some modifications in recent years. Nonetheless, these changes remain subordinated to the philosophical framework that strives to sustain an alternate Arab Israeli identity, alienated from its historical, cultural, and national past.[63] The emphasis put on the issue of loyalty to the state, stressing the uniqueness of the Israeli Arabs as a community separate from the rest of the Palestinian people, is sufficient evidence of the ideological and political intentions of the Israeli Ministry of Education. Sami Mari long ago demonstrated that the Arab education system "is a tool by which the whole minority is manipulated by a powerful reward and punishment system, based on the quality of political behavior rather than the merit of Arab teachers."[64] Examinations of the contents of the Arab education system have found that it aims at creating a submissive Arab, who is willing to accept his inferiority against the superiority of the Jews, consequently weakening and eliminating the Arab-Palestinian identity.[65]

A study recently conducted by this author on the field of civic education in Arab schools showed that the main goal of this education is the promotion of Israeli patriotism and acceptance of the political system rather than nourishing civic consciousness and active citizenship. Arab children learn about the Israeli political system as democratic, bearing liberal values, but without much reference to their secondary status. Furthermore, Arab children are exposed to the formal structures of the Israeli political system without much reference to its practices. The gap between the formal structure and the daily translations of its policies is never explained, something that generates cognitive dissonance in most Arab children. This type of education creates the illusion that discrimination against Arabs in Israel is only a temporary flaw rather than an institutionalized policy applied to them by virtue of the identity of the Arab children as Palestinians per se. This identity is misrepresented in civic education in order to justify the status quo and legitimize the system, which deprives the same children of basic financial resources to study in conditions similar to their Jewish compatriots. The misrepresentation of Arabs in the contents of school textbooks is echoed in the physical condition of Arab schools when compared with Jewish ones.[66]

An important policy outline that has not been seriously addressed in the literature is the Israeli media policy toward the Arab community. Although coercive measures have dominated Israeli policies toward the Arab population from 1948 until today, this does not and should not mean that other means of manufacturing consent were not also implemented. Most studies of state-minority relations in Israel belittle this dimension of Israeli policies, despite the fact that some do relate to it, albeit indirectly. For instance, the treatment of Arab leadership presented by Lustick in the early 1980s demonstrates the attempts made by the state to co-opt leaders who help to pacify the population and to control its behavior. Furthermore, the educational policies mentioned earlier are aimed at manufacturing consent and lead to deep changes in the collective imagination of the Arab community. These studies do not pay attention to the role of the media as a means of achieving consent. They do not address the information policies directed toward the Arab community and especially its elites via the media. Thus the following chapter draws attention to the media policy of the state toward the Arab community and the means utilized to foster the process of manufacturing consent within it, as a background review for the presentation of the empirical data drawn from the survey conducted recently.

THREE

Israeli Media Policies toward the Arab Minority

Like other hegemonic regimes, the state of Israel transformed the media into one of its principal socializing mechanisms, second only to the education system, seeking to manufacture consent among the Israeli public. In the early years of the Israeli state, the Hebrew press, both the party-affiliated and the privately owned, and the Voice of Israel Radio were tightly connected to the information organs that operated in the Prime Minister's Office, the Foreign Ministry, and the Israeli Defense Forces (IDF).[1] Despite internal differences, the Hebrew media institutions have been completely loyal to the leadership of the state in regard to security and foreign policy. They serve as an organ of the hegemonic elite to promote the state's interests as defined by state leadership.[2]

The same policy of manufacturing consent soon applied to the Arabs who have remained in Israel. Major attempts were made to unite all information organs into one centralized bureau in the Prime Minister's Office. These attempts were not successful, although very effective information organs, such as the Information Center, the Government Press Office, and the Government Advertising Agency, were established and have remained until this very day. The Information Center, which was transferred to the Education Ministry in 1955, issued publications on various issues, including on the Arab community in Israel, aimed at educating the public in Israel and abroad. The Information Center maintained close ties with security and other information institutions issuing information that supported the major attempts to justify the establishment of the Israeli state and to reflect its self-confidence.

These various efforts, which targeted both external and internal audiences, were especially relevant for controlling and resocializing the Arab community that remained in Israel after 1948. The raison d'être behind the informative efforts made by state agencies toward the Arab minority has been that the genesis of the state of Israel forms a new category in the history of the region that should be accommodated and accepted. Palestinian history was suspended, and a new historical image began to unfold that sought to transform the Palestinian population into Israeli Arabs.[3] The information apparatus of the Israeli state operated within and in concert with the military government that actively restrained civil and political activity in the Arab community as part of the effort to forcibly inculcate a new, government-dictated "perception of reality." These military and information agencies worked rigorously to inculcate awareness and acceptance of the new reality throughout the Arab population for the purpose of quashing dissent.

The official information policy therefore attempted to construct an Arab collective memory divorced from its cultural environment and historical past.[4] Moreover, this policy aimed at extolling the cultural supremacy of Jewish society, while implying the cultural, economic, and social backwardness of Arab society. All these ploys were contrived to justify the cultural, political, and military colonization of Arab society and its geographic space.

As a result of the 1948 war, the Palestinians lost control over their national and cultural institutions. During the war, the Arab political, cultural, and economic elites were exiled, and all Arab urban centers were destroyed by the Israeli army.[5] As a result, the majority of Arab public institutions collapsed, including those vehicles of mass communication that had developed up to then.[6]

Since the first decade of the twentieth century, the number of journalists active in Palestine has continually increased.[7] Many newspapers were published, principally in the major urban centers, such as Jerusalem, Jaffa, Haifa, and Acre. These newspapers expressed the feelings of the Palestinian people as they anticipated the approaching threat, posed primarily by Zionist immigration and settlement in Palestine. Palestinian newspapers reached other Arab countries as newspapers from neighboring countries reached the major cities of Palestine, especially the coastal cities, which were connected via the regional rail line. Among the most widely disseminated newspapers of that era were *Filisteen, Al-Karmel,* and *Al-Difa'a.*[8]

In the wake of the war, a deep cultural and communication vacuum suddenly appeared that severed the local population from Palestinians and Arabs living in neighboring countries, as well as from the surrounding Arab landscape. This isolation intensified the population's sense of crisis and powerlessness. Geographic factors exacerbated the predicament: Because the majority of Arabs remaining in Israel were rural peasants, scattered in isolated areas, they became totally dependent on the information that the

Israeli propaganda machine disseminated, excluding those few who owned radios. The latter were among the few remaining well-to-do traditional families who had much to lose should they reveal any negative sentiments toward the new state.

All Palestinian newspapers that were published during the British mandate period, except *Al-Ittihad,* the organ of the Communist Party, ceased operations after the defeat of 1948. The extensive network of newspapers and the lively public sphere that had characterized the large Palestinian cities vanished. The sudden disruption of social and political communication in Palestinian society and the massive displacement of thousands of people led to a communicative vacuum that could not have been filled or exploited by *Al-Ittihad,* especially when we take into consideration that the Communist Party, which supported the establishment of the state of Israel, was closely scrutinized and its Arab members were strictly watched.[9]

Therefore, due both to the pressure the government exerted on the oppositional Communist Party and to the fact that only a small percentage of the Arab population was literate in Arabic, the party's newspaper, *Al-Ittihad,* had limited influence, often reduced to a very small circle of readers. In the atmosphere of fear and defeat, especially in light of a developing collaborator culture—that is, Arab citizens who collaborated with the Israeli military and the General Security Services (Shabak)—most members of Arab society did not dare to openly show that they listened to radio programs from Arab countries or that they read *Al-Ittihad.*[10]

Most Palestinians at the time still believed that their presence in their homes and villages was a temporary matter and that their ultimate fate would be similar to that of their brethren who had been expelled and who had to find refuge in remote places.[11] Evidence drawn from interviews with refugees reflects the sense of fear and suspicion that characterized Palestinians in general and the Palestinian population that remained in Israel in particular.[12] Historical evidence published recently demonstrates that the fears of the Palestinians who became citizens of Israel was not imagined.[13] The Israeli government contemplated the expulsion of residents of various villages and Arab residential areas from Arab cities even after the armistice cease-fire with all Arab states.[14]

As we discussed in chapter 2, the coercive organs of the Israeli state implemented an intensive policy of surveillance orchestrated by the Israeli security services, which scrutinized all aspects of Arab life, especially those aspects that have to do with employment, political organization, and freedom of speech. One of the main goals of the surveillance policy was to create total dependence of the population on the state through its geographic, economic, and cultural marginalization. For that purpose this population was cut off from its brethren and the Arab cultural landscape extending beyond Israel's borders for a long time. Their minority status has been controlled by a military government, residual mechanisms of which continue to be employed today, such as control of the education and official communicative systems. The military government was imposed in order to ensure total hegemony of state authorities over all dimensions of Arab life.

One of the main dimensions of the control system of the cultural life of the Arab population was aimed at divorcing this population from its past and from its natural geopolitical space.[15] The state followed policies known from the colonial culture of world empires and adopted a strict policy of renaming places and spaces.[16] It sought not only to uproot the physical connection of Arabs with their homeland but also to delete their historical memory of their environment.[17] The Israeli state was, and still is, very aware of the centrality of space as a central mechanism of subjective consciousness.[18] Since its inception, the Zionist movement has invested much energy in reframing the meaning of space, enfolding Palestinian memory and replacing it with Jewish narratives. This policy became one of the major raisons d'être of the Israeli education system. The remapping, as a major Zionist project, was wonderfully described by Meron Benvenisti, who followed the decision-making process that led to the renaming of places in order to establish what he called the "Jewish Map."[19] The renaming policy was not only an official effort. It characterized initiatives of Jewish settlements that sought to purify and legitimize their presence on the ruins of demolished Arab villages. The study of Noga Kadman demonstrates how not only the state but also the liberal kibbutzim contributed to the erosion of Palestinian presence from their environment by physical as well as symbolic policies.[20]

One of the major columns of the construction of the Arab Israeli subject that is to replace the Palestinian subject has been resocialization through education and propaganda. The Education Ministry took control of the Arab educational system. The Prime Minister's Office, especially the advisor on Arab affairs, took care of the informative dimension. Information was to be dispersed by various means, including the media.[21] The goal was mostly psychological rather than informative. It aimed at demonstrating that the newly established state could not be defeated and that "good Arabs" have a better chance to live in peace and prosperity than "trouble makers."[22]

For the purpose of passing information to the local Arab public and especially to its elite, various information organs were established by different state-related institutions, such as the Arab Unit in the Histadrut (General Federation of Labor). One of the best examples of such information organs was the daily *Al-Yom,* which began publishing in 1948 out of the offices of the now defunct *Filisteen,* a Palestinian newspaper published before the war. The daily was later integrated into the Arabic Press House, which issued several publications that included a daily newspaper, *Al-Yom,* two biweeklies,

Al-Yom for Our Children and *The Echo of Education,* a monthly, *Al-Hadaf,* and, in the 1980s, the quarterly *Lika'a.* Some of these publications are still published today. The Arabic Press House also issued the books for the Arabic schools and thereby controlled the contents that socialized Arab youth.

The publications of the House were major tools of the propaganda efforts of the Israeli state in which the Histadrut, in cooperation with the Information Center at the Prime Minister's Office, played a major role. These two institutions shared the monies won from the Islamic Waqf (Islamic Endowment Money) and invested them in what has been presented as services to the community, such as publications in Arabic. Such policies are still valid today, since the Waqf is still under the direct auspices of state agencies, mainly the Custodian of Absentee Properties.[23]

In order to enforce these information policies, Arabic speakers were needed, especially those experienced in journalism and media work. Many of the leaders of the Jewish community in pre-1948 Palestine spoke Arabic. However, the number of those able to get involved in the propaganda establishment was limited. Therefore, there was a need for integrating experienced journalists from among the newly immigrated Jews from the Arab world. Although many of the Jewish immigrants from Arab countries did not come out of Zionist motivations, some of the most educated were invited to work in various governmental agencies, including the Information Center and the Arabic Unit of the Histadrut.[24]

Unlike most studies of the location of Oriental Jews in Israeli society, culture, and politics in the early years of the state, the examination of the role of Jewish intellectuals of Oriental origin, especially from Iraq, demonstrates their central role in setting up the control and surveillance mechanisms in Arab society. Although some studies demonstrate the critical stance that intellectuals of Oriental origin had taken vis-à-vis Zionist policies in the late 1940s and early 1950s, these voices were few and very soon had almost disappeared.[25] Intellectuals from Arab countries, especially those who had journalistic experience, were immediately integrated into the Information Center and the Histadrut propaganda machine, mainly Arabic Press House, and into the Arabic department in Voice of Israel Radio and later into the Israeli television. Many of those who won a job at that time continued working there for many years to come, shaping the character of the Israeli Arabic media system. This system began losing its appeal only recently, something that reflects on its ability to influence the Arab public sphere in Israel, in the Palestinian territories occupied in 1967, and in neighboring Arab countries for a long period. It is impossible to imagine the success of such a media system without the role that intellectuals of Oriental origin played in establishing its infrastructures and developing its contents.

Al-Yom employed Jews from Arab countries who spoke Arabic as a first language and had some journalistic experience.[26] One of these leading figures was Menashe Zaarur (Abu Ibrahim), who used to be the editor of *Al-Bilad* newspaper (The Country) in Bagdad before immigrating to Israel. Another important figure was Meir Garah, who worked for the Information Center in the Prime Minister's Office and functioned as the link between the Center and the prime minister's advisor on Arab affairs, on the one hand, and the newspaper editorial board, on the other. Nissim Ragwan, who published several books in English and Arabic, wrote once a week in *Al-Yom* and later became its editor. Ragwan had worked as a journalist for the *Baghdad Times* in the 1940s and used his experience in order to promote the influence of *Al-Yom* daily in Arab society. He became a central figure in the Israeli information machine directed toward Arab society.[27] Those and many others were well aware of Arab culture and soon became very influential agents of the state propaganda machine, disseminating information in Arab society that aimed at reconstructing its collective imagination and reshaping it historical memory.[28]

The newspaper functioned among other things as a stage on which Arab leaders in the Arab lists close to the dominant party, Mapai, could express their attitudes and promote their worldview. Some Arabs were employed by *Al-Yom,* and their task was to reflect attitudes in the Arab community, mainly those that were sympathetic to the state. In some cases, Arab journalists or columnists in the newspaper were encouraged or even pushed to write against the spirit of critical opinions and ideas expressed in the opposition newspapers, *Al-Ittihad* and *Al-Mirsad,* concerning governmental policies toward the Arab population.[29] Columns, such as *Afwah Al-Nas* (The Mouths of the People), which appeared in the newspaper for several years, aimed at presenting daily social issues in a creative form that counterbalanced criticism expressed by Arab journalists or politicians in other Arab sources.[30] Various journalists, such as Mustafa Marar and Najib Susan, who became well-known authors in Arab society wrote in the newspaper and presented authentic Arab positions that balanced between criticizing governmental policies and simultaneously presenting a positive model for imitation in Arab society, a model that conceives of Israel as a viable and rational state that enables debate and is tolerant of criticism.[31]

Al-Yom disseminated ideas and opinions among the Arab community, creating the sense that Israel is a phenomenon to be taken for granted, one that should be feared and respected. The contents of the newspaper, as well as evidence provided by people who operated it, demonstrate the Machiavellian line that the newspaper adopted in regard to the relationship between a new occupier and an occupied population.[32] It sought to propagate a frame of mind that accepts Israel as a *fait accompli* that cannot be overturned and should be feared, lest it be forced to adopt fierce policies.

Simultaneously, the newspaper was opened for Arab voices that reflected the efforts made by the state to improve the living conditions of its Arab citizens. The burden for the miserable situation of the Arab population was projected onto the "irresponsible" Palestinian and Arab leadership, which had pushed the population to pay a heavy price, but that served its own narrow interests. The newspaper presented its worldview in a very sophisticated way in order to avoid antagonizing the Arab public.

The following statement made by one of the people in charge of the newspaper concerning its role demonstrates its dominant purpose at the time:

> In opposition to the common stand, I do not see any problem or repercussion, also from the standpoint of the Arab reader, of the newspaper being a governmental one. There is no sense in trying to hide the connection of the newspaper to the government. . . . The orientation of the newspaper should be . . . as the broadcasts from the Israeli Arabic Radio, concerning foreign policy and positions regarding Israel. Special emphasis should be put on information on the Arabs of the state and the treatment of their special needs." (G-5498/12)

Al-Yom was distributed in all large Arab residential areas, in both cities and villages. People in charge of the newspaper searched for different ways to persuade Arab citizens to buy it on daily basis, aiming for a stable pool of readership. One method involved using connections that functionaries in the newspaper had with officials in the various governmental ministries to put pressure on Arabs, who needed various permits from the ministries, to read the newspaper on daily basis. Another method used was to approach different government functionaries, seeking to get their sympathy to financially support segments of Arab society in order to facilitate *abonnement*.[33] Another method was to look for potential readers among the Arab educated elite. For instance, the manager of the newspaper approached the Hebrew University asking for the names of Arab students, in order to contact them and encourage them to read the newspaper.[34] Another important phenomenon that is well documented in the history of the newspaper is the effort made by the people in charge to convince large Israeli merchant houses to advertise in the newspaper in order to encourage consumerism in Arab society. Two simple examples from the files of the newspaper in Israeli government archives are sufficient to illustrate the efforts made by directors of the newspaper to merge its particular interests, to increase its income from advertisement, and the general interest, to transform Arab society into consuming society. The first example is the attempt made to persuade the Israeli tea company, Wissotzky, to compete with local merchants and introduce new habits of drinking tea and advertise their products in the newspaper.[35]

The second example is the letter sent to the manager of the Israeli cigarette company, Dobik, to advertise their products in the newspaper in order to increase their usage in Arab society.[36]

Despite the efforts made to enable *Al-Yom* to continue publishing, it was closed in 1967. It was replaced in 1968 by *Al-Anba'a*, which continued *Al-Yom*'s agenda, but in a more sophisticated form, in order to better succeed in penetrating Arab society and setting its public agenda.[37] Most of the editors and journalists who had worked for *Al-Yom* continued to operate *Al-Anba'a*. They had to face new challenges after Israel occupied the Palestinian territories in the 1967 war. They sought to penetrate Palestinian society in the newly occupied territories, which was influenced by the many media outlets in these territories as well as from the Arab world. This was a task that demanded a more sophisticated policy of concealing the newspaper's official affiliation with the government. Therefore, the editors of *Al-Anba'a* sought to establish the impression that the newspaper was a mouthpiece of the average person, founded to serve its readers and address their problems.[38] Nonetheless, one should note that the aim of the newspaper was to facilitate the framing of reality in a way that would promote the interest of the government to penetrate Arab society and control it.

Like *Al-Yom, Al-Anba'a* was an establishment newspaper, financially supported by official sources. Many of the documented meetings of its board of directors reflect the financial linkage of the newspaper and the difficulties it faced in guaranteeing the support of the government.[39] The newspaper made efforts to expand its distribution and utilized the personal relationships between its leaders and governmental officials to exert pressure on those Arab citizens who were close to the ruling Labor Party and to governmental offices to read the newspaper. The leaders of the newspaper tried to win the trust of leaders of the Palestinian community in East Jerusalem and turn them into regular readers. Meetings with influential figures were initiated in order to penetrate Palestinian society and compete with local newspapers, mainly *Al-Quds,* daily.[40]

The goal behind *Al-Anba'a* was, first, to establish an image of an open public sphere into which multiple Arab voices could come and participate in the debate concerning the relationship of the state of Israel with its Arab neighbors, including the Arab minority inside the state.[41] Second, people in charge of the newspapers were eager to facilitate the acceptance of the state of Israel as a *fait accompli* that should be respected for its willingness to integrate the Arab population in building the country in the spirit of the Israeli declaration of independence. The newspapers propagated the idea that Israel was one state among many that had won their independence in the late 1940s and should therefore be conceived of as part of the wave of decolonization that had hit the world after World War II. When it came to internal Israeli affairs, the newspaper highlighted constructive measures taken toward loyal Arabs and ignored policies that aimed at land expropriation and detainment of national activists. It encouraged sympathetic Arabs to write articles that pinpointed the progress in Jewish-Arab relations, especially the eager attempt of the state officials to solve local problems in the Arab villages. The directors of the newspaper were willing to go as far as claiming that "the newspaper shall form an open stage for the expression of opinions that do not go along the official state policy, but the newspaper should make sure that the last word would be according to the spirit of governmental policies." It was agreed that the newspaper "emphasizes how Israel solves its internal problems," something that reflects the search for manipulative ways to convince the Arab readers that Israel is strong and that they should expect that their problems would be solved if they filed a complaint.[42] Third, the newspaper aimed at encouraging Arab citizens to adopt a conciliatory line to solve their problems with the state. As one of the people in charge of the newspapers stated, their aim was to support the rise of "quiet Arabs."[43]

Taking into consideration the ferocious military government, which imposed harsh policies, and the maneuvering space given to Arab citizens, the presence of a media system in Arabic created the façade of an open and liberal public sphere. This façade was facilitated by a confidence in loyal voices, which would emphasize efforts made by the state to help solve the problems of the Arab population, such as road building, infrastructures for water and electricity, as well as schools and healthcare facilities. Arab officials in the various state organs, especially school principals and Histadrut functionaries, became active opinion leaders who promoted the plans of the state to penetrate Arab society from its cultural gate. These became a solid stratum of symbolic collaborators that provided the state with the internal sympathetic voice it needed.

Al-Anba'a experienced severe economic problems with the decline of the Histadrut and the beginnings of privatization and liberalization of the Israeli economy led by the first and second Begin administrations. The withdrawal of the official support of the Histadrut led to the closure of the newspaper in 1984.[44] By the time it was closed, however, the purpose of its existence was redundant. Despite its limited number of readers, the Arab population had by then accepted the rationale of the newspaper, namely, that the Arabs are a minority inside a Jewish state. It is hard to claim that this political result was an outcome of the policies adopted by the newspaper. Nonetheless, one cannot ignore its role as a disciplining mechanism vis-à-vis the Arab population. By the mid-1980s, most Arabs viewed their Israeli citizenship as a given and had internalized their minority status in a state dominated completely by a Jewish majority.[45] As Bishara has demonstrated, the Arab political discourse inside Israel was Israelized, despite the dissenting voices of some small political movements.[46]

Al-Ittihad, the mouthpiece of the Israeli Communist Party, was an important player in the Israeli Arabic public sphere. Despite the fact that it was a weekly in its initial years and then began to appear twice a week, until it was turned into a daily in 1984, it played an important role in forging opinions and confronting ideas propagated by *Al-Anba'a*. It was widely read by Communist Party members and supporters, whose numbers increased steadily. This newspaper became a unique voice, articulating what had been conceived by the leadership of the Communist Party as the Arab population's heart and soul. It served as a platform for the intellectuals and cultural commentators excluded from the Israeli press. Despite the fact that *Al-Ittihad* began daily publication in 1984 and served as a school nurturing generations of Arab journalists with nationalist political leanings, it never succeeded in garnering broad popular support. It generally remained limited to social circles close to the Communist Party.

One can observe several reasons for the limited circulation of *Al-Ittihad*, one of which is the fact that it was delegitimized by the Israeli authorities and its readers were conceived of as dissenters who were targeted by Israeli security authorities. In a situation where the Israeli authorities controlled the maneuvering space of Arab citizens, especially their ability to access the job market, being singled out by Shabak as a dissenter was a heavy price to pay.[47] Another reason for the limited circulation of *Al-Ittihad* was the fact that it expressed the viewpoint of a political party in a social reality where fierce competition raged over political support. The Arab lists affiliated with the governing Mapai Party fought the Communist Party and its newspaper on a daily basis. They functioned as agents of fear and intimidation in Arab society in order to win support. The leaders of these lists became mediators between state agencies and the Arab public and therefore had a major influence on the chance of solving daily problems. These leaders have special traditional power in a patriarchal society, and their propaganda "war" against the Communist Party and its followers influenced the status of *Al-Ittihad*. Another reason for the limited circulation of *Al-Ittihad* was its heavy focus on political issues, especially the Israeli-Palestinian conflict. After 1967, it diverted much of its attention to the occupation policies in Palestinian society and to the international efforts made to promote negotiations between Israel and the Arab world. As a result, its main audience was drawn from the politicized segments of Arab society, which is numerically small. Like party-affiliated newspapers all over the world, *Al-Ittihad* began losing readership to the rising commercial private newspapers that provided soft news and entertainment information, as we shall see in the forthcoming chapters.

The weekly *Al-Ittihad* and the daily *Al-Anba'a* remained the leading newspapers in the Arab language that drew some attention from Arab elites until the early 1980s. These two newspapers attracted a relatively large number of leaders in two antagonistic elite groups that began emerging in Arab society. The readers of *Al-Ittihad* came from the elite circles affiliated with or close to the Communist Party. This elite group supported the establishment of the state of Israel and called for the full integration of Arab citizens on equal footing.[48] Part of this elite went so far as to call for the drafting of Arab youth into army service, based on the belief that Israel was going to develop into an egalitarian democracy.[49] When Israel maintained the military government and persecuted Arab Communist leaders, the tone of the media organ of the party began to change. *Al-Ittihad* gradually became the platform of pro-national Communists who balanced between internationalism, as a basic value that ought to be promoted, and national affiliation, as cultural identity that ought to be respected.[50] It reflected the shifts taking place within the Communist elite, which grew continuously and became a vocal opposition to Israeli policies toward the Arab minority.[51]

In contrast, the readers of *Al-Anba'a* belonged to what have been called the accommodative leaders.[52] Although many of the readers of *Al-Anba'a* did not read it out of choice, especially schoolteachers, a group of Arabs had become used to its presence. Since *Al-Anba'a* sought to give voice to those Arabs who believed in Israel's endeavors to improve the living conditions of the Arab community, it drew its readership from among ambitious leaders. These were strong propagators of the official ideology that established a connection between good behavior and improving conditions. This connection proved to be incorrect, especially against the background of the harsh suppression of political activists and the massive confiscation of Arab land. As a result, the readership of *Al-Anba'a* declined until it folded in the early 1980s. This does not mean that the elite who had identified with *Al-Anba'a* have vanished from the Israeli political and cultural scene. This elite, who experienced major changes, remained part and parcel of the Arab social and political scene, most apparent in their support of Zionist political parties.[53]

The presence of *Al-Ittihad, Al-Yom,* and later *Al-Anba'a* encouraged other political movements in the Arab community to issue their own publications. As a result, some people in the Arab community were exposed to other local Arabic national publications, such as the newspaper circulated irregularly by Al-Ard in the late 1950s and early 1960s and the newspaper of the Abna'a Al-Balad (Sons of the Village) movement, *Al-Raya,* which was circulated in small numbers in the late 1980s. These publications reflected the rising pluralism in Arab society and marked a flowering of the domestic Arab public sphere in which authentic opinions engaged in debate regarding various topics that concerned Arab society in Israel.[54] However, despite the importance of these publications in terms of content, they never enjoyed widespread distribution, mainly because of policies of the Israeli authorities toward them. Al-Ard publications were never legalized, so they had to come out as sporadic and separate onetime publications, a production format that allowed the publication to forgo the procurement of licensing required under Israeli law. The efforts of Al-Ard to acquire a license to issue a regular newspaper were rejected by the interior minister, who is empowered to legalize the publication of newspapers in Israel. The leaders of Al-Ard found ways to overcome the legal limits put on their efforts to issue a newspaper but only for a short time. The entire movement was targeted and declared illegal in November 1964 by the defense minister, based on the authority granted to him by the emergency regulations of 1945.[55] His decision was declared legal by the Israeli Supreme Court, thereby putting an end to an important effort made by Arab leaders to raise an authentic voice in Arab society in the Israeli public sphere in general and the local Arab public sphere in particular.

Al-Ard publications, together with several other party newspapers—e.g., *Al-Mirsad,* published by Mapam, the United Labor Party—succeeded in attracting many Arab journalists, who presented ideas that challenged political positions close to the state propaganda line. Rashed Hussein, Fawzi Al-Asmar, Rasmi Biadseh, Muhamad Watad, and other Palestinian novelists and poets were active journalists in *Al-Mirsad,* turning it into an attractive newspaper that managed to partially express the needs of Arab society without challenging the Israeli system of cultural control. They wrote columns and reports that challenged official positions, as expressed in *Al-Yom,* on the one hand, and the positions presented by prominent figures in *Al-Ittihad,* such as Emile Habibi and Emile Tuma, on the other. The mere existence of *Al-Mirsad* reflected the sophistication of the cultural surveillance of the Israeli control system, which enabled some outlet for Arab critical ideas, while confining it within the conceptual framework that legitimated the Jewish state. The authorities thereby managed to project an image of a liberal state without losing their ability to exercise control and surveillance policies.

Local broadcast information has been available in Arabic since 1948. The Israeli radio broadcast news in Arabic twice a week in order to counterbalance the news from the Arab world. It was only after 1958 that Kol Yisrael (Voice of Israel) initiated a regular radio channel, composed of news and other limited programming in Arabic. This broadcast was run by Oriental Jews who were proficient in Arabic, had some journalistic experience, and were submissive to the information policies dictated by the Prime Minister's Office. This radio service still operates, and until recently, a considerable portion of Arab society listened to its broadcasts.

The Israeli radio station in Arabic has played a major role in providing both basic information and a comprehensive interpretation of reality to the Arab public. It gave the Arab community the sense that it represents their interests by offering programs in which Arab citizens were able to communicate their problems. One of the well-known programs was *Jayeb Le Salam* (Bringing Me a Hello), based on a format in which Arab citizens voiced their concerns and sent their regards to refugee relatives living in the Arab world.[56] These programs sought to form a "bridge" between Palestinians who remained in Israel and those who had become refugees. Another important program was *Ibn Al-Rafidayn* (Son of Mesopotamia), which was edited and moderated by Daud Al-Natur, an Iraqi Jew, who spoke to his listeners in an Iraqi accent, presenting a special perspective on Middle Eastern reality. According to some sources, these programs were used by Israeli intelligence to pass codified messages to agents operating in the Arab world.[57] Another program that used creative methods to disseminate the hegemonic ideology of the state was *Between the Citizen and the Authorities,* which enabled Arab citizens to call and discuss problems they had with the state authorities. The person in charge of the program, who presented himself under an Arabic name, Zaki Al-Mukhtar, but was an Iraqi Jew (Yitzhak Ben Ovadia), used to contact the authorities and try to solve the problem on the air or at least to establish a contact between the citizen and the people in charge in that particular governmental office. Such programs were oriented toward drawing Arab citizens closer to state authorities and giving them the sense that Israeli radio was concerned with the difficulties that Arab citizens faced daily.

In the last decades and as a result of the need to compete with alternative radio stations from Arab countries, such as Sawt al-Arab in the past and Ajyal from Ramallah today, with radio stations from Europe broadcasting in Arabic, such as the BBC or Monte Carlo, or with local radio stations, such as Radio Ashams, Israeli radio in Arabic has introduced some changes in its programming. It has opened up to new voices and integrated new cultural programs that aim at attracting an audience from the younger generation. In the last few years, Arab journalists and reporters were promoted to leading positions in the radio station. This change has strengthened the authentic Arab voice in the various programs of the station. Notwithstanding these changes, the radio is still dominated by Jewish managers of Oriental origin, whose primary aim is to guarantee that the radio serves Israeli national interests. This is especially true when it comes to transmitting the voice of Israeli officials and introducing the official Israeli understanding of the Israeli-Palestinian conflict. When it comes to programs dealing with state-minority relations inside Israel, there is a good deal of freedom of speech, which is balanced by voicing different opinions that represent different positions regarding issues of concern to the Arab public. The pluralistic façade manages to present the station as liberal and open without having to adopt Arab national positions. The outcome is guaranteed by the composition of the team of journalists who work in the radio, who are mostly accommodative and loyal to the official understanding of Israeli Arab citizenship.

Since the late 1960s, Israeli television has employed a similar strategy. The Israeli Broadcasting Authority (IBA)—an ostensibly public body that manages and monitors domestic public television production—was for quite a long time a department in the Prime Minister's Office. It used transmissions in Arabic to shape the Arab population's media agenda and public opinion. As was stated on the website of Israeli radio (Sawt Israel), "Sawt Israel in Arabic acted in its initial days to disseminate Israeli propaganda in order to counteract Arab radio stations."

As a result of the geopolitical changes initiated by the 1967 war, in tandem with the technological advances and transformations that overtook the Israeli media, the conditions of Arab society within Israel's media space altered, but not necessarily for the better. As noted, no autonomous electronic Arabic media institutions were in existence. Israel's expansion into the West Bank and the establishment of the IBA altered the media environment. The dwindling number of Arabic-language newspapers published by Zionist political parties did not mean that a serious change in Israeli media policies was taking place. Control of the collective Arab memory continued to occupy the attention of those in charge of Israeli media policy and practice. This policy received added impetus when Israeli television was introduced within the framework of the IBA. The Israel Broadcasting Authority Law (1965), the institution's legal foundation, expounds on the official position regarding the Arab audience. Section 3 of the law refers to Arabic-language broadcasts to be conducted for the benefit of "Arabic-speaking residents," as well as to promote and support mutual understanding and peace with neighboring countries.[58] The law's wording refers not to "Arab citizens" but to "Arabic-speaking residents," as determined by state policy. That is, the establishment of this media channel was not targeted at filling the needs of Israel's Arab citizens, but was rather to ensure the Arab population's loyalty and control by means of a hegemonic media regime.

In time, Arab society adapted itself to Israel's media map. This process was driven by increasing levels of education and integration into Jewish Israeli society, observed in the ubiquity of spoken Hebrew among the Arab population. Yet, like other accommodations, the spread of Hebrew was not by choice; it was the outcome of total political and economic dependence on state institutions and the Jewish economy. The number of Arab readers of Hebrew-language newspapers increased, as did the number of

Arab listeners to Hebrew-language radio broadcasts. Arab viewers of news broadcast on Channel 1, the sole Israeli channel operating until the early 1990s, increased as well.

Similar to trends in media consumption surfacing elsewhere and in Jewish society in particular, radio and television became the principal sources of information about events transpiring locally and internationally. The strength of Kol Yisrael radio and Israeli television broadcasts in Arabic derived from the fact that they devoted much of their programming to local Arab affairs and were the only media outlets to do so. Local Arab affairs did not interest any media institution in the Arab countries, giving Arabic-speaking Israeli media outlets the ability to become the "voice" of the Arab population and hence win the loyalty of most of the Arab audience.

The only competitors to these sources of information originated in the Arab world, primarily Sawt al-Arab (Voice of the Arabs) radio broadcasts from Cairo and television broadcasts from Jordan and Egypt and, until the civil war erupted in 1975, from Lebanon. The attraction of Egyptian and Lebanese television broadcasts decreased, however, with the decline of Nasserism and the outbreak of the Lebanese civil war. Jordanian television thus became the primary Arab provider of programming to Arab viewers in Israel, for many years serving as the only bridge linking Arab society in Israel to the Arab world prior to the satellite era. Since Jordanian television broadcasting was state controlled, it tended not to relate to political affairs that could be of interest for the politicized strata in the Arab society in Israel. Despite the fact that cultural programs were of interest to the Arab audience in Israel, the political news was narrow and mostly limited to the activities of the Jordanian king, something that drew no genuine interest in Israeli Arab society.

Before we move ahead to have a closer look at the recent communicative behavior of the Palestinian minority, it is important to shed light on the roots of the double consciousness and the hybrid collective behavior that characterize this society in the communicative realm. The patterns of communicative behavior that characterize the Palestinian minority, which asserts its in-betweenness, is not a sudden phenomenon that emerged only recently. Deeply rooted, it began emerging in the early years of the Israeli state, resulting from existential necessities that, given the circumstances during the years of the military government, are fully understandable. The instinctive search for survival in circumstances in which hundreds of thousands were exiled and thousands were killed was a very strong impulse, something that has been widely proven by the behavior of defeated communities in various places today.

When examining the existential reality of the Palestinians who remained in Israel, one senses the effort made to balance between nationalistic pride and love for the land, which were captured in Arab poetry and literature, and the need for accommodating the new reality imposed by the defeat of 1948. For most Palestinians in Israel, fear and a sense of capitulation were expressed in their resignation to the rules of the new political game, even if this was only considered to be a default preference. As already mentioned, state mechanisms of surveillance, orchestrated by the military govern-ment, which sought to strengthen the role of the clan and ethnic leaders in Arab towns and villages, encouraged the development of behavior pat-terns expressing the overall population's de facto "reconciliation" with the new reality. In this context, it is important to point out that most Palestin-ians who remained on their land were villagers characterized by patterns of thought that were traditional in nature. Therefore, in light of the fact that the political, cultural, and economic leadership of the Palestinian nation-alist movement did not remain within the physical territory of Israel, the local traditional leadership became the central focus. Social structure and official policy served as fertile ground for the construction and implanta-tion of a collective consciousness characterized by the principles of accom-modation and adaptation to the new reality. These efforts, promoted by the state, contradicted attempts made by local national leaders to resist clien-talism, the strengthening of local and familial loyalties and the consequent elimination of national patriotism.

Instinctive attachment to the homeland and intuitive devotion to the place produced patterns of thought and behavior that combined national patriotism with a certain reluctant acceptance of the new political reality. In many cases this patriotism was camouflaged by universal ideologies like Communist internationalism or appeared in a humanitarian and cosmo-politan guise. This was expressed by ambivalent political behavior and in complex literary works that formulated clear statements discreetly or even cryptically.

Many Palestinians in Israel wanted to maintain the two worlds—the old Palestinian and the new Israeli—simultaneously. The tension between the need for a sense of belonging—which was partially generated by the absence of ontological security, re-created on a daily basis in political-eco-nomic reality—and the burden of survival gave rise to patterns of hybrid collective behavior. For example, many Palestinians in Israel accepted the convention that voting for Knesset candidates appearing on the Arab lists, which were associated with the Mapai Party (the predecessor to the current Labor Party in Israel), was the best way to advance the Arab population's interests.[59] This belief was translated into political reality, the sincere hope being that it would convince the authorities of the Arab's good intentions and cause them to show him compassion.[60]

One manifestation of such hybrid collective conduct can be found in the celebrations of the Israeli day of independence that took place in Arab towns and villages, on the one hand, and the struggle against state policies of surveillance and control by insisting and emphasizing traditional patterns of social solidarity and economic cooperation, on the other. It became a common notion that Israeli state leaders, including army officers, were welcomed in big receptions by accommodating traditional leaders in Arab villages that sought to convey their loyalty to the state. The Israeli flag decorated most streets of these villages that lacked basic roads, electricity, and running water. This pattern of behavior was augmented by a trend in works of literature and journalism that praised Israeli reality, produced primarily by Arab educators employed by the Ministry of Education. The peak of this process was the poem, which nobody endorses anymore, although it is widespread knowledge that it was written by Jamal Kaawar, celebrating Israeli Independence Day as a national day for Arab citizens:

In my country's independence day / the crooning birds start singing
Happiness spread over in all villages / between the plain land and the valley.

Another example that illustrates this trend in Arab efforts to reconcile Israeli policies and meet official expectations of loyalty and obedience is the poem written by Sami Mazigiet:

A beam sparkled in the Middle East / flash lighting the gloomy night
Is this a comet in the sky / pointing pagans to the place of the manger?
Or is it Israel whose light shines / like a sun illuminating the Western sky?[61]

The sense of precariousness with regard to security and the constant fear of the authorities' arbitrary hand prompted many Palestinians to resign themselves to the perception that being accepted by the state and achieving any kind of integration into it was the best technique to guarantee survival. They did not necessarily accept the Zionist ethos or act out of a conviction that the state was also theirs. Nevertheless, in the absence of an established intellectual, political, or cultural elite, over time this technique became the strategy that led a majority of Palestinians to live within the conventions of the hegemonic Israeli national discourse, albeit without adopting its ideological and normative underpinnings. In an endeavor to survive, Israeli Palestinians integrated components of their national and cultural identity with their new identity as citizens of the state. On the one hand, they voted for the Mapai lists of Knesset candidates and hosted state leaders, including security officials, while, on the other, they listened to the speeches of Egyptian president

Gamal Abdel Nasser—whom they idolized—on Sawt al-Arab (Voice of the Arabs) radio broadcasts from Cairo. Azmi Bishara expressed this consciousness well when he said, "The 'Israeli Arabs' are without a doubt the artisans of 'catering,' but also artists of the game of reality and the stage."[62]

Parallel to the accommodative collective conduct that reached absurdity have emerged other patterns of collective behavior that are a much more sophisticated blending of resistance with pragmatic behavior that guaranteed survival. Those who put the deepest imprint on Palestinian behavior patterns in Israel and embodied the aspiration to strike a better and more dignified combination between the Palestinian past and Israeli reality of the present were the earlier mentioned growing Arab elite affiliated with the Communist Party. These leaders were Arab patriots as well as realistic politicians. They sought to develop a new type of civic patriotism based on class affiliation that overcomes the negative implications of narrow ethnic nationalism common among most Jews in Israel. They also sought not to yield to the submissive behavioral patterns that characterized part of the traditional leadership of the Arab community and some Arab intellectuals who were employed by the Ministry of Education to promote an Israeli Arab political identity affiliated with the Jewish state. Arab Communist leaders sought to develop a political ideology and ethos that could balance between their national and cultural identity and their new civic affiliation. They sought this goal in the pages of their publications, the leading of which was *Al-Ittihad*.

Arab Communist leaders maintained national slogans that were redefined to accommodate the Arab presence in Israel. While utilizing Arab national imagery, they sought to establish clear boundaries between the new reality of the Arab citizens of Israel and the rest of the Arab world. Although this process was not necessarily completely international, it did lead to the development of a new ambivalent political discourse that escaped the tight confines of space, place, and identity. The Communist Party that produced the emerging Arab political and intellectual elite in Israel promoted a cultural identity that is proudly Palestinian-Arab and a political identity that is Israeli. It introduced the political slogan of "two states for two nations," stressing the Green Line as the legitimate political border for the state of Israel. Simultaneously, Arab party leaders viewed themselves as an integral part of the progressive Arab forces that admired Arab culture but did not fall into the trap of chauvinist nationalism. The acceptance of the slogan of two states for two peoples became the central marker that differentiated the party from Zionist parties in the Israeli political system. Inserting this slogan into the discourse of the party was the purest expression of acceptance of Israeli citizenship, on principle, as the legal-political framework in which Arabs in the future would struggle for their civil rights as Israelis. Within this framework Palestinians in Israel became "the Arab public in Israel," a depiction that blurred national affiliation as a central mobilizing mechanism and as a source of romantic affiliation. This did not mean dismissing the Palestinian national affiliation, but rather neutralizing this identity as a central motivating force of political struggle. To compensate for this change in the party's political discourse, the Palestinian right of self-determination in the West Bank and Gaza Strip was heavily emphasized in the publications of the party. The Palestinian struggle for independence was given constant headlines in *Al-Ittihad,* and Palestinian culture and history won much attention in the literary works published in *Al-Jadeed.* This emphasis on Palestinian affairs has led to the constant nationalization of the Communist Party, leading to what has been termed by some analysts as national Communism.[63]

Arab Communist leaders expressed their patriotic positions in a universal civic language. They propagated the interests of the Arab community in Israel while downplaying its nationalist sentiment and favoring a civil worldview. Their faith in their Marxist-Leninist thinking allowed them to bridge the gaps between the political reality in which they lived and the political discourse that they espoused. This perhaps explains the statements of Communist leader Tawfik Toubi when he said that "Communist Party membership is fostering man's most inner virtues—unbounded devotion and willingness for self-sacrifice for matters of the people and the working class, undaunted readiness to fight while maintaining modesty and integrity of character."[64] Although Toubi does not name the people to whom he is referring, it is unreasonable to assume that he was speaking of a people other than the Israelis. Israeliness was viewed as a possible civil identity that Jews and Arabs can share if they swear allegiance to the legacy of the working class as formulated in the Marxist tradition.[65] The political discourse of the party denounced both Zionism and Arab nationalism as antagonistic to brotherhood and unity of "nations." They envisioned a civic state based on universal values in which Jews can have a refuge from external threats.

In a political speech, startling at the time, to the 13th Congress of the Communist Party, Emile Habibi claimed: "In defense of the Arab-Palestinian nation's right to self-determination and the right of the refugees to return to their land, our party defends the right of the people of Israel to self-determination and a peaceful life, freedom and security in its homeland."[66] Habibi's speech expresses his worldview regarding the conditional moral relationship between Palestinian and Jewish rights of self-determination. What is interesting in the context of this speech is his strategic location as speaker in relation to Israel, on the one hand, and to the Palestinian people, on the other. In his speech Habibi uses the concept "our country," referring to Israel. He, for instance, asked, "What good comes to our country or any other in the Middle East from being dragged after [the chariot of imperialism]?" In another context he says, "Many parties exist in *our country*, parties turning right and parties turning left." As was already said, Habibi's expression "our country" refers to Israel, which according to his belief is supposed to be a country/state for both Arabs and Jews equally. Hence he claims:

> Our party is proud to have captured the support of the Arab masses on our land. This support proves that the path of our party is the path of peace, brotherhood—the future of Israel. Our Arab nation is proud to support the Communist Party, despite the means of oppression and terror it faces. This is proof of the maturation of our nation's consciousness, its readiness to fight, and its faith that democratic powers will be victorious in our land. This is proof of our nation's devotion to Jewish-Arab brotherhood, which the Communist Party has built and established, and to the confidence that Jews and Arabs can live in a *shared homeland* in equality, brotherhood, and peace. (emphasis added)[67]

Despite Habibi's strategic stand on civil discourse within the state's framework, he attacks Israeli policies and demands a return to the United Nations partition plan of 1947. Habibi's position reflects his civic patriotism, as evident in the following:

> The Communists, because they are Communists, feel maximal responsibility for the nation's future. The Communist Party is the conscience and dignity of the nation. Therefore, the label Jewish and Arab Communists give the path within their party's framework as the only way to settle the Israeli-Arab conflict is conclusive proof that this plan expresses the true interests of the two nations and is the program of patriots with the heaviest sense of responsibility toward the nation and its future. The Communists are patriots who proudly withstood all chauvinistic incitement and police terror.[68]

This political stand, reflected in Habibi's political discourse, accepted Arabs in Israel as part of the "Israeli nation," while simultaneously demanding the right to self-determination for the Palestinians according to the partition plan, and it expressed his honest patriotic feelings. The primary concern of the Communists was to liberate the Arab population inside Israel from the yoke of the military government, achieve equality between Arabs and Jews, and establish a shared civic culture of Israeliness. On the other hand, there was a consistent demand for Israeli recognition of the rights of the Palestinians to establish a state alongside the state of Israel, to which would be returned territories captured by Israel in the war of 1948 and to which homeland refugees could return.

These demands, expressed repeatedly by the party's Arab leaders, especially in *Al-Ittihad,* became a bone of contention between Jewish and Arab leaders in the party, until it finally split in 1965.[69] Arab leaders were not fond of the growing intimacy between Jewish Communists and state leaders. This growing intimacy led Arab leaders to suspect some of their Jewish comrades and raise questions concerning their loyalty to a civic model of the Israeli nation.[70] The final split in 1965 could be seen as an attempt of the Arab leaders of the party to assert the civic option, especially when the process of abolishing the military government was reaching its peak. With the termination of the military government in 1966, Arab Communists became more and more immersed in the daily battles over the authorities' policies of discrimination and oppression against Arab citizens of the state. The fight for civil equality became the embodiment of their patriotism, of their commitment to a civic model of citizenship that respects the equal access of all citizens to state institutions. They invested much of their effort toward achieving distributive justice for their constituency. This battle was conducted on two central spheres. The first was in the Israeli Knesset, and the second was in the pages of the party's publications.

More than anything else, the party slogan of "Israeli patriotism and proletariat internationalism" captioned the civic model that characterized the Communist leaders' worldview. Arab activists in the party stood at attention for the singing of the Israeli national anthem before the Israeli flag at the party congress. In demonstrations, the party arranged for Israeli flags and red flags to be hoisted side by side. Arab party members identified with the party slogans, which had Israeli nuances, from an idealistic belief that the moral basis on which Israel rested was based on a brotherhood of nations, which also necessitated the creation of a Palestinian state alongside Israel. The "protest" policy, on which the party prided itself, rejected the Zionist characteristic of the state and the signs of capitalism that had begun to appear in its economy.

The Communists believed in a state that would express the Jewish nation's right to self-determination without harming the moral right of the Palestinian people to establish their homeland and return the refugees to their homes. The class perception of the Israeli-Palestinian conflict drove many Arabs with a strong patriotic awareness to believe that there was no clash of issues in Jewish-Arab cooperation based on the Communist Party platform.

The power of the Communist Party arose from the fact that it was the lone non-Zionist party that openly criticized the government's oppressive policies and demanded equal rights for Arab residents. Arab support for the party began rising when it was targeted by the authorities as a result of its critical voice vis-à-vis the government, mainly after the Kufur Kassem massacre and the Sinai War in 1956. The constant criticism that appeared in *Al-Ittihad* and the magazine *Al-Jadeed* was interpreted as a patriotic stand by an increasing portion of the Arab public and reinforced support of the party during Knesset elections. Arab leaders in the party saw themselves as representatives of Arab society in the Knesset and acted according to a sense of patriotic mission. The party won an increasing majority of the Arab votes in Knesset elections and dominated the Arab political scene in the 1970s and 1980s.

Communist leaders saw themselves as the intellectual vanguard of Arab citizens in Israel. They were compelled to fight government discriminatory policies. But they also "rejected irresponsible infantile revolutionary extremism," as Tawfiq Zayyad said in a contribution to the *Journal of Palestine Studies* in 1976.[71] They claimed that "irresponsible Arab chauvinist statements, threatening Israelis with destruction, played into Zionist and imperialist propaganda prior to the June 1967 war."[72] Therefore, moderation and "muddling through" was seen as the right path to follow in order to achieve a just solution to the Palestinian problem and bring Israel to recognize "the right of Arabs to exist and to develop on their land and in their homeland."[73]

The battle of the Arab Communists contained a strong cultural dimension that strove to preserve Arab cultural tradition and the population's nationalistic identity through various means, the main one being the opening of the newspapers and the magazines of the party as a platform for Arab authors and poets. In the absence of an independent Arab press, *Al-Ittihad* and *Al-Jadeed* became the primary forum for Arab cultural productions, opposing the various government means of mobilization among the Arab educated strata. The media organs of the Communist Party became a major platform for critical voices vis-à-vis state policies toward Arab society and the nucleus of an Arab public sphere that set a worldview contentious to official state positions concerning the cultural and political orientation of the Arab minority. This public sphere grew tremendously in the 1980s when various numbers of privately owned Arabic newspapers were established, feeding the growing pluralism in Arab society. The following chapter follows these developments, seeking to characterize the Arabic public sphere in Israel from the 1980s until today.

Arab Media Space in the Jewish State

Seeking New Communicative Action

The state of Israel has acted vigorously but unsuccessfully to dissociate the Arab population from its cultural space and historical past.[1] Arab society has not yielded to Israeli efforts but instead has developed various strategies to cope with this situation.[2] The struggle for survival has been complex and varied. One of the first stratagems applied was the development of an oppositional public sphere. As illustrated in the previous chapter, this public sphere was rather narrow under the military government. It has experienced major changes in the time since then.

To understand the emergence, differentiation, and pluralization of the Arab public sphere in Israel, it is necessary to differentiate between various historical periods, based on the changing characteristics of the media institutions and the communicative behavior, especially media consumption, in each period. Historically, it is possible to differentiate between the period in which the press and the radio were the main media institutions available in Arab society and a period when television took their place. In addition, one should differentiate between a period in which party-affiliated newspapers versus state-affiliated newspapers dominated the journalistic scene and a period when the latter vanishes and a new media scene emerges in which party-affiliated newspapers compete with private newspapers that are not politically committed but are seeking profit. Accordingly, it is possible to differentiate between four periods in which major changes took place. These periods are continuous and do not reflect interruptions in the development of media institutions. Periodization will facilitate our understanding of the forces active in shaping the Arab public sphere and help us follow the major changes. It is important to note that the Arab media scene after 1948 is in no sense a continuation of the journalistic scene that characterized Palestinian society before that year.

The Initial Stages of the Arab Public Sphere, 1948–67

The Arab public sphere between 1948 and 1967 was quite restricted. Limitations on freedom of expression that were imposed by the military government and the fear of expulsion suppressed voices that might have expressed the views and attitudes of the Arab minority. The difficulty that Al-Ard experienced in getting permission to issue a newspaper reflected a major effort by the Israeli authorities to stifle Palestinian national voices. The military government did not tolerate any Arab political organization that propagated the Palestinian affiliation of the Arab minority or criticized the Israeli discriminatory policies on this ground. Arab citizens of the state did not enjoy the freedom of expression that characterized the Jewish public, and so Arab publications issued by Arabs faced major distribution difficulties and were forcefully closed when they challenged the limits set for them by the military government.

Arab media space was mainly occupied by the newspaper *Al-Ittihad*, affiliated with the Communist Party, and other party-sponsored publications, such as the quarterly *Al-Jadeed*. These newspapers offered a platform for the criticisms voiced by Arab intellectuals and political leaders.[3] The elite close to the party were the best educated among the Arab population, and most read *Al-Ittihad* and *Al-Jadeed*. Most of what has been categorized by the Palestinian novelist Ghassan Kanafani as "resistance literature" was published in *Al-Ittihad* and *Al-Jadeed*.[4] Governmental pressure was tremendous, and these newspapers were closed or threatened with closure on numerous occasions. Censorship was common, and coverage of state policies that violated the basic human rights of Palestinians was softened. The *Kol Ha-Am* affair and the ruling of the Israeli Supreme Court defined a new relationship between state authorities and the newspapers and journals of the Communist Party.[5] Since that ruling, the policies of censorship and control of information have had to change. New means of surveillance were introduced in order to limit the influence of the *Al-Ittihad,* one of which was the intensive delegitimation of the Communist Party and the public intimidation of its supporters.[6]

In the late 1950s and early 1960s, part of the Arab public was exposed to the publications of Al-Ard (The Land). This movement emerged from the remnants of the national Palestinian leadership that had remained inside Israel. The founding gathering of the movement was convened in 1959, led by Mansur Kardush, Habib Kahwaji, Saleh Baransi, and Sabri Jiryis. Its emergence marked the failure of the Israeli control mechanisms to uproot or silence national activity in the Arabic community. Al-Ard leaders applied to the interior minister for an operating permit in accordance with the 1933 press ordinance. The military governor refused. Since issuing a onetime publication did not require a permit, the leaders of Al-Ard tried to bypass the governor's decision by issuing publications under various names, such as *Al-Ard, The Good Land,* and *The Smell of the Land,* which were edited randomly. Circulation was rather limited. Nonetheless, these publications reached the educated Arab elite in various locations.[7] When Al-Ard was declared an illegal organization by the Israeli defense minister in 1964, the publications died away. Attempts to institutionalize the movement as a political party and run for Knesset elections in 1965 were unsuccessful, and Al-Ard leaders were administratively detained.[8]

During the 1950s, but especially after 1956, some Arabs listened to Sawt Al-Arab, the Cairo-based radio station, especially for news about the policies adopted by Arab states to solve the Palestinian problem. Arab citizens listened in particular to the speeches of Egyptian president Gamal Abdel Nasser, who was considered a hero. This pattern of communicative behavior spread with increased access to media technology, such as transistor radios, which were easily affordable and which enabled people to tune into such broadcasts from home.

Notwithstanding this behavior, the Arab public sphere was limited, and only a small number of Arab citizens had access to newspapers and radio broadcasts. This was influenced by the fact that most Arabs were unable to read.

Adapting the Arab Public Sphere
to the Emerging Regional Reality, 1967–85

The geopolitical transformations following the 1967 Six-Day War also played their part. After 1967, the Arab population in Israel acquired access to the Palestinian population in the West Bank and the Gaza Strip. The involuntary reunification of the two parts of the Palestinian people who were living on the homeland soil had a deep impact on them. They became aware of the strong national and patriotic sentiments among the Palestinian population of the newly occupied territories. The interaction between the two communities quickly resulted in a rise in national sentiment among the Arab population in Israel.[9]

Due to the Israeli-Egyptian peace agreement, contact between Arab society and Arabs abroad, particularly in Egypt, also became possible. Thousands traveled to Egypt and were exposed to the richness of Arab cultural heritage and to the solidity of Arab tradition manifested in various ways in Egyptian society. These processes, which counteracted Israeli government influence, reduced the effectiveness of Israel's efforts to control the content of the public debate.

On the other hand, by 1967 the Arab population had experienced Israeli rule for nineteen years. The level of education among Arab youth was on the rise, and a growing number of Arabs were acquiring knowledge of the Hebrew language. This process has eased the entrance of educated Arab citizens into the Israeli job market and facilitated the integration of Arabs into the Israeli public sphere. Moreover, Arabs who worked in Jewish towns began having access to Hebrew newspapers, radio stations, and television programming.[10] Simultaneously, the Arab search for strategies that could challenge Israeli control and surveillance policies continued. *Al-Ittihad* became a central media tool for promoting counterhegemonic opinions, which reached a turning point with the outburst of the Land Day events on 30 March 1976. The success of the Arab Communist leadership at mobilizing the Arab population and the rise of the clarifying voice of *Al-Ittihad*, as compared with the official daily newspaper *Al-Anba'a*, led to a concomitant rise in state control policies, which aimed at stopping the growing power of the Communist Party and, after 1977, of Al-Jabha in Arab society. In this context, the first Begin government declared illegal the Nazareth rally, which was supposed to gather Arab political forces to protest the peace agreement with Egypt and government policies toward Palestinians in the occupied territories. Begin also threatened to close *Al-Ittihad*.

In response, *Al-Ittihad* became a daily newspaper in 1984. The Communist Party had won the support of a growing number of voters in the elections of 1977 and 1981, and it needed to communicate with them on a daily basis. There was also a growing challenge to the newspaper, manifested in the rise of a new private weekly (*Assennara*) owned by a well-known journalist, Lutfi Mashour, who had long worked for the official newspaper, *Al-Anba'a*. Despite the fact that *Assennara* began as an advertisement blat, it still represented a new development in the Arab media scene that could draw readers and present news that challenged the discourse of *Al-Ittihad*.

In 1972, a new extraparliamentary Arab movement emerged, founded by Muhammad Kewan from the Um Al-Fahem village in the Triangle area and named Abna'a Al-Balad (Sons of the Village/Homeland). Although Abna'a Al-Balad did not issue its own publication until 1987, it did use pamphlets. The movement flourished mostly among university students. Its activity on campuses seriously challenged the monopoly that the Communist Party had had on the representation of the Arab national voice in Israel. The challenge of the Abna'a Al-Balad movement differed from that of the Arab lists affiliated with the dominant Zionist Mapai Party. Abna'a Al-Balad spoke a national language that sought to empty the discourse of the Communist Party of substantial meaning. The debate between Abna'a Al-Balad and the Communist Party, and later with Al-Jabha, has enriched the Arab public sphere and intensified the competition for dominance over Arab public opinion.

Meanwhile, Israeli television began broadcasting in Arabic. Although the programs in the Arabic language were reduced along the way, until they were set for only ninety minutes in the early evening hours, they won a wide audience. Soon television viewers outnumbered newspaper readers. Therefore, the Israeli authorities began shifting their investment from *Al-Anba'a* to ensure that Israeli television in Arabic met expectations, namely, by introducing programs that fell within the ideological and political framework set by the Israeli foreign ministry.

The people appointed to deal with managing the Arabic department in Israeli television were mainly Jews of Egyptian origin who had had some experience with broadcasting and program production. Salim Fatael and Shlomo Inbari were appointed as members of the founding committee that established Israeli Television Broadcasting, and they became central figures in setting up the programs in Arabic.[11] Several Arab journalists were hired, but they initially remained outside policymaking circles. Their reports attempted to mirror debates taking place within Arab society in Israel as well as to reflect some of the political processes in the occupied Palestinian territories. This coverage gave priority to voices and events that promoted Israeli control and surveillance policies, instead of representing the authentic needs of Arab society, something that led many Arabs to watch Arabic television programs for pragmatic reasons only, so as to know about developments taking place in the political system, the economy, education, and other daily issues.

The Rise of Two Schools of Journalism, 1984–92

Major changes occurred during the 1980s. In 1984, *Al-Anba'a* vanished. As a result of economic difficulties, especially the decline of the economic power of the Histadrut, resulting from the privatization policies led by the Likud government, and due to the rise of alternative media organizations, especially television, the newspaper lost its efficacy and therefore its financial backing. Since the newspaper could not have continued based on its own revenues from advertisements, it had to be closed.

By the mid-1980s, an extensive network of Arabic-language newspapers had been developed. Weeklies such as *Assennara* (1983), *Kul al-Arab* (1987), and *Panorama* (1988) began to compete with the Communist Party–affiliated newspaper, *Al-Ittihad*. These developments have markedly changed the Arab public sphere and influenced media consumption patterns. Since no previous studies have examined patterns of newspaper reading in Arab society in Israel, it is hard to trace the exact impact of these weeklies. Notwithstanding this difficulty, it is possible to discern that the rise of these newspapers has led many more Arab citizens to start reading newspapers in

Arabic and thereby to have access to information and know about developments that were not previously available to them.

The Arabic weeklies, especially *Assennara,* have introduced a new school of journalism that is not politically or ideologically committed but is motivated by profit and therefore willing to publish any piece of information that might translate into revenue. Because it seeks to reach all segments of Arab society, it brings forth a wide spectrum of voices that are not always in concert. This pattern of journalism is different from that which had been known in Arab society, and therefore it managed to draw new readers into the expanding public sphere. In turn, the new newspapers have led to a pluralizing of the Arab public sphere, especially when we consider the fierce competition between the private newspapers, something that will be addressed later.

Simultaneously, the private newspapers commercialized the Arabic media scene in Israel and introduced a new journalistic model, according to which the news is a vehicle that promotes profit-making, and therefore media coverage is subject to new economic considerations. This change is particularly important because party-affiliated newspapers were not a profitable venture, and therefore their editorial lines and the news they produced were never determined by economic calculations or profit considerations.

Assennara began as a marketing vehicle for a large Nazareth advertising company. Lutfi Mashour, the owner and first editor, had worked for *Al-Anba'a* and written for Hebrew newspapers, such as *Maariv.* He also owned an advertising firm that worked with Israeli governmental agencies and with Israeli commercial companies that sought to advertise in Arab society. Mashour introduced a new journalistic model that resembled the commercial Israeli Hebrew newspapers, such as *Yedeot Aharonot* and *Maariv.* He was the first in Arab society in Israel to understand the major social and economic changes taking place in Israel in general and in Arab society in particular. His venture was risky economically as well as on the journalistic level. But his speculation was not misplaced. Arab society was ready for commercial newspapers, and *Assennara* managed very quickly to become a vibrant newspaper that established a balance between social, political, economic, and cultural news and advertisements.

In 1985, upon winning two seats in the Israeli Knesset, the Progressive List for Peace began publishing a newspaper, *Al-Watan.* This weekly lasted until 1993. After being published regularly, the newspaper began lagging behind and appeared intermittently until it vanished in 1993. The main reason behind its decline was the failure of the PLP to enter the Knesset in the 1992 elections. Mentioning this weekly is important because it clarifies the fact that Arab political parties begin publishing a newspaper upon their establishment, something that will be illustrated more thoroughly later, and when they find out that the costs of propagating the ideology in a newspaper are much higher than the gains, they tend to give it up, especially if they do not have their own financial resources. The second point to make in this context is the difficulty in publishing a party-affiliated newspaper despite the support of the party. As we shall see, the chances for the survival of private newspapers are much higher than for those affiliated with political parties, especially in an economic environment that is heading toward a neoliberal consumer market.

Assennara's success as a private commercial weekly paved the way for the foundation of two similar weekly newspapers. *Kul al-Arab* (All the Arabs) was founded in 1987 as a common venture between an Arab businessman and the owners of the most widely read Hebrew newspaper in Israel, *Yedeot Aharonot*. This venture followed the success of *Assennara* and was an attempt to share the profit that was accumulating in the Arab commercial market. The liberalization of the Israeli economy and the improving growth rate had opened new economic opportunities in Israel. This economic process impacted Arab society especially in respect to the turning of this society into a consumer society, especially for Jewish commercial firms. *Kul al-Arab* presented a similar journalistic format to that of *Assennara,* but with two important differences. The first was that *Kul al-Arab* was less sensational and confrontational in its coverage of internal Arab affairs. Its owner, who came from the Arab business circles, searched for a better relationship with this elite and did not have a serious journalistic background that might have resulted in a more investigative and sensational journalistic style. The second was that *Kul al-Arab* sought to present itself as a more nationally responsible and even more socially representative newspaper. Therefore, its discourse maintained a balance between its national commitment and commercial interests, something that put it closer to the party-affiliated newspapers, despite the fact that it was founded as a commercial undertaking. The less sensational editorial line could have been a factor in the success of the weekly and its ability to overtake *Assennara* in terms of circulation within a short period of time.

Panorama, a third widespread commercial private newspaper, began publication in 1988. It was established by Bassam Jaber, an Arab journalist who had worked for Israeli radio and television for several years. The newspaper, which was located in the Triangle area and focused on news of that area, soon reached a wide readership and established itself as a central private weekly. *Panorama* further pluralized the Arab public sphere and carved an editorial line that is different from *Kul al-Arab* and *Assennara*. The owner of the newspaper turned it into one of the leading newspapers in Arab society by launching a highly developed website and a portal in Arabic oriented toward the younger generation. This quickly became the most popular website among the Arab population

These three weeklies gradually dominated the Arab newspaper market. No substitutes for *Al-Ittihad,* the three represent a different type of press, one that strives to adapt itself to the competitive market conditions now characterizing the local as well as the global economy. The three newspapers entered into a fierce competition and sought to present news and analysis that set the public agenda in Arab society. But, because they were commercial newspapers, the space given to advertisements sometimes equaled the amount of space given to news.

Arab society, located at the margins of the Israeli economy, has adopted economic patterns of behavior that are considerably influenced by norms dominant in Jewish society. Improvement in the quality of life of Arab society in Israel, accompanied by the growth of a large lower middle class, has enabled the spread of consumer culture. The three private weeklies referred to provide clear indications of this trend. They are more commercial than informative. Their format is similar to that of popular Israeli newspapers, such as *Yediot Aharonot* and *Maariv.* Tabloids in character, they present news with a sensational twist. They do not conduct their own in-depth reporting, but mostly publish short reports, some of which are obtained from recognized news agencies or from the electronic media, especially the internet. Despite these limitations, their distribution is relatively wide, especially when compared with party-affiliated newspapers. The three newspapers have thus successfully restructured the Arab media landscape, which is distinct from the Hebrew media landscape both in language and in the subjects addressed. The three newspapers adopted a very simple formula by which they combined soft political news with much infotainment. They were oriented to the average Arab reader without much focus on news analysis or investigative reporting.

A market spirit and profit considerations inform the management of the three weeklies. Their status as privately owned enterprises, free of any ideological commitments, has turned them into "supermarkets" for news seekers. Notwithstanding their commercial bent, the owners profess to represent the interests of Arab society, each according to his/her style and outlook. The language of national consensus that leaps from the pages of the commercial press should, however, be considered, at least partially, as a mechanism for the accumulation of wealth rather than as an ideological commitment. Content analysis of the texts appearing in the newspapers indicates that they do represent Arab society, but rather superficially. The language of national commitment and the demands voiced for the rights of Arab society as a national minority tend to be motivated by pragmatic interests. Indications of this attitude can be seen in the space allotted to official announcements emanating from the Government Publications Bureau (Lapam). The latter controls the government publications market, which serves as an important source of income for Arab newspapers due to the weakness of the Arab advertising market. In order to obtain advertising contracts, the Arab press often yields to the Bureau's demands. The Bureau utilizes its economic power to pressure Arab newspapers into softening nationalistic language and minimizing criticism of governmental policies. This acquiescence allows the Arab commercial press to benefit from close to 1% of all official advertising expenditures in Israel, including its share of the rather paltry government publication budget.[12] This tiny piece of the advertising pie fuels the raging competition by the commercial press in the Arab sector, a phenomenon increasingly blatant in recent years.

To the journalistic media scene developing in Arab society in the 1980s one should add *Al-Raya*, a weekly that began in 1987 as the mouthpiece of the Abna'a Al-Balad movement. It belonged to the ideologically and politically committed journalistic school and propagated the national worldview of Abna'a Al-Balad. *Al-Raya* was closed in 1989 by military order.[13] in December 1989 the movement issued *Al-Midan* weekly, this time not under the name of the movement but rather using the license of a private journalist. The weekly was closed in 1991, as a result of losing the private license it had managed to acquire. Since the movement did not have its own license to issue a newspaper, it began using the method known from Al-Ard experience, issuing onetime publications in order to avoid the need for an official permit.[14] The publications propagated a Palestinian national view and sought to promote the ideology of the movement, which believes in a secular democratic state in all historical Palestine. Since Abna'a Al-Balad did not have its own financial resources to support the newspaper, and since it had to compete with the financially stronger private newspaper and with *Al-Ittihad*, *Al-Midan* was unable to win a broad audience. It remained limited to a very small circle of readers.

In the late 1980s, the number of Arabic-language newspapers published steadily increased. The newspapers were mostly private, which reflected the rising view among Arab entrepreneurs that media and advertising are good avenues for business and profit. Most of these newspapers, which will be listed later, did not last long or did not manage to overcome limited circulation, mainly in the largest Arab city in Israel, Nazareth. On the other hand, several newspapers were founded by political parties that were also newly established. The party-affiliated newspapers contributed to the already tense situation in Arab society and marked both the rise of new political forces and the fragmentation of Arab political society.[15]

In 1989, the rising Islamic movement began publishing *Sawt al-Haq wal-Hurriya*. This newspaper, which is still published, expresses Islamic views on local, regional, and global realities and assesses those realities based on the principles of Islam. In 1997, the National Democratic Assembly Party started the weekly *Fasl al-Maqal*. This expresses the voice of the Palestinian national movement in Israel and has a small circulation. The weekly faced financial difficulties on several occasions, which once led to its closure for few months. It still forms a platform for debates with other political parties and movements.

Several other private newspapers appeared: *Al-Midan* (1994), *Al-Ain* (1999), *Hadith al-Nas* (1999), *Al-Akhbar* (2001), *Al-Ahali* (2004), *Al-Fajr al-Jadeed* (2004), and *Enwan Raese* (2008). Some ceased after a short time, and some are in limited circulation today. Some have an electronic version only. In addition, a chain of local newspapers and monthly magazines began supplying the Arab public sphere with additional platforms on which information and opinions could be expressed.

One of the strongest explanations for the constant fluctuations in the Arab print media scene is the disparity in economic growth between Jewish and Arab societies in Israel. Most of the economic wealth in Israel is held in Jewish society. The Arab economy has become marginalized and totally dependent on the Jewish economy. Therefore, most of the investments in advertising, the main source of income, come from Jewish firms. These firms invest only a small share of their expenditures in the Arab press, either because they believe that Arab society is not sufficiently a consumer society or because they know that Arab citizens are exposed to the Hebrew media and thereby to their advertisement there. Although these conventions are slowly changing, one cannot speak of fundamental change. The growth in advertising volume, when combined with the continuing marginality of advertising in the Arabic press, has accelerated competition and made the battle for advertising, circulation, and reputation highly aggressive. For instance, the three most widely read Arab weeklies, *Kul al-Arab, Assennara,* and *Panorama,* are engaged in a bitter struggle over market share. These transformations affect Arab society as much as they are affected by Arab society. These developments explain why an analysis of the Arab public's attitudes toward events transpiring in its environment, processes fed by the media's transformation, is so important, perhaps even more important than the attempt to understand specific patterns of Arab media consumption.

Radio and television have also undergone enormous changes. The liberalization of the Israeli economy brought about the media's empowerment and turned it into a separate market niche. Numerous regional radio stations have joined *Galei Zahal* (IDF Airwaves) and *Kol Yisrael* as a consequence of Israel's Second Broadcasting Authority Law (1990). A considerable number of illegal radio stations have also sprung up. At the close of the 1980s, cable television was introduced, adding a long list of channels to the media system. Israel has therefore witnessed a revolution in radio and television broadcasting since 1992, something that influenced Arab society as well.

The Satellite and Internet Revolutions, 1992–Present

The print media was not the scene in which the most developments occurred in the Arab media. Technological changes led to a revolution in the broadcast media in the Middle East, particularly in Israel. In 1990, Israel moved from having one official television channel to becoming a satellite regional power. In that year the Second Authority for Television and Radio was founded, which enabled the establishment of several regional radio stations and a new private television channel. In 1992, Channel 2 began broadcasting on a regular basis. Although this channel offers only a few Arabic programs, it has drawn a large number of Arab viewers, especially to its news broadcasts. In 2002, Channel 10 began broadcasting, thereby raising the number of national television stations to three. Channel 10 also managed to draw some Arab audiences, despite the fact that only a tiny portion of its broadcast time is in Arabic.

Based on the law of the Second Authority for Television and Radio, Radio 2000 began operating in 1998. Established by several Arab and Jewish entrepreneurs and broadcast from Nazareth, it did not last long. As a result of differences between the owners, the station stopped broadcasting regularly and began losing its listeners. As a result of its coverage of the October 2000 events, in which Arab demonstrations in Israel were fiercely crushed by the police, the license of the station was withdrawn, and it was closed in 2000. Three years later a new private Arabic radio channel was established.[16] Although Radio Ashams was established by an Arab and a Jewish entrepreneur, it was later fully owned by the Arab partner, who had bought all its shares. It broadcasts various programs and news in Arabic and makes a fundamental contribution to the enrichment of Arab public sphere in Israel.

With the development of television satellite services, the number of regional Arabic channels available to the Arab public became enormous. Although exposure to Jordanian and Egyptian television had begun in the early 1970s, only official channels were received. In contrast, since the early 1990s the Arab audience has been exposed to dozens, perhaps hundreds, of private Arabic-language television channels. Among the most notable is Al-Jazeera, the Arabic equivalent of CNN, which has become the most widely watched channel by the Arab population in Israel. Many channels offer family programming: MBC, ART, Orbit, Rotana, and other networks and their affiliates. Availability of these broadcasts has inaugurated a revolution in the media consumption patterns of Arab society in Israel.

Yet, despite these changes, Arab society does not enjoy the status of partner in the determination of policy pertaining to radio or television, neither in Israel nor in the Arab world. Without such participation, neither broadcasting system takes account of its unique needs. This led one of the prominent Arab journalists in Israel, a previous editor of *Kul al-Arab,* Zuhair Andrawus, to write an article in 2000 entitled "Give Us an Arab Television."[17] This call was directed at Israeli officials, asking for a TV channel operated by Arabs and meeting the needs of the Arab population.

The liberalization of the Arab media space and the utilization of technological developments are paralleled by the rise in the number of Arab internet websites available to Arab citizens. The three commercial newspapers, *Kul al-Arab, Assennara,* and *Panorama,* have websites to provide up-to-date news that cannot be contained in the weeklies. Other websites were developed by party-affiliated newspapers, such as *Arabs48* by the National Democratic Assembly Party and Al-Jabha by the Democratic Front for Peace and Equality. There are hundreds of local, regional, and international internet Arab websites.

This media reality has changed the Arab public sphere, giving it a very open and pluralistic character. The number of media resources available has become enormous, something that cannot be compared with earlier years. The ability to consume contents has grown rapidly. The access to local newspapers in Arabic and to Israeli Hebrew newspapers has grown enormously. The number of radio and television stations has also grown. However, one should not forget that the growth in the number of media institutions and contents to which Arab society in Israel has access does not obviate, by any means, the fact that the influence of this society on content, especially when it comes to television channels, and their representation in most of these channels is very limited or even nonexistent.

This multiple media scene raises questions regarding the media behavior of the Arab public. What is read, heard, and viewed, to what extent, and why all become important avenues to explore. Since we have already assumed that the communicative action and media consumption of social groups can reflect social beliefs and modes of thinking, on the one hand, and can have influence on future behavior, on the other, the explication of these actions and consuming patterns form an essential venue of research, especially in the case of a homeland national minority living in an ethnic state. This sociopolitical context turns the understanding of communicative behavior and consuming patterns into an opportunity for understanding minority-state relations and the strategies that minorities develop to cope with their minority status. For that purpose I turn in the coming chapters to the research I have done on this matter.

FIVE

Arabic Print Media and the New Culture of Newspaper Reading

The changes in the media structure, which were initiated either by private Arab citizens or by political parties, especially in the print media, have been translated into collective communicative behavior and patterns of media consumption. Shedding light on the communicative behavior of the Arab minority in each of the media forms is an important issue to explore. There are well-known differences between newspaper reading patterns and television viewing.

The following analysis is based on two sets of data. The first is a representative survey among a random sample of the entire Arab population in Israel. The second is a selective survey of representatives of the different elites within the Arab minority. The two surveys, conducted in different periods, posed the same questions, aiming to enable a deep examination of the assumption set forth in the introduction of the book and facilitate comparisons that are of analytical and theoretical importance. The following analysis will be selective and does not utilize all the data available from the surveys. It delves into the patterns of newspaper reading relevant for this book. For reasons of space, it does not analyze the ratings of all newspaper reading, but rather takes the most widespread newspapers, according to the data, and delves deeper into their patterns of reading.

Newspapers were the first means of communication to provide Arab citizens of Israel with an independent voice, a platform from which to express themselves politically and culturally in their native language, with limited governmental interventions. Thus patterns of press reading, satisfaction with the press, and trust in its messages are important indicators of the politics of contention of the Arab community in Israel.

The data made available by the general survey shows that the Arab public in Israel has developed a unique culture of reading newspapers, adapting to the structure of the Arab newspaper industry. Responses to the question regarding frequency of reading newspapers revealed that 9.3% of the population of the survey read Arabic newspapers daily; 45.3% read these newspapers on the weekend. Another 25.1% of the respondents who read Arabic newspapers do so infrequently, and 20.3% do not read Arab newspapers at all.

Various factors can account for the differences in the number of people who read newspapers daily and those who read them on the weekend. Before we delve into explanations, it is important to pay attention to the factors that explain the patterns of reading weekly newspapers, on the one hand, and the factors that explain the low percentage of readers of daily Arabic newspapers, on the other. These factors are not necessarily identical, although some may overlap.

The first factor explaining the difference between daily (9.3%) and weekend (45.3%) reading of Arabic newspapers has to do with the supply structure. The dominant Arab newspapers are weeklies, a format dictated by financial factors and the availability of advertising revenues. The Arab public has become accustomed to awaiting the weekly newspapers, which are mostly distributed for free in gas stations. Another factor that can explain the gap is the fact that the public *habitus* of newspaper reading has been constructed so as to primarily look for and consume "soft" news. The weeklies cannot compete with the electronic media and daily newspapers in transmitting "hard" news (current events). Specializing in "soft" news is, consequently, a strategy adopted by all weeklies to overcome their own limitations, turning this type of news into the most widespread type of news consumed by the Arab newspaper-reading public. Concentrating on this type of news has turned the weekly newspapers into tabloids, publishing superficial stories with sensational titles and large photos. They may be considered "supermarkets," selling a wide range of news items in small doses, written in simplistic language. This approach creates a sense of superficiality and lack of seriousness. Although it can be argued that the lack of daily newspaper reading habits in Arab society may prevent expansion of the daily Arabic-language press, the character of existing publications is one of the principal factors preventing any change in reading patterns. Yet the weekly press evidently reflects its Arab readers' preferences for light news on weekends. That is, it allows Arab readers to feel informed about what is happening without requiring them to invest any special effort in obtaining that information. The entertainment value of these weeklies is thus an important factor in their circulation among Arab consumers, just as it is in other national markets.[1]

Yet another factor is the informative value of the reports printed in the daily press. The two daily newspapers, *Al-Ittihad* and *Al-Fajr al-Jadeed,* the latter of which has since ceased regular publication, did not fulfill the Arab public's media needs for information. The fact that *Al-Ittihad* is affiliated with the Communist Party may put off many potential readers and limit its readership to party supporters. In addition, *Al-Ittihad* has become a very slim newspaper in recent years, no longer having the capacity to provide a wide range of news items and analyses. Its financial difficulties have likewise hampered its ability to compete with new media and technological challenges. In contrast, the low percentage of *Al-Fajr al-Jadeed* readers can be attributed to the fact that it was a new actor in the Arabic press industry, entering the stage at a time when newspapers were seriously challenged by news websites.[2] Moreover, its limited journalistic resources, the absence of a skilled, professional staff, and a dependence on secondary sources of information such as the Internet damaged its credibility. It may therefore have been difficult for the newspaper to attract a wider readership.

Another explanation of the differences encountered in newspaper reading has to do with the objective and subjective aspects of the print environment. One major feature of this environment is the inability of the daily press to compete in a timely fashion with the significant increase in the number of electronic media providing breaking news. As Meyer has indicated, the future of newspapers is at risk as a result of the rise of modern telecommunication technologies.[3] The daily press cannot compete with electronic news websites that are updated constantly. To that one should add that the Arab population in Israel is exposed to the daily Hebrew press, which provides news on Israeli and international reality. The daily Hebrew-language press attracts 17.4% of the Arab population. This availability certainly has negative repercussions on the circulation of Arabic-language dailies.

Under such circumstances, we may ask, why don't the weeklies expand their operations and publish daily, an option that might raise their revenues? The answer to this question can be inferred from the experiences of *Assennara,* which started publishing a second edition on Tuesdays for some time. This experiment was very short-lived because the second edition was unprofitable. We may therefore conclude that the weekly readership patterns that initially represented responses to the structure of newspaper supply later served to reinforce that structure, perpetuating a pattern of low daily newspaper reading. If this conclusion is correct, competition from the electronic media only reinforces that pattern.

Another factor affecting reading patterns is the fact that the weeklies fulfill the Arab population's need to be informed about events in its immediate environment, primarily local Arab society. Such information cannot be received from any other source, with the exception of Radio Ashams, which began broadcasting only in 2003. The weeklies compete with the dailies over local coverage. They make major efforts to remain one of the main sources of information on social and cultural issues in Arab society. The fact that *Al-Ittihad* is an ideologically committed newspaper that provides news analysis reflecting the party's worldview and the fact that *Al-Fajr al-Jadeed* was too thin to be able to provide an overview of major events in Arab society turn the weeklies into the main source of news on Arab society.

Another important explanation for the low percentage of Arab readers of daily newspapers is linked to transformations in media consumption due to the increasing significance of broadcast media. Since it has become a common commodity, television has captured a steadily increasing share of the media market around the world. This phenomenon is based on the electronic media's capacity to provide up-to-date information in a timely fashion and to transmit multiple stimuli simultaneously, without demanding any special effort on the part of consumers. With the advent of television, the picture reached a pinnacle of popularity, leaving the printed press in an inferior position. Radio and television consumption does not require any skills beyond a basic understanding of one's native language, and in the case of television, even that is not always necessary.

The general survey data reveals that, although 9.3% of the adults in Arab society read newspapers daily, 52% listen to the radio daily and 81.7% watch television daily. This distribution demonstrates Arab society's reliance on the broadcast media for its news and entertainment. Thus, in response to a question regarding the medium that the interviewees rely on most to obtain news, 75.3% of the respondents replied "television." Only 9.9% said that newspapers are their primary source of news, and 10.6% stated it was radio. The remainder, 4.2%, indicated that their main source of news was the internet. This low percentage of those who acquire news on the internet could be explained by the fact that the internet requires reading skills, computer access, and operating skills, which are relatively uncommon among the adult population.

This presumption is illustrated by examining the answer to the same question in the selective survey. The data on the Arab elites regarding sources of news demonstrates that the responses are divided almost equally between television, radio, newspapers, and the internet. Whereas 26% of the respondents claimed that they acquire news mostly through television, 32.8% said it is through the radio, 25.6% through newspapers, and 24.5% through the internet. This distribution reveals that newspapers and the internet form a more central source of news among the elites than among the general public. This gap could be explained by the higher average level of education and higher socioeconomic status among the elites. Higher education is translated into higher reading skills, and the higher economic status is translated into more access to computers and technology.

A noteworthy difference concerning reading newspapers was found in the percentages of respondents stating that they do not read any Arab newspapers (20.3%) and those stating that they do not read any Hebrew newspapers (36.7%). The findings show similarities in the rates of respondents uninterested in reading newspapers, whether in Arabic or Hebrew. Of those who stated that they do not read Arabic newspapers, 50.3% indicated a lack of interest or time; 45.7% indicated the same reasons for not reading Hebrew newspapers. If we add those uninterested in reading newspapers to those who read infrequently, the total indicates that almost 45% of the Arab public is uninterested in the print media. This high percentage of nonreaders does not meet the expectation that one may have in regard to the fact that the Arab population is a national minority coping with daily political, economic, and social difficulties, forced to protect itself from discriminatory government policies, and therefore expected to display more interest in the press. The high percentage of nonreaders could be explained, partially at least, in addition to the reasons we suggested earlier, by the lack of match between the expectations of some of the general public and the information provided by the newspapers. As mentioned, the public has to choose between party-committed daily or weekly newspapers that provide hard news and commercial weeklies that are dominated by soft news and advertisements.

Two important comments are warranted regarding illiteracy as a reason for not reading newspapers. One pertains to the difference between the high level of literacy among the respondents who do not read newspapers and the level of illiteracy reported in the sample. Of those who do not read Arabic newspapers, 39.6% said it was due to illiteracy, but only 8.1% of the total sample reported that they are illiterate. That is, the majority of Arabs in Israel are literate, yet a large percentage are uninterested in reading newspapers. A similar pattern, though at even higher proportions, is observed among those stating that they were not literate in Hebrew. Among the group that does not read newspapers, 49.4% stated that they were not literate in Hebrew, but only 18.2% of the entire sample stated that they were not literate in Hebrew. The percentage of the Arab population literate in both languages is high. Hence illiteracy alone cannot be the principal factor causing the low percentage of newspaper reading. On the other hand, it may be true that mere literacy is not sufficient reason for reading newspapers; nonetheless, it plays a major role. When looking at the selective survey among the elite, we see that 43.2% read an Arabic newspaper daily. Besides the fact that people in leading positions are generally more interested in the news, the fact that this interest is translated into reading newspapers, as much as listening to the radio or watching television, reflects the notion that high literacy is inherently related to habits of reading.

The second comment refers to the difference in the percentages obtained for those who do not read Arabic-language newspapers because they are not literate in Arabic and those who do not read Hebrew newspapers because they are not literate in Hebrew. Although the difference is almost 10% (39.6% and 49.4% for Arabic and Hebrew newspapers, respectively), if we take into account the fact that Arabic is the respondents' native language and that Hebrew is considered a foreign language, we must conclude that the difference in percentages is relatively low.

We may interpret this small difference as indicating that the Arab population in Israel is mostly bilingual, and the percentage of those speaking both languages equally well is higher than the percentage of those who speak only Arabic. This finding demonstrates some of the changes taking place in Arab society in Israel. The language barrier, which is perceived by many as the main obstacle to integration of the Arab population into Israeli society, is disappearing. More and more Arabs speak Hebrew fluently and exhibit patterns of linguistic behavior characterizing bilingual people.[4] Language difficulties can therefore no longer explain the socioeconomic gaps between Arab and Jewish societies.

Furthermore, there are another two salient aspects of newspaper reading patterns indicated by the data. The first has to do with the significant percentage of the Arab population that reads both Arabic and Hebrew newspapers. This data is reflected in the fact that 75.1% of the selective survey on the elites read Arabic and Hebrew newspapers. This high percentage mirrors the cultural pattern that has been emerging among the Arab minority, in general, and its elite, in particular, manifested in utilizing the structure of opportunities available in the press in order to extract whatever information is needed to enable the best possible forms of coping with their status. According to the selective survey, the number of those who read only Arabic newspapers amounts to 18.3%, whereas the percentage of those who read only Hebrew newspapers is 5.2%. The gap between those who read newspapers in one language and those who read newspapers in two languages speaks for itself in regard to the double consciousness hypothesis. One could claim that this pattern of newspaper reading is based on instrumental needs of the elite and its efforts to survive the inherent split reality in which it has to function. Although this could be true, one cannot escape the accepted notion that the media plays a major role in constructing consciousness, and therefore this pattern of newspaper reading must have an impact on this process.

The second salient aspect of newspaper reading patterns indicated by the data is that a large proportion of Arabic newspaper readers read more than one newspaper. It seems that newspaper readers are not satisfied with one source of information when it comes to newspapers. They seek to get various views. However, the need to read more than one Arabic newspaper might reflect the weaknesses of Arabic weeklies and their inability to gain the trust of their readers, reflected in the search for other sources of information. The conclusion that may be drawn is that many members of Arab society in Israel read more than one Arabic newspaper precisely because newspaper quality is poor and because readers adopt a more active stance when consuming the print media, something that is supported by the data that will be presented later.

Weeklies are usually acquired in gas stations free of charge. This may influence reading patterns, especially the fact that many people read more than one newspaper. Would the reading of more than one newspaper continue if Arabic weeklies were sold from newspaper stands rather than being given away at gas stations? The relevance of this question increases if we consider the fact that among the same respondents, few read more than one Hebrew newspaper. That is, it appears that the majority who read the Hebrew press are satisfied with one exclusive source. This observation supports our conclusion that the level of trust in Arabic newspapers among Arab readers is not especially high. Data on the Arab public's trust in the Arabic press, presented below, supports this argument.

In order to deepen our understanding of the media consumption culture exhibited by Arab society in Israel, the interviewees were asked why they read newspapers.

The principal reason given is to obtain news (80.9%). This finding indicates that those who read newspapers view them as an important source of news. They are not satisfied with the news obtained from television or radio, and thus they make sure that it is upgraded by the press. Arabic newspapers are a major source of information on events pertaining to Arab society in Israel that cannot be obtained from any alternative source other than Radio Ashams. Expanding their horizons was a reason given by 67.4% for reading newspapers. This segment of consumers appears to take advantage of the fact that most Arab newspapers cover a wide variety of subjects, from some "hard" weekly news to "soft" entertainment news. News analysis (57.1%) and improvement of language skills (57.1%) tie for third place in importance. These factors support the claim that newspaper readers view the deeper analysis of events to be one benefit of newspapers not readily obtainable from the broadcast media.

Similar to other newspapers, Arabic weeklies are divided into niches, by topic. Not all subjects enjoy identical treatment in the various newspapers. Usually each newspaper has a clear policy that determines its layout. For example, the daily newspapers give greater space to political news than they give to cultural issues. Furthermore, most general newspapers, including the weeklies, exhibit clear preferences in the placement of items, so that political news precedes economic news, and both take precedence over cultural news. Studies indicate that the order in which subjects appear in newspapers and the degree to which they are stressed will affect their readers' assessment of an issue's salience.

This observation raises several questions concerning the importance attributed to various topics by the newspaper-reading public. The extent of association between the agenda of the newspaper reader and the salience that readers attribute to specific topics becomes an important issue. Much research has been done to explore this issue from the perspective of theories of agenda setting and that agenda's effect on the media-consuming public. Although the data of the two surveys does not focus on agenda-setting, questions were put to interviewees that attempted to elicit responses regarding Arabic-language newspaper readers' preferences for the different sections of the newspapers they read, based on research indicating that newspaper readers exhibit varying preferences for specific sections. A list of topics was therefore presented to the interviewees, including politics, economics, social news, culture, sports, religion, health, and editorials. Respondents were then asked to rate their preferences for the sections focusing on each category of news. Although we cannot state with any certainty the level of association between a newspaper's agenda and the reader's order of preferences, based on the literature, we can nonetheless posit some hypotheses about this association.

It is important to note at this stage that in preliminary interviews held with journalists who write for the weeklies, the poor working conditions and the meager resources available for investigative reporting became evident. These conditions influence the nature of the items reported in the weeklies. Still, the goal of increasing circulation has steered weeklies toward providing news unobtainable from other media sources. Writers and editors have consequently stressed the importance of local news, particularly on political and social matters, as the main topics reported in the weekly newspapers.

The distribution of Arab readers' preferences for the various newspaper sections supports previous assumptions. A large percentage of respondents (between 54.6% and 93.4%) are interested or highly interested in all but two sections of the newspaper; less than 40% express interest in sports and editorials. The section dealing with social topics was ranked first (93.4%), followed by the section dealing with cultural topics (88.1%). Health issues were ranked in third place with 83.3%.

These interests in newspaper content resemble the publication policy of the Arabic weeklies expressed in their coverage and layout of topics, as a previous content analysis of the commercial newspapers has indicated.[5] The findings thus support those theories that suggest an association between media policies and the reading public's preferences for various topics.

Considering the fact that the social and cultural news in these weeklies displays a drift toward entertainment and in many cases gossip, the findings indicate that the Arabic newspapers fulfill their readership's expectations for local Arab news, an area neglected by other media. Due to their inability to compete with the hard political news addressing Israeli national and regional politics in the Hebrew press and television, the weeklies have stressed the provision of soft news and items ignored by the other media. This, in turn, appears to have affected the level of interest that consumers display in the topics covered by the Arabic newspapers.

Despite the fact that politics was expected to be the topic of highest interest to Arabs, the data indicates politics as ranking only fourth in readers' interest, with 76.5% indicating that they are interested in political news. This finding requires explanation. A possible logical explanation would be the pattern of news coverage in the Arabic newspapers. As stated, these weeklies cannot compete with daily newspapers regarding political news. Therefore, they tend to concentrate on presenting news on local political, social, and commercial matters; however, since they do not invest in a professional journalistic team, they tend to be superficial in their coverage of these issues. For economic reasons, these newspapers lack writers with established reputations or political commentators capable of providing daring, coherent analyses that might raise readers' interest in their columns. As a result, the weeklies tend to provide news based on economic calculations of gain and loss, a tendency that limits their ability to develop an investigative journalistic tradition.[6] This leads Arab readers to obtain hard news on national matters from other media outlets.

The fifth topic in readers' interest is religion (68.9%), followed by economics (54.6%). Sports attract relatively little interest and are ranked seventh with 40.4%. The low level of interest in sports can be explained by the Arabic weeklies' inability to compete with alternative sources of information on this topic. Television and the daily Hebrew press provide more immediate and comprehensive sports coverage. At the bottom of the scale are editorials, including commentaries (30.4%). Almost 70% of Arab newspaper readers are uninterested in reading editorials, and 81.5% are uninterested in commentaries. This data may be explained by the fact that these newspapers do not present positions written by prominent columnists. The same tendency emerges in the selective survey in which we find that interest in local news is higher (78.9%) than interest in national news (46.9%). Also here we find that the interest that readers show in the editorials and commentaries is relatively low, 12.2% and 37.6%, respectively.

The low reader interest in commentaries of the editors may be accounted for by the fact that Arabic newspapers have no effect on Israeli policy and decision makers. As a result, the opinions and analyses of the editors of these newspapers appear to have no great value. Editors and columnists have not managed to fulfill their traditional role as opinion makers who influence the public agenda concerning subjects they believe to be significant. Nevertheless, one cannot help but emphasize the readers' broad interests in various topics in the Arabic newspapers, something that would not have existed were these newspapers not there. The fact that news in various fields is provided by the Arab newspapers enriches the Arab public sphere and enables debates based on common knowledge that is not provided by any other source of information in the media scene available to the Arab public.

Reading Patterns, Satisfaction, and Trust of Arabic Press

In preparation for this study, preliminary interviews with Arabic newspaper readers were conducted. These interviews clearly showed that the Arab newspaper consuming public reads more than one newspaper. A very high percentage of respondents mentioned two or three newspapers. Although such a reading pattern could be anticipated with respect to weeklies, this finding compelled us to explore the reasons behind this pattern. Various explanations can be offered for this behavior. As mentioned earlier, one assumes that Arab newspaper readers try to balance their sources of information by looking at more than one paper. This explanation is reinforced by the in-depth interviews conducted with various focus groups.[7] Nevertheless, the availability of weekly newspapers (as indicated earlier, they are distributed gratis at gas stations) should be taken into account as a significant factor contributing to this behavior. Another factor to be considered is that reading Arab newspapers on weekends has become part of the culture of leisure in the Arab community. Many readers noted that the principal reasons for selecting newspapers included availability (40%), habit (18.3%), and entertainment (29%). In contrast, 26% stated that they chose a specific newspaper because of how it reported news about Arab society, while 19.2% stated that an important reason for reading Arab newspapers was their reflection of the general atmosphere in Arab society and 20% mentioned the newspapers' objectivity.

As indicated earlier, the interviewees in the research were asked to name the newspapers they read most, according to importance. The interviewees were given the opportunity to name up to three newspapers. Therefore, when analyzing the data we established a hierarchy of three consecutive ranks. The analysis that follows compares the readership of the newspapers in the three rankings. This analysis was considered the best way to mirror the patterns of newspaper reading in the Arab community in Israel and do justice to the different newspapers, especially because of the possible financial implications that the data could have on advertising revenues.[8]

The data shows that the ratings of Arab newspapers change according to readers' preferences; thus, a considerable difference exists in readers' first, second, or third choice. Certain newspapers were ranked in first place by numerous respondents whereas others were ranked as first by a small or negligible percentage of readers. Thus reading patterns of Arab newspapers can be divided into four main categories. The first includes *Kul al-Arab* and *Assennara,* which have relatively large readerships. Of those who read Arabic newspapers, 29.5% ranked *Kul al-Arab* in first place and 26.1% ranked *Assennara* in first place. In the category of moderate readership, 15.8% ranked the daily *Al-Ittihad* in first place and 13.5% ranked *Panorama* in first place. In the third category, containing newspapers with low circulation, 4.6% of the respondents ranked *Sawt al-Haq wal-Hurriya* first, 2.1% ranked *Al-Mithaq* first, 1.7% ranked *Al-Osbua' al-Arabi* in that position, and 1.4% ranked *Akhbar al-Naqab* first. The fourth category is characterized by newspapers with extremely low readerships: 0.9% ranked *Al-Ahali* first and 0.6% ranked *Hadith al-Nas* first. *Fasl al-Maqal,* which reappeared in mid-January 2005 after the research had begun and after a recess in publication, was ranked first by 0.4% of the respondents, whereas only 0.2% ranked *Al-Akhbar* first.[9]

When we compare the data of the general survey with that of the selective survey, we notice that the Arab elites demonstrate a slightly different pattern of newspaper reading. The newspaper that understandably ranked first with 38.8% was the daily *Al-Ittihad. Kul al-Arab* was ranked second with 20.1%, which means that this newspaper is leading the list of the weeklies, similar to the data of the general survey. *Panorama* ranked third with 16.4%, and surprisingly *Al-Mithaq* ranked fourth with 8.4%.[10] *Assennara* ranked fifth with 7.5%, seriously different from its ranking in the general public. This low ranking could be explained by the sensationalist orientation of the newspaper regarding the Arab elite in Israel. The initiative of the newspaper to publish a column written by one of the central leaders every week did not help the newspaper improve its ranking among the elites. *Fasl al-Maqal* ranked in sixth place with 4.2% among the elites, and *Sawt al-Haq wal-Hurriya* ranked seventh with only 2.8%.

The rankings of some newspapers in the general survey vary when we consider the second preferences of their readers. These changes derive primarily from the requirement that readers rank the newspaper according to importance. The percentage of respondents ranking *Kul al-Arab* in second place rose to 34.9% among all those who read Arabic newspapers. *Assennara* and *Panorama* also rose slightly in rank, to 27.4% and 14.9%, respectively. In contrast, *Al-Ittihad* descended drastically in rank, with only 4.9% ranking it first among newspapers in the second preference category. This decline indicates that *Al-Ittihad* remains the first choice of its loyal readers, perhaps due to familiarity, and that it is the second choice of a much smaller group of readers. This trend in the changing rankings of newspapers when going from first to second preferences continues for newspapers with limited circulation. For example, *Sawt al-Haq wal-Hurriya* declined to 2.6% of the respondents, whereas *Hadith al-Nas* rose to 2.2%. These changes indicate the considerations guiding Arabic newspaper readers, who display loyalty to the newspapers they consider most important and turn to other newspapers only after they have completed reading their preferred newspaper.

A similar pattern was observed when ranking third-order preferences: *Kul al-Arab* declined to 19.4% and *Assennara* to 19.8%. Despite these declines, both newspapers maintain wide circulation. A more glaring change occurred in the ranking of *Panorama*. That newspaper jumped to 28.9% in the third preference ranking, which indicates that it enjoys wide circulation and has numerous readers but only as a second or third choice. Compared with this increase, the data indicated a steep decline in the readership of *Al-Ittihad,* which was ranked far above *Panorama* in the first-order of preference category but received very low rankings in the second and third preference categories, 4.9% and 6%, respectively. *Sawt al-Haq wal-Hurriya,* which was ranked 4.6% in the first preference category, declined to 2.6% in the second preference category, but ascended to 4.2% in the third preference category. These shifts indicate varied patterns in reader preferences. Some readers prefer a specific newspaper, but do not limit themselves to reading it exclusively, and yet a larger percentage of readers may choose the same newspaper as a third rather than second alternative.

These findings indicate the advantages of providing a choice of alternatives when inquiring into Arab newspaper reading patterns. A research design that had presented only one choice to participants would have misled us in regard to newspaper reading patterns in Arab society. Such a research design would have overlooked the tendency of Arabs to read more than one newspaper and would thereby have led to wrong conclusions concerning the culture of newspaper reading. The possibility of choosing more than one alternative clearly revealed that the percentage of people exposed to a given newspaper is usually greater than the percentage of those indicating a newspaper as their first choice. Even if a given newspaper is preferred by a certain percentage of readers, this does not detract from the importance of other newspapers to those same consumers, or to a portion of them. This also explains why the cumulative percentage of readers preferring a newspaper in any category exceeds 100% on occasion. This is accounted for by the fact that readers of a given newspaper are also counted as readers of other newspapers.

Another significant question examined has to do with the diverse newspaper reading among the Arab public. Examining the ranking has helped to reflect the structure of the Arab media space and the way in which it is influenced by the competition between the newspapers. However, this information is not sufficient if we do not go further to examine the exact alternative newspapers that Arab readers choose, especially since we know that the average reader reads more than one specific newspaper. This information may explain specific patterns of newspaper reading and shed light on the reasons for changing preference rankings. Within this context, it is important to note that the competitive wars waged between the newspapers take on a different coloration when the study's findings are analyzed; the fact is that readers of one newspaper are also the readers of another. For example, the data of the general survey demonstrates that 68.4% of those who ranked *Kul al-Arab* in first place also read *Assennara*. Although they might have ranked *Assennara* in second or third place, these readers could be interested in both newspapers equally, attitudes that would explain the high percentage who read both newspapers. The figure also shows that 44.9% of *Kul al-Arab* readers also read *Panorama,* a figure which indicates *Assennara's* advantage over *Panorama* among readers of *Kul al-Arab.* Furthermore, a relatively large percentage (23.2%) of *Kul al-Arab* readers also read *Al-Ittihad.* Yet fewer of those who ranked *Kul al-Arab* first read other newspapers to any significant degree.

The data indicates that 76.6% of those who ranked *Assennara* in first place also read *Kul al-Arab.* More readers who ranked *Assennara* in first place ranked *Kul al-Arab* in second than vice versa. This difference may explain the sharp increase for *Kul al-Arab* among those who ranked this newspaper second as compared with those who ranked it first. As noted earlier, 29.6% of Arab newspaper readers ranked *Kul al-Arab* as their first preference, whereas 34.9% indicated that they read this newspaper. Among those who ranked *Assennara* first, 37.9% responded that they also read *Panorama,* while 18.4% noted that they also read *Al-Ittihad.*

Among those who ranked *Panorama* first, 79.8% also read *Kul al-Arab.* This finding indicates a difference in preferences between readers of the two newspapers. While readers of *Panorama* ranked *Kul al-Arab* as their second choice, readers of *Kul al-Arab* did not rank *Panorama* as a second choice to the same extent. A similar pattern, although with varying percentages, is discerned with respect to the relationship between *Panorama* and *Assennara*: 60.2% of *Panorama* readers also read *Assennara,* but only 37.9% of *Assennara* readers also read *Panorama.* This difference partially explains the position of *Panorama* as the third choice for readers of *Kul al-Arab* and *Assennara.* The differences in the findings underscore the achievements of *Kul al-Arab* and *Assennara* with respect to readership, as well as the failure of *Panorama* to make much headway despite its success in penetrating the market and becoming a widely circulated commercial weekly.

The same trend can be observed among readers of *Al-Ittihad*: 77.2% who ranked *Al-Ittihad* first also read *Kul al-Arab*. In contrast, only 52.8% of those who ranked *Al-Ittihad* first also read *Assennara*, whereas 25.6% read *Panorama*. These findings support the conclusions regarding differences between newspaper readers in general and illustrate that while the commercial weeklies constitute the main alternatives in readers' eyes, the differences in consumers' rates that do exist favor *Kul al-Arab*, which maintains its dominance as the most popular newspaper in Arab society.

Among the readers who ranked *Sawt al-Haq wal-Hurriya* first, 44.7% also read *Kul al-Arab*, 41.8% *Assennara*, and 11.4% *Panorama*. A relatively high percentage (18.9%) of *Sawt al-Haq wal-Hurriya* readers also read *Al-Mithaq*, which is identified with the faction of the Islamic movement that competes with the same faction that issues the weekly *Sawt al-Haq wal-Hurriya*. Moreover, 9.3% of *Sawt al-Haq wal-Hurriya* readers also read *Al-Ittihad*, which is identified with the Communist Party, whose ideology is secular and critical of religious belief that is promoted by *Sawt al-Haq wal-Hurriya*. The data demonstrates that unlike the readers who placed other newspapers first and who read mainly another one or two of a limited number of newspapers, the readers who placed *Sawt al-Haq wal-Hurriya* first in their ranking exhibit greater plurality in their reading patterns of other newspapers.

The obvious advantage of the commercial newspapers when compared to the party-affiliated newspapers can be deduced from the preceding figures. The percentage of those who ranked party newspapers as their first choice and still read commercial newspapers is much greater than the percentage of readers of commercial newspapers who also show interest in party newspapers. This difference indicates that most commercial Arabic newspaper readers are content with their source of news. However, this should not necessarily imply that the level of public trust or satisfaction with those newspapers is higher than the trust in party-affiliated newspapers. The preference given to commercial newspapers may be related to availability or convenience rather than to satisfaction from or trust in the content of these newspapers.

The data presented earlier based on the selective survey shows a different picture. Among the elites, interest in the party-affiliated newspapers is higher than their interest in commercial newspapers. This data meets the expectation, since the elites are expected to be more politicized. Both surveys clearly demonstrate that the Arab public sphere is rich. The various newspapers, which compete for the same readers, provide a wide range of knowledge in various fields. There are many debates taking place in the pages of the newspapers, and every one of these seeks to win the attention of the readers. An important conclusion to consider at this point has to do with the fact that the general Arab public has adapted its reading patterns to the structure of the Arab newspaper market, which is predominantly a weekly market.

Careful examination of the reasons for reading a specific newspaper can be expected to reveal the variables or characteristics that link newspapers with their readership and thus contribute to our understanding of the media consumption culture of Arab society in Israel. We assumed that ideological as well as practical factors might explain the observed newspaper reading patterns. Other causes for differences in reading patterns may also be associated with the contents offered and availability. The interviewees were asked to list not only the names of the newspapers they read but also the reasons for reading a specific newspaper. Based on our review of the research literature, we provided a list of twelve possible reasons and asked the respondents to select three. The findings do indeed enable a more penetrating look into the culture of newspaper reading of the Arab population in Israel.

According to the available data, there are three primary reasons for choosing a particular newspaper: objectivity, availability, and habit. The factors of availability and habit are straightforward, but objectivity is a complex concept that takes on different meanings with different readers. However, it is important to note that in Arabic, the language used in the interviews, the concept's interpretations are rather limited and tend to focus on a more tangible meaning, that is, substance oriented coverage.

Analysis revealed that the reasons for reading newspapers affiliated with a political party are different from those given for reading commercial papers. The most salient reason for choosing the two party newspapers was their objectivity, with 40.9% assigning that reason for choosing *Sawt al-Haq wal-Hurriya* and 39.7% for *Al-Ittihad*. In contrast, the principal reason for choosing the commercial newspapers was availability. Of those who read *Kul al-Arab*, 23.7% cited objectivity as the reason, as did 21.3% of those who read *Assennara* and 25.4% of those who read *Panorama*. On the other hand, availability was indicated by 26.6% of *Kul al-Arab* readers, 32.8% of *Assennara* readers, and 36.5% of *Panorama* readers. Habit was the reason given by 20.1% of those who preferred *Kul al-Arab,* 27% of *Assennara* readers, and 17.5% of *Panorama* readers. These differences support the hypothesis that the relationship between readers and the party-affiliated newspapers is based on different factors than those motivating the relationship between readers and the commercial newspapers. As can be seen from the figures, a reader who chooses a specific newspaper develops certain expectations of that newspaper. While readers of the party organs expect those newspapers to supply them with substantial news, they do not expect the same level of substantiality from the commercial newspapers. The availability of a commercial newspaper is apparently enough of a reason to read it. The fact that Arab commercial newspapers are available, especially through their distribution at gas stations, increases the number of readers. If availability were to be restricted and the commercial newspapers were not free, one could speculate that the readership of these newspapers might decline.[11] The figures given above reflect the possible gap in the attachment of readers to the newspapers they read. Despite the fact that party-affiliated newspapers are less read, their readers are still more loyal to them when compared with the loyalty of the readers of commercial newspapers.

Analysis of the separate indices revealed the specific factors that differentiate between the newspapers in each category. Objectivity was rather consistently indicated as the most important factor determining the choice of a party-affiliated newspaper as opposed to a commercial newspaper. Small, statistically insignificant differences were found between the responses listing objectivity as a factor in reading the three commercial newspapers, *Kul al-Arab, Assennara,* and *Panorama* (23.7%, 21.3%, and 25.4%, respectively).

A considerable difference was found for habit as a factor for reading the various newspapers. Again, habit was most salient with respect to the reading of commercial newspapers. Readers of *Assennara* (27%) most often listed habit as their main reason, followed by readers of *Kul al-Arab* (20.1%), *Panorama* (17.5%), *Sawt al-Haq wal-Hurriya* (13.6%), and *Al-Ittihad* (12.3%). The relatively high proportion of party newspaper readers who listed habit as the main factor determining their reading makes this factor particularly relevant for understanding media reading habits in Arab society. Habit as the cause for continued reading of a newspaper is a phenomenon known from research in other societies. However, habit is not a strong factor in explaining the differences in reading between commercial and party newspapers among Arab readers.

The differences in the data obtained between the various commercial newspapers do not enable unequivocal conclusions to be drawn. Nonetheless, if we compare the data and then compare commercial and party-affiliated newspapers, a clear difference appears in the factors determining the relationship between commercial newspapers and their readers. Clearly, the reading of one or another of the commercial newspapers is not necessarily dependent on their contents; the main factor is availability. Distribution affects the level of commercial newspaper readership. The findings thus point to a weak relationship between commercial newspapers and their readers; in other words, these newspapers have failed to establish significant emotional or ideological links with their readers. The basic determinant of reading remains pragmatism. But who would read these commercial newspapers if they had to pay for them? Answering this question demands further research.

In order to deepen our analysis of the Arab public's attitudes toward Arabic newspapers, we examined the level of the Arab public's trust in the news, reported by the various newspapers' readers. The general survey participants were asked to indicate how much they trusted the newspaper they had ranked as their first preference into categories ranging from very high to very low trust. The most obvious result of the ranking is the finding that the Arab newspaper readers place less trust in commercial newspapers than in political party publications.

The data confirms that readers tend to trust party newspapers more than commercial newspapers. While the dominant positions among readers of *Al-Ittihad* and *Sawt al-Haq wal-Hurriya* are high and very high, respectively, the dominant position among readers of the three commercial newspapers is moderate. The differences in trust ratings demonstrate the slight skepticism with which readers view the commercial press. These findings were consistent regardless of whether the newspaper was ranked first, second, or third. Thus the average level of trust in the party newspapers ranked in all three preference categories was regularly higher than the average level of trust in the commercial newspapers. *Sawt al-Haq wal-Hurriya* was rated first in trust by readers, regardless of its preference rank; *Al-Ittihad* was rated second. Most *Sawt al-Haq wal-Hurriya* readers (78.2%) claimed that they very highly or highly trust what they read in that newspaper, and 70.7% of *Al-Ittihad* readers claimed the same. In contrast the three commercial newspapers, *Kul al-Arab, Assennara,* and *Panorama* received ratings of less than 50% when it comes to very high and high levels of trust.

Contrary to expectations, a comparison of the data on trust with the data on the distribution of the different newspapers demonstrates that the level of trust in a newspaper does not affect readership. Despite the high level of trust in the party newspapers and the moderate level of trust in commercial newspapers, the public prefers to read commercial newspapers to a significant extent. This pattern confirms the results of other research recently conducted on this subject.[12] The first possible germane factor explaining this phenomenon is the availability of the commercial newspapers. Large numbers are distributed gratis at gas stations to drivers who purchase a specific amount of gasoline. This distribution tactic spurs their acquisition and reading. But interviews with over 100 students, chosen randomly, show that this exact form of distribution turns the relationship between readers and specific newspapers into something occasional and pragmatic.[13] Readers do not develop any attachment or loyalty to a specific newspaper. Most students admitted that they view the newspaper as a gift for being loyal to the gas station rather than to the newspapers themselves. A second possible explanation for the gaps in trust for the party-affiliated versus commercial newspapers among their readers has to do with the political and ideological affiliation of the readers. These readers are usually loyal to the party and therefore to its newspaper as well. This explanation is insufficient, however, since it cannot explain the widespread distribution of commercial newspapers, despite the low level of trust in them. This leads us to the third explanation, and that is the fact that the commercial newspapers provide news items that cannot be found elsewhere, such as local news from the Arab community. As a result, they meet readers' needs irrespective of the deepness or thoroughness of the news they provide. A fourth possible factor contributing to the relatively low trust in commercial newspapers may be the fact that these newspapers are "supermarkets" for news, a characteristic that prevents development of a high level of attachment and thus trust.

Another variable explored was reader satisfaction with the scope and quality of coverage. The survey participants were asked to indicate their satisfaction with the newspapers they read regarding coverage of the following subjects: Arab political leadership, the Israeli government's policy of demolishing Arab houses, and coverage of Arab protests against the government's discriminatory policies. These topics are of importance to the Arab public and reflect readers' views concerning the forms in which Arab newspapers represent central Arab issues.

The first issue examined was satisfaction with coverage of the Arab society's political leadership. The data demonstrates that 24.1% of the research participants assigned a midpoint level of satisfaction (neither satisfied nor dissatisfied). In contrast, 22.2% said they were moderately satisfied, 6.8% were very satisfied, 15% were moderately dissatisfied, and 9.2% were very dissatisfied. Another 22.6% responded that they did not know, equivalent to having no opinion. Combining the categories to achieve a clearer picture of the results indicated that low and very low levels of satisfaction were expressed as frequently as high or very high levels combined. This data mirrors a relatively low level of satisfaction characterizing the Arabic public's assessment of Arab newspapers' coverage of its political leaders. This finding is particularly salient given that there are a relatively large number of party-affiliated newspaper readers among the respondents. On the other hand, the data reflects a certain type of normal curve when those who had no opinion are taken out. This interpretation allows one to say that the average readers of Arabic newspapers accept the way in which their political leadership is represented in the newspapers. This data becomes even more important when we add that a content analysis examination of the commercial newspapers' coverage of Arab leadership showed that their representation is relatively low.[14] Arab leadership is marginal on the agenda of the commercial newspapers. The general survey shows that the readers of commercial newspapers are relatively content with this coverage. This position should raise questions regarding the Arab leadership's behavior that does not lead to more coverage, as well as to a general indifference toward these leaders on the part of readers.

Regarding Arab newspaper coverage of the Israeli government's policy of demolishing houses in Arab areas, opinions were once again not very decisive. A total of 30.9% of the participants in the survey noted that they were satisfied or very satisfied with coverage, whereas 31.4% said they were not very satisfied or totally dissatisfied. However, if we add those indicating a midpoint level of satisfaction to the percentage of those dissatisfied, we can conclude that the majority of readers were not particularly satisfied with coverage. These findings are understandable if we consider the meager coverage by most, particularly commercial newspapers. That is, although the Arab press criticizes this policy and provides coverage of such incidents, it toes the general line set by the Hebrew press: the issue is raised only in connection with specific cases of policy implementation. In a content analysis survey of the three most popular commercial newspapers, *Kul al-Arab, Assennara,* and *Panorama,* we found that the newspapers published very little on this topic. Out of thousands of articles published during a five-month period, the survey found only forty-one related to this topic. This means that each edition of these newspapers had less than one article on the average on the topic. When the size of these articles was examined, we found that the average articles that dealt with the issue of house demolition took up 25% of a page. The small number of articles, their brevity, and the fact that they appear only when the authorities demolish a house makes the marginality of this topic in the agenda of the commercial newspapers even more apparent. Having said that, it should be noted that, in contrast to the Hebrew press, which emphasizes the legal aspects of the event and provides a platform for government spokesmen as opposed to Arab stakeholders and victims, the Arab press focuses on the human aspects and the grave infringement to basic human rights that this policy represents. Arab commercial newspapers do represent the interests of the Arab community and criticize the authorities heavily for this policy.

Arabic readers were also not satisfied with the coverage of Arab protest activities against Israeli government policies in various areas. Although 33% stated that they were satisfied or highly satisfied with the topic's coverage, one can see that 45.4% expressed direct or indirect dissatisfaction. One should note that 21.7% expressed a midpoint position that represents a certain measure of dissatisfaction. The data, which represents the ambivalence of the Arab public, demonstrates that the Arab readers of the Arab newspapers are split and do not take a firm position reflecting satisfaction with the coverage of protest activities.[15]

The general survey participants were asked to indicate how they perceived the Arab newspapers' role in the public debate on the major issues affecting Arab society. The Arab press in Israel claims to provide a platform for the Arab population, which is forced to defend its rights daily and remains the object of discrimination by the government and other residents of the country in which they live. As research on the minority press in other parts of the world has revealed, minorities usually expect their newspapers to actively defend their rights and advocate positions that strengthen the minorities' positions on crucial issues.[16] These conclusions apply even more strongly in cases where the minority press is published in a separate language. In other words, the minority press functions as both a vehicle for maintenance of cultural identity and a means for recruiting members for collective action.[17] Hence its readers expect this press to do more than express community hopes, dreams, and interests. Obviously, if the minority press intends to strengthen its position and attract a broader readership, it has to meet its public's expectations.

Following this argument, several questions were posed to the interviewees that sought to explore the extent to which the Arabic press reflects the range of opinion found in Arab society, deepens the reader's sense of belonging (community), and defends the community's rights. Responses to these questions represent measures of the Arab readership's satisfaction with the press as a minority advocate. Although a wide variance of opinion was expressed, the general level of satisfaction with the Arab press in these areas was not high. A midpoint level of satisfaction was the most prevalent response among interviewees; that is, readers of Arabic newspapers are skeptical regarding the accuracy with which these newspapers articulate the range of opinions found in Arab society. Although 40% of the respondents agreed significantly or fully with the statement that Arabic newspapers express the full range of opinions in Arab society, 34.5% expressed ambivalence. When adding this answer to those that disagreed or totally disagreed, we reach 57.4%, implying that the Arab public would like to see greater pluralism represented in the Arab press.

A similar pattern emerges regarding the role that the Arab press plays in providing readers with a sense of belonging or membership to the community: 27% of Arabic newspaper readers expressed a midpoint level of satisfaction, whereas 46.2% expressed a positive opinion (agree or highly agree) when asked if the Arab newspapers support communal identity. In contrast, 52.2% expressed midpoint to very low satisfaction. In other words, a considerable proportion of newspaper consumers view the Arabic press as positively supporting a sense of belonging and Arab identity. However, the majority of respondents appeared to have doubts about the Arab press's effectiveness in these matters. Such a position can be interpreted as critical with respect to the public's expectations of the Arab press as fulfilling a more patent role in building national identity and reinforcing internal solidarity. Nevertheless, we may also suggest that some respondents did not view the press as an institution whose task it is to reinforce a sense of belonging, a position expressed in negative responses to the question asked in this regard.

The slight skepticism alluded to by the responses regarding how well the Arab press provides a sense of community recurred, but more emphatically, in responses to the question regarding the extent to which the Arabic press expresses the needs and interests of Arab society. On this issue, too, the most popular response was the midpoint choice; that is, the respondents appear to be a bit skeptical of the role that the Arab press plays in this area. The findings indicate that 50.1% of the Arab public is dissatisfied to some degree with the way that the Arab press voices communal needs and interests. Stated differently, the Arab public would like the press to represent the interests and needs of Arab society. Nonetheless, one notes that 47.5% expressed a firm positive view with regard to the role the press plays.

The survey respondents also expressed slight dissatisfaction with the role that the Arab press plays in defending Arab rights. Although a considerable percentage of the respondents (46.3%) agreed to a great or highly great degree with the statement that the Arab press defends the Arab minority's rights, more than 50% expressed a midpoint to very low level of satisfaction. The trend observed in these responses clearly indicates that the Arab press does not meet the expectations of a large segment of the Arab public, nor does it fulfill the roles that many of its readers have assigned to it.

In order to verify that the Arab public's expectations of the press are not exaggerated, and thereby ascertain whether the public ignores or underestimates the functions that the Arab press does fulfill, interviewees were asked to indicate whether they agreed to a series of negative statements about the Arab press. The findings indicate that, in contrast to the criticism leveled against the Arab press on the specific issues surveyed, the consensus was almost unanimous that the Arab press does not necessarily play a negative role. For example, the research participants were asked to indicate whether the Arab print media represents official Israeli positions. The most common response was rejection of this possibility, with 33% decisively rejecting this statement and an additional 19.7% moderately disagreeing with the statement. Alternatively, a considerable minority (21.5%) stated that they significantly or fully agreed with the statement, a result that should raise questions and concern among newspaper publishers, especially when considering the latter's attempts to enlarge their readership circle.

A relatively large proportion of the respondents adopted a midpoint position regarding Arab press's expression of official Israeli positions. When this stance is added to those who significantly and fully agreed with this proposition, it indicates considerable discontent and implies expectations of change. The cumulative percentage of respondents who expressed midpoint to total agreement with the statement was 42.8%. This relatively high percentage is indicative of public suspicion or dissatisfaction with the Arab press.

A decisive majority of the respondents (78.8%) did not agree with the statement that the Arab press plays a negative role in Arab society, such as encouraging internal social or ethnic strife, despite their criticism of the press's deficiencies in the area of advocacy. We may conclude that this finding reflects the Arab public's dissatisfaction with the role played by Arab newspapers. At the same time, this view reinforces Arab society's pragmatic view of the press and the predominantly commercial character of the Arabic weeklies.

The general survey participants were asked to describe their trust in the Arab and Hebrew presses. While 35.4% stated that the Arab press was more credible, only 19% stated that the Hebrew press was more credible. This gap indicates that a considerable proportion of newspaper readers take a decisive position. Yet 23.2% stated that they trusted both presses equally. This is almost half the percentage of respondents who expressed clear trust in either press (54%). In contrast, only 3.6% stated that they distrusted the Arab and Hebrew presses equally. A significant percentage (18.8%) said they had no opinion.

These findings indicate that the criticism leveled against the Arab press by its readers has not greatly affected the public's trust in those newspapers when compared with the Hebrew press. Nonetheless, if we take into account that only 35% of the general survey participants replied to this question, the responses continue to reflect a high level of skepticism. The relatively low percentage of responses serves as a further warning to Arab newspaper publishers, editors and journalists.

A decisive difference has always existed between political party newspapers and the commercial press.[18] Party newspapers function to spread ideology and recruit adherents for the political parties that sponsor their publication. Commercial newspapers, in contrast, generally seek to make profit. Thus the two types are based on different ideological and economic foundations. Despite these differences, both inherently aim at setting the public agenda and influencing their readers' viewpoints.

Although this is not the place to expand on these issues, it is important to note that the party press, in the form of the Communist Party newspaper *Al-Ittihad,* existed prior to the establishment of the state of Israel. The commercial press only appeared on the scene in the early and mid-1980s, when the weekly *Assennara* began to publish, and thereafter gained a wide circulation in the Arab community. Hence *Al-Ittihad* and *Assennara* were trendsetters that introduced two new schools of journalism and heralded the founding of other party and commercial newspapers in the Arab community. Newspapers representing these two schools have continued to address different audiences despite their attempts to expand their circulation.

The available survey data demonstrates that there are differences between the party-affiliated and commercial newspapers in the average amount of time devoted to reading them. While differences in the amount of time spent in reading the various commercial newspapers was relatively small, a larger difference was found between the amount of time devoted to the party newspapers and the time spent reading all three commercial newspapers. *Assennara* readers devoted an average of 1.37 hours weekly to reading, *Kul al-Arab* readers spent an average of 1.19 hours weekly, and *Panorama* readers devoted an average of 1.099 hours weekly. In contrast, readers stated that they devoted an average of 3.139 hours weekly to reading the party newspaper *Al-Ittihad*, while *Sawt al-Haq wal-Hurriya* readers spent an average of 1.59 hours weekly.

The findings presented so far demonstrate that a major change took place in the Arab public sphere manifested in the emergence of new patterns of newspaper reading among the Arab population in Israel. One can speak of the rise of a plural press structure in the native language of the Arab minority, which is for the most part owned by it and represents its needs and interests. Within the print media space, one can speak of two schools of journalism that have developed and have given the Arab readers the possibility to choose between different sorts of newspapers. The party-affiliated newspapers offer more hard news and committed views on the surrounding social and political environment. The commercial newspapers offer the average reader a broad spectrum of news formulated in a softer language that is easier to digest. Both forms of newspapers are read by the Arab public thereby having some impact on shaping public opinion and constructing the characteristics of the Arab public sphere. Based on the data analyzed, one could conclude that the Arab public has developed a clear pattern of newspaper reading that conforms to the structure of the press, which is divided not only between party-affiliated and commercial but also between daily and weekly press. Furthermore, the Arab public has crystallized diverse opinions on the newspapers and their contents. It was found that factors such as habit, availability, and objectivity play a role in favoring one newspaper over another. The issues of trust and satisfaction were also found to be important factors influencing patterns of reading. These findings reflect the richness of the Arab public sphere and the emergence of a special culture of newspaper reading among the Arab minority in Israel. It has also been made clear that the level of trust of Arabic newspapers is higher than the trust of Hebrew newspapers, something that reflects a patriotic attitude among the Arab minority. This attitude will be better elaborated when we examine patterns of reading of Hebrew newspapers and the measure of trust that Arab readers have toward Hebrew media in general, something that we turn to in the next chapter.

SIX

Resisting Cultural Imperialism

Alienation and Strategic Reading of the Hebrew Press

Before beginning our analysis of consumption of the Hebrew press by the Arab public in Israel, it is important to note that Hebrew is a foreign language for Arabs. Although a significant number speak Hebrew, it is not their native language. It is more than likely that this fact has a considerable impact on the way Arab society relates to the Hebrew press. Very few issues of importance to the Arab community are reported by the Hebrew press. Furthermore, when such reporting does appear, it is usually negative.[1] The coverage tends to present Arabs as lawbreakers who shirk their legal obligations to the state.[2] This type of reporting serves Jewish society's need to know about what is happening in the minority population, yet the same articles do not attempt to express the opinions, positions, processes, or state of mind of this minority as an integral segment of Israeli society. Although such images doubtlessly affect readership among the Arab population, this particular issue was only indirectly examined in this study. The focus has been on the reading patterns and attitudes of the Arab population. This chapter deals with these reading patterns and attitudes toward the Hebrew media.

Before we examine Arab reading patterns and attitudes toward the Hebrew media, it is necessary to recall that they cannot be understood out of context. The Arab minority in Israel is an indigenous national minority whose status was determined by war. It is a suppressed minority that for a long time had the sense that its future in the Israeli state was not self-evident. The Arab minority belongs to the Palestinian people who lost their homeland and their right to statehood and who pay the price of Jewish sovereignty. The hegemonic Jewish culture and the dominance of the Hebrew language in the Israeli public sphere automatically translate into the suppression of the native culture and language of the Arab minority.

The Hebrew media, in general, and the press, in particular, directly express the cultural and linguistic hierarchy in Israel. The Hebrew language is not only foreign to the average Arab citizen; it is also the language of the suppressor, notwithstanding the fact that most Arab citizens in Israel are bilingual. They speak, read, and write Hebrew daily, and the selective survey shows that 75% of Arab elite read both Arabic and Hebrew newspapers. Although the survey did not delve into Arab feelings toward the Hebrew language and culture, there is no doubt that the feelings of the average Arab citizen toward the Hebrew language and Jewish culture have major effects on reading the Hebrew press and consuming Hebrew media.

The Arab minority has demonstrated various forms of resistance to Jewish hegemony in Israel. Since 1948 there have been attempts to resist the efforts made by the Jewish majority to establish its hegemony over every aspect of life inside Israel. Although without much success, the Arab minority showed dissatisfaction and suspicion. It used linguistic, cultural, folkloristic, literary, and other means to protect its authentic culture and language. The poetic and literary works of Arab citizens, which have become very well known since the 1960s, are a good example of the efforts made to resist the Israeli control system.[3]

Arab resistance to Israeli control and surveillance has taken various forms. These forms can be followed in the political, legal, cultural, and linguistic fields.[4] The patterns of Hebrew media consumption are best understood when located in this context. As mentioned, Hebrew is a foreign language for the average Arab. Moreover, the fact that Hebrew newspapers are not regularly distributed in every Arab neighborhood is an important factor that determines patterns of Hebrew newspaper reading in Arab society.

The Arab public is exposed to the Hebrew press together with the Arabic press. Yet the general survey shows that only 17.4% of the Arab population reads Hebrew newspapers daily, with another 45.9% reading the Hebrew press irregularly. It was also found that 36.7% do not read any Hebrew newspaper. Lack of knowledge of the language (49.4%) and lack of interest (45.7%) were the main reasons cited.

When asked about their newspaper preferences, the interviewees indicated the three major dailies, *Yediot Aharonot, Maariv,* and *Haaretz.* Most preferred *Yediot Aharonot,* thereby resembling the reading habits of Israel's Jewish society. Of those who did read Hebrew newspapers, 84.7% rated *Yediot Aharonot* in first place, 12% preferred *Maariv,* and 2.3% liked *Haaretz* best. As for second place, Arabs preferring *Yediot Aharonot* fell to 19%, and those preferring *Maariv* increased to 59.9%; that is, *Maariv* is considered a substitute for *Yediot Aharonot* in case the latter is not available. The preference rating for *Haaretz* also rose to 13.2% among the newspapers in second place; that is, *Haaretz* is the less-preferred substitute for *Yediot Aharonot.*

This data should not lead to the conclusion that a considerable proportion of the Arab public reads two Hebrew newspapers; rather, the findings indicate which newspapers are likely to serve as alternatives. Thus, if readers cannot obtain *Yediot Aharonot,* they are much more likely to choose *Maariv* than *Haaretz.*

When looking at the selected survey among the Arab elite, one views similar patterns of reading, but with a slight difference in favor of *Haaretz.* *Yediot Aharonot* remains the leading newspaper with 69.6% ranking it in first place. But the second newspaper is *Haaretz* with 25%, and *Maariv* comes in third with 5%. This data reflects the fact that *Haaretz* is more widely read among the educated elite, despite the fact that it cannot compete with *Yediot Aharonot.* Examining the second priority set by the interviewees demonstrates that *Maariv* is a substitute for *Yediot Aharonot.* Whereas *Yediot Aharonot* went down to 36% as second choice, *Maariv* went up to 35% as second choice. This data shows clearly that when people cannot get *Yediot Aharonot,* they choose to read *Maariv* rather than *Haaretz.* The latter maintains its rating as second choice also with 23.4%, meaning that *Haaretz* has stable readership.

The findings also show that the average amount of time devoted to reading Hebrew newspapers is different from the average amount of time devoted to reading Arabic newspapers. Based on the findings, among those who read Hebrew newspapers, it became clear that an average of 2.16 hours per week were devoted to reading *Yediot Aharonot,* 1.81 hours to *Maariv,* and 2.05 hours to *Haaretz.* The data demonstrates that the average time devoted to reading Hebrew newspapers is greater than the average time devoted to reading Arabic newspapers. In all likelihood, the main reason for this finding is that the Hebrew newspapers are dailies; hence their readers are accustomed to reading them every day. In contrast, most of the Arabic newspapers are weeklies, and the political news they report is not sufficient to cover political affairs seriously. What remains to be read in the Arab newspapers on a weekly basis is local news, pertaining to Arab society, and general news, primarily in the areas of entertainment and leisure.

The perception of the Arab public of the Hebrew newspapers that represent Israel's dominant Jewish majority and its language becomes a very important factor if we wish to understand the communicative behavior of the Arab minority in Israel. Arab society is a deprived indigenous minority that must cope with discriminatory policies on the part of the majority society, with the latter taking advantage of the minority's resources at the same time that it prevents this minority's enjoyment of any equality. The Hebrew media, particularly the print media, are integral components of the majority's efforts to control this minority. Therefore, examination of the trust placed by the minority in the majority press and the positions it takes can bring into focus various dimensions of the convoluted relationship between the two groups. In order to fulfill our purposes, questions similar to those posed about readers' perceptions of the Arabic press were presented to the interviewees. Several major issues were selected, with the respondents asked to express their level of satisfaction with the coverage by the Hebrew press. The issues chosen were coverage of Arab leaders in Israel, the house demolition policy, and Arab protests against government policies. In addition, the respondents were asked to indicate which source they believed when the Arab and Hebrew medias reported on the same event, given the different points of view of Arab society. The survey elicited responses worthy of special attention.

In general, high levels of distrust and dissatisfaction were indicated. Arabs are highly critical of the Hebrew media, an attitude that reflects their severe alienation from Israeli society and their disappointment with the Hebrew media. Despite their critical view, Arabs have neither abandoned nor entirely boycotted the Hebrew media. Reading Hebrew newspapers daily is widely practiced, as is listening to Hebrew radio broadcasts and watching Hebrew television programs. The Jewish public does not have alternative media sources in Hebrew, whereas the Arab public has access to media originating in the Arab world. Thus a considerable segment of Arab society supplements its Arabic media consumption with sources from beyond Israel's borders. Arab consumption of the Hebrew press is based on the need to know what is happening daily in its immediate environment, especially the positions, debates, and arguments developing among the Jewish majority. Since the Arab minority is totally dependent on its Israeli environment relating to economic well-being, education, land and housing policies, politics, policing, and education, they need information about these issues. This need does not automatically translate into trust or sympathy. The data of the general survey demonstrates that the respondents expressed low confidence in the Hebrew press in general.

Among those who read Hebrew newspapers, the highest level of trust was placed in *Haaretz:* 88.8% of those who read that newspaper said that they placed high or very high trust in it, with another 11.1% stating that they placed moderate trust in that newspaper. In contrast, 54.7% of *Yediot Aharonot* readers stated that they placed high or very high trust and 38.6% stated that they placed moderate trust in that newspaper. As to *Maariv,* this newspaper enjoyed moderate trust among 56.8% of its readers and high or very high trust among another 40.9%. This data demonstrates again that trust does not influence the rates of newspaper reading. As indicated by other researchers, people consume mass media despite their distrust in it.[5]

Respondents were also asked their reasons for choosing a specific Hebrew newspaper. The findings show that among readers of *Haaretz,* 62.5% stated that objectivity was their principal reason for choosing that newspaper. In contrast, 21.8% of *Yediot Aharonot* readers listed objectivity as their main reason, with only 17.8% of *Maariv* readers indicating this reason. Yet 26.7% of *Maariv* readers mentioned availability as an important reason for reading that newspaper, compared with 21.2% of *Yediot Aharonot* readers. Not a single *Haaretz* reader mentioned availability. These differences indicate that *Haaretz* enjoys high levels of trust among its readers despite the relatively low readership. Moreover, the data showed that *Yediot Aharonot* readers assigned almost equal weight to its availability (21.2%) as they did to its objectivity (21.8%). *Yediot Aharonot* readers also indicated that habit was an important reason for reading that newspaper (12.5%), which helps explain *Yediot Aharonot*'s high readership. Alternatively, depth of analysis was given as an important reason for reading the newspaper by 17.8% of *Maariv* readers.

An important indicator of the relationship between the Arab community and the Hebrew media was the public's level of dissatisfaction with the coverage of Arab leaders in the Hebrew press: 47.8% said they were dissatisfied or strongly dissatisfied. Only 8.4% expressed satisfaction, with another 13.4% expressing a midpoint position, and 30.4% stating that they did not know (or had no opinion). The Arab public is fully aware of attempts made by the Hebrew media to delegitimize Arab leadership based on a broader official policy.[6] Being aware of the media images of Arab leaders makes the level of satisfaction rather low.

Arab leaders are rarely covered in the Hebrew press. In content analysis sampling six months of the most widespread Hebrew newspapers, this author found that only 4.1% of the 713 news items on Arab society mentioned Arab leaders on the local or national levels. This low percentage is reflected in the dissatisfaction of the interviewees. A similar trend was observed regarding satisfaction with coverage of house demolitions. The Israeli government's policy of destroying houses in Arab areas is one of the most painful issues. Every year, dozens of Arab homes are bulldozed. This policy is part of a broader official policy aimed at impeding infrastructure development and other housing-related issues, especially in the Naqab area.[7] Coverage in the Hebrew press is minimal and is usually totally reliant on official sources, thereby demonstrating the legitimacy of the state action and ignoring the human dimension of such policies. The Hebrew press reduces every decision of the state to a onetime event, eliminating the ability of the readers to view these decisions as a general policy that is usually directed against Arab citizens and almost never against Jews. Furthermore, this coverage policy contradicts the tradition in the Israeli press where violations of the law by individual Arab citizens are usually generalized and set in a historical context that demonstrates their collective and intentional character.

Against this background, the data shows that 55.7% of the readers of Hebrew newspapers were dissatisfied with the coverage of this policy, with only 5.6% indicating approval. The main source for this critical view is the above indicated coverage policy of the Hebrew press, which reflects the official police position—the Arab homeowners involved are treated as criminals endangering state land.[8] The dissatisfaction among Arab readers reflects their awareness of the emphasis that Hebrew newspapers, especially *Yediot Aharonot* and *Maariv*, put on the legal aspects exclusively, while never addressing the serious harm done to basic civil and human rights.

An almost identical picture is repeated with respect to Hebrew press coverage of Arab opposition or protests against the government's discriminatory policies. Experience has shown that the state's reaction to protests by Arab citizens is quite different from its reaction to Jewish protests. The most recent traumatic example was the police response to the protests held in October 2000, when the main roads in Wadi A'ara in the Triangle and in Galilee were temporarily blocked by demonstrators. During those events, the police fired directly into the Arab crowd and killed 13 protesters. In contrast, the Israeli police did not respond with violence when Jewish settlers blocked the country's main arteries, especially the Ayalon highway in Tel Aviv, in protest to the 2005 disengagement plan. The efforts made by the police to evacuate the demonstrators never approached the level of violence that characterized the October 2000 events, irrespective of similar behavior. The coverage in the Hebrew newspapers of these parallel events demonstrates the dichotomous treatment of social protests, depending on the identity of the participants.

Therefore, the data shows that 52.1% of the Arab respondents were dissatisfied with Hebrew press coverage of Arab protests, and only 4.8% were satisfied. This data reflects the level of alienation separating Arab society in Israel from the Hebrew media, in general, and the Hebrew press, in particular. As mentioned earlier, the Hebrew press reflects the suppressive mentality that dominates the Israeli policies toward the Arab minority. Justifications of state policies, through format, genre, style, discourse, narrative, etc., turn the Hebrew press into an ideological apparatus of the state vis-à-vis the Arab minority.

In order to make this point even clearer, the interviewees were asked to express their opinion regarding which newspapers—Arabic or Hebrew—they were more likely to believe or trust when both reported the same incident. To elicit the responses, the following scenario was presented:

The newspaper *Kul al-Arab* reported an incident in which an Arab citizen was shot and killed in the Triangle by a member of Israel's Border Police. The *Kul al-Arab* article stated that the policeman did not appear to have any reason justifying the use of live ammunition. The Hebrew newspaper *Yediot Aharonot* also reported the incident but explained the policeman's motivation, writing that the Arab citizen had endangered the policeman's life.

As noted, the research participants were asked to state which newspaper they trusted more for an accurate account of the incident. More than half (51.4%) placed greater trust in the Arab newspaper, *Kul al-Arab,* while only 8.4% trusted the report in *Yediot Aharonot.* Neither newspaper was believed by 9.2% of the respondents, although 14.4% responded that it depended on the case. This difference clearly indicates the Arab public's low level of trust in the Hebrew press in cases where an alternative Arab source is available.

The data regarding the comparison between the Arabic newspaper and the Hebrew one obliges a reconsideration of the attitudes presented earlier. When interviewees were asked about the general level of trust they placed in the newspapers they read, which were named, they tended to be generous and express a relatively high level of trust. When the interviewees were asked to compare the reporting of the same event provided by two specific newspapers—one Arabic and one Hebrew—there is clear preference for the version in the Arabic newspaper. However, the crux of the message transmitted by the comparison lies in the high level of suspicion revealed in matters pertaining to the coverage of events that touch upon the relationship maintained between official Israeli institutions and the average Arab citizen. Bitter experience with the police, especially if we take into consideration the Land Day ceremonies, the Nakba memorial day, the October 2000 events, and the coverage of the police violence in the Hebrew press, greatly increased the skepticism felt by Arab citizens vis-a-vis the Hebrew press.[9] The Hebrew press acts in such events as a mouthpiece of the state and frames the events from the standpoint of the official representatives of the state.[10] Therefore, when news reflecting the relationship between Arab citizens and the Israeli police is reported in the press, the tendency of most Arab citizens is to question the Hebrew press reports and believe the Arab press reports. This tendency recurs with respect to television reporting.

The Arab public's critical view of the Hebrew press is reinforced when the data on attitudes toward Hebrew press coverage of other issues is examined. Respondents were asked whether Hebrew press coverage of Arab social issues was objective. The distribution of answers regarding the Hebrew media's level of objectivity demonstrates that the dominant response was that the Hebrew media lacks objectivity in the coverage of social issues current in Arab society. Among the respondents, 48.9% stated that the Hebrew media is either not objective or extremely not objective. Only 16.7% answered that the Hebrew media is objective or extremely objective. The midpoint view was expressed by 23.8%, with another 10.6% replying that they did not know (had no opinion).

In addition, the respondents were asked to assess the objectivity displayed by the Hebrew media regarding internal social conflicts in Jewish society for purposes of comparison with the Arab media consumers' perceptions of coverage of their own society. The data indicates that almost half (46.6%) believed that the Hebrew media was objective or very objective in the coverage of social conflict within the Jewish society, while only 14.3% stated that the Hebrew media was not objective. Among the respondents, 20.1% stated that they did not know (had no opinion).

The difference in the Arab media consumers' views of the Hebrew media reflects the unfairness that the Arab public attributes to the Hebrew press in its coverage of matters important to Arab society in Israel. Thus the Arab public believes that the Hebrew media is fair only in its coverage of issues important to Jewish society. In effect, the Arab respondents were conveying that they perceive the Hebrew media is biased. This view supports and further explains this community's alienation from and disappointment with the Hebrew media.

This alienation is reflected in the data concerning the question of representation. The interviewees were asked to express their view as to the extent to which the Hebrew press represents Arab citizens of Israel. Most (58.4%) indicated that the Hebrew media does not represent them. Only 18.2% thought that it did, and 17.4% did not express an unequivocal opinion. Only 6% said that they did not know (or had no opinion). Arab citizens who read the Hebrew press tend to have unambiguous opinions of how this press relates to their society, and thus they tend to make more definitive assessments of the extent to which that media represents or, more precisely, does not represent them. These responses therefore provide additional indicators of the degree to which Arab society is marginalized in the Hebrew media.

This data acquires added salience when we consider the findings regarding the extent to which Arab media consumers perceive the Hebrew media as representing official positions. Although today's leading Hebrew newspapers were founded as private newspapers and have consistently functioned from that position, their relationship with the state, formed through informal as well as formal administrative and institutional arrangements, has created an impression of partnership, if not co-optation. This relationship could be demonstrated by the policy and activities of the Council of Editors, the forum of daily newspaper editors that essentially regulates newspaper policy. The relationship between the Hebrew media and defense institutions has been particularly blatant. Since the early 1990s, the Hebrew media has been part of the commercial market. All secular party-affiliated newspapers have closed. The main three newspapers are privately owned, and one expects them to become a public sphere where opinions, conformist as well as dissenting, are expressed. However, the private newspapers have accommodated the official policy of the state, especially when it comes to security and foreign policy. In research conducted by Daniel Dor concerning the media coverage of the Israeli army's Operation Defensive Shield, it was made clear that the Israeli Hebrew media has shown a very high level of loyalty to the official discourse of the army.[11] The Hebrew media agreed not only to submit to the military's orders on the "combat field," as if the curing of public unrest were a war, but also to express only the army's viewpoint. The information that was released to the public was censored and expressed the interest of the army to convince the public that suppressing the Palestinian unrest should fall under the rules of war in which every means is legitimate.

The data demonstrates that a clear majority of the respondents (64%) felt that the Hebrew media represented official government policy; 8.7% did not agree with that statement, and 13.7% said they did not know (had no opinion). One can therefore conclude that Arab readers of the Hebrew press do not believe that this press operates as a free and open arena, divorced from state dictates, as many liberal media critics would have us believe. Instead, they view the Hebrew media as part of the state's ideological apparatus—a mechanism for expressing Israel's goals and furthering its interests. Based on these findings, one can conclude that Arab society does not expect much from the Hebrew media. It does not view it as an arena in which they could express their views and raise their demands of the state.

When examining the data of the selective survey, one notices that the same attitudes toward the Israeli media are prevalent among the Arab elite. For instance, 51.8% of the respondents claimed that the Arab population is underrepresented in the Israeli media, and 55.3% of them claimed that the Israeli media does not keenly report the needs of the Arab society. Moreover, 54% of the interviewees claimed that the Israeli media does not provide the Arab society with programs that correspond with its needs and expectations. When comparing the coverage of negative phenomena in Jewish and Arab societies, 50% of the interviewees have claimed that these phenomena are not covered equally in both societies; 52% claimed that the Israeli media is negatively biased toward Arab society, and 50% rejected the claim that the Israeli media is able to represent them. This data demonstrates that the Arab elite has the same sense of alienation from the Hebrew media and is aware of the negative framing of Arab society in the reporting of news relating to it or to its relationship with state institutions and officials. Despite the fact that the Arab elite relies on the Israeli media, in general, and the Hebrew press, in particular, for news and analysis, it is not ignorant of the negative role that this media and press play when it comes to the relationship between the state and the Arab minority. It is fully aware of the negative role that the Hebrew media play in state-minority relations, and it experiences such a negative role not only through the contents and forms of coverage of the Arab society but also through the fact that this elite is not able to access the Hebrew media and transmit its attitudes and point of view to the Jewish public.

There are no media sources in Hebrew outside of Israel. Therefore, the misrepresentation of Arabs and the negative coverage offered by the Israeli press have a strong framing impact on the Jewish public, setting its agenda along the lines defined and determined by state institutions and officials, leading to what could be seen as indoctrination.

Unlike the firm positions taken by liberal thinkers of public debate and deliberation, where one expects the media to be protective toward minority opinions and to be the agent that enables them to influence the public agenda, the media, even when it is private and plays according to the rules of the game accepted in the market, could become a strong, effective repressive force, silencing dissenting voices.[12] This conclusion is reminiscent of the model presented by Wolfsfeld concerning how the conflict is waged between social actors over who sets media agendas. He identifies a deep association between the news value of social actors and their dependence on the media.[13] The penetration of media agendas by political actors is thus dependent on their news value as determined by their positions, resources, organizational capacities, and behavior. The higher the news value of a political actor—whether a leader, a party, or an institution—the more dependent the media are on the actor. Furthermore, the lower the actor's news value, the greater the actor's dependence on the media. Indeed, the higher a given actor's position, the greater the actor's resources, the more effective the organizational infrastructure, and the more attention-getting the behavior, the greater the probability that a political actor will deeply penetrate media agendas. According to Wolfsfeld's model, a political actor's salience in a given media agenda is not fortuitous. The political actor's penetration reflects the media's attitudes regarding the position held, the resources and organizational capability available, and the explicit behavior observed.

The data reflecting the Arab public's level of interest in Hebrew cultural programs shows the degree of alienation the Arab public feels from the Israeli media's programming, primarily cultural programming. A high percentage (62.5%) of the respondents indicated that they were not interested in Hebrew films and television series. A much smaller percentage (17.8%) responded that they were interested, with 11.8% stating that they were moderately interested, and only 7.9% stating that they were very interested in this type of programming. These findings essentially repeat the trends previously reported. They capture the deep sense of alienation felt by Arab society. The discriminatory policies and the Hebrew media's negative role within the context of state-minority relations are sufficient to explain these findings. It should be added that Hebrew films and television series are inherently foreign to Arab society, both culturally and linguistically, which further reinforces the Arab population's sense of alienation and isolation from mainstream Israel's Jewish culture and society. Furthermore, Hebrew films and television series reflect the views dominant in Jewish society concerning their Arab neighbors. Arabs are either completely ignored or represented in negative terms that turn them into aliens in their own homeland. This treatment leads to much of the alienation of the Arab minority from its Israeli environment and its antagonistic attitudes toward Israeli culture. It is translated into the emerging new patterns of communicative behavior of the Arab minority, which follows daily practical news, but abandons that Israeli cultural arena and lands in the Arabic public sphere, broadcasted via satellite on hundreds of television channels and via the Internet. This pattern of differentiated communicative behavior can best be demonstrated through the consumption of electronic media, something that we shall address in the next chapter.

SEVEN

Electronic Media and the Strategy of In-Betweenness

When examining the communicative behavior and media consumption patterns of the Arab community in Israel, one observes its meaningful attempts to maintain a foot in two available media spaces. Arabs listen to local Hebrew and Arabic radio stations broadcasting from inside Israel. Television viewing patterns are distributed between Israeli-Hebrew channels and satellite TV channels from Arab countries. This pattern demonstrates the double location and the in-betweenness of the Arab community as a strategy to overcome its structural marginality. It also demonstrates how national minorities utilize all means available to them to cope with their minority status and overcome the limitations imposed on them as a result of their location. They seek to protect their cultural and national identity without renouncing the means available to them through their citizenship. The globalization of media institutions, especially emanating from what they conceive of as their kin nation states, enables minorities to be in direct contact with their culture.

This pattern of behavior, which is clearly manifested in the consumption patterns of broadcast media, is conceived to be a form of contention against structural limitations set by stronger political or cultural actors. Instead of accommodating the cultural and political reality set by the hegemonic Israeli state, the Arab minority strives to "cross" the Israeli boarders and to enjoy the cultural life available in the Arab world. Arabs in Israel share with Arabs in the Arab world the same communicative space, despite the fact that this world is not easily accessible to them. While it is true that since the signing of the peace agreement in 1979 Arab citizens of Israel have been able to visit Egypt, and that they have been able to visit Jordan since 1995, still their daily life is conducted in Israel. This reality is overwhelmingly Judaized; the Hebrew language and Jewish culture are heavily facilitated by state agencies, which enable them to occupy all available public spaces in Israel. Effective political deliberation, like cultural production, is strongly and closely contained by the Jewish majority, which seeks hegemony over all public spaces, official and unofficial. Major state resources are invested in strengthening Jewish and Hebrew culture, rendering Arab local culture marginal. This strong discrepancy is reflected in the resources invested in Arabic radio and television and in the support that Arab producers and artists receive from the state, as compared with their Jewish compatriots.[1]

Access to Arab media space compensates for the lack of daily contact with Arab social and cultural centers. The data presented below substantiates the claim that Arab citizens of Israel share media space with other Arabs and experience the same broadcast contents. This is best illustrated by the patterns of viewing television contents and by the positions presented by Arab citizens of Israel concerning the influence of Arab satellite television networks on their attitudes and behavior. I first present the patterns of consumption regarding radio stations and then those regarding television stations. I also deal with Arab attitudes toward the impact of Arab satellite television channels on the self-perception of the Arab community inside Israel.

Radio

Radio holds a central place in Arab media consumption patterns. It was the first electronic media outlet to be received by the Arab public. As early as the 1950s, the Arab community showed a tendency toward contending Israeli informative hegemony by listening to the Arab radio stations from Arab countries, especially Sawt al-Arab from Cairo. This station broadcasted the political speeches of the charismatic Egyptian leader Gamal Abdel Nasser. Various people in the Arab community, which at that time lived under military rule, used to listen to Sawt al-Arab secretly in order to overcome the political and cultural barriers set by the Israeli government. It is in this context that one must understand the rationale behind the founding of Kol Yisrael (Voice of Israel) in Arabic in the late 1950s. This radio station was established as an ideological apparatus of the Israeli government in order to penetrate Arab society and set its political agenda. It was and still is a tool for nurturing "Arab Israeli" political identity. Since its inception, it has functioned as an extension of the state's propaganda apparatus—one of the mechanisms used to control the Arab public's political agenda and resocialize Arab society in line with Israeli interests.

The hegemony of Sawt Israel in Arabic (Voice of Israel) over the media agenda of the Arab community has diminished with the technological developments of the 1980s and 1990s. Many legal regional radio stations were established, including Radio 2000. This station was initiated by three

Arab businessmen, in accordance with the law of the Second Authority of Television and Radio passed by the Knesset in 1990. In 1998, it began broadcasting local Arabic cultural programs and news. The station ceased operations, ironically enough, in the year 2000, due to internal differences among the station owners and attempts made by the Israeli authorities to limit its operation. After three years, a new legal Arab radio station was established, Radio Ashams, which has since won a high percentage of the audience. Being very innovative and creative, addressing the authentic needs of the local Arab community, Radio Ashams has managed to establish itself as the most popular station among Arabs. At the same time, there are several Arab radio stations that broadcast illegally. These attract a small audience, as the data presented in the following pages shows.

Due to the variety of accessible stations, the study attempted to discern patterns of radio consumption, including the stations listened to, and the frequency and time of listening. Participants in the research were asked to rank the radio stations to which they listened according to number of hours and types of programs. Similar to the questions asked about the press, respondents were asked to rate the three principal radio stations to which they listened by order of preference.

The findings show that just over half the respondents (52%) listened to the radio. Of those who listened, 54% said they listened to the radio mostly at home, 36.7% tended to listen while driving, and 9.3% listened primarily at work. In addition, the majority of listeners spent 1–2 hours daily tuned in to the radio. It was also found that consumption patterns varied by radio station, whether in Arabic or Hebrew. For example, among listeners to Radio Ashams, 50% also listened to Sawt Israel in Arabic and 33.3% to Reshet Bet in Hebrew (the main public Hebrew station of the official Broadcasting Authority). Moreover, listening patterns varied between entertainment stations, which broadcast mostly music, and general stations, which integrate news and entertainment. The data indicates that a considerable portion of Arab radio consumers listen to illegal stations, similar to the pattern found in Jewish society in other studies. The Arab public also listened to non-Israeli stations. To illustrate, Radio Monte Carlo enjoys a number of Arab listeners, as does Radio Ajyal, broadcast from Ramallah in the occupied West Bank.

The participants in the research were asked to rank up to three stations they listened to most. The data shows that Sawt Israel in Arabic, Radio Ashams, and Reshet Bet have the most listeners and most favorable rankings. Among listeners, 24.7% ranked Sawt Israel in Arabic, 18.8% ranked Radio Ashams, and 17% ranked Reshet Bet in first place. The same stations were also ranked in second place—Sawt Israel in Arabic (20.1%), Radio Ashams (18%), and Reshet Bet (8.6%)—and third place—Sawt Israel in

Arabic (11.4%), Radio Ashams (7%), and Reshet Bet (9.6%). When the available data are calculated according to average exposure, the results show that among all radio listeners, 40% were exposed to Sawt Israel in Arabic, 31.5% to Radio Ashams, and 24.8% to Reshet Bet. We should note, however, that these percentages do not directly indicate the frequency (number of hours) with which listeners tuned into the specific stations.

As indicated by the data, a large number of radio stations have captured relatively small segments of the listening audience. These included Al-Qura'an al-Kareem (religious), (10.5%), Gali Tzahal (8.4%), Radio Monte Carlo (7.3%), Al-Shatea' (6.4%), Ajyal (6.4%), Sawa (4.7%), Al-Salam (4.7%), and Al-Amal (4.6%).

As mentioned, despite the high rate of listening to Sawt Israel in Arabic, the relatively new station, Radio Ashams, followed it in first and second place rankings. The consistently high rates indicate that Radio Ashams has managed to attract a permanent audience in a short time. If we take into account the fact that Radio Ashams is not received fully in the Negev, that it is most popular among younger age groups, and that Sawt Israel in Arabic is popular among all age groups, we can anticipate that Radio Ashams listening rates will grow even further in the future.

When it comes to the data on the elites from the selective survey, we notice that 40.7% stated that they listen most to Reshet Bet. The second station in the first choice, which won 26%, is Radio Ashams, and the third is Sawt Israel in Arabic with 10.6%. When looking at the second choice ranking, we notice that Reshet Bet goes down to 16.7%, meaning that it does not manage to maintain its ranking among the whole Arab elite. Nonetheless, the number of Arab elites exposed to Reshet Bet is relatively high, reflecting the engagement of these elites in Israeli public life and their dependence on information related to their Israeli environment. This rating of Reshet Bet does not reflect sentimental positions or the identification of the Arab elites with the contents of the station, since when looking at the measure of trust and satisfaction from the station, we notice that they are relatively low.

When we look at the radio station that receives the highest rating as second choice, we find Radio Ashams, which has 27% of the listeners. This data demonstrates that the percentage of people exposed to the station is much higher than what seems to be the case if we limit ourselves to the first choice. Radio Ashams has managed to become very established among the Arab elites and win their trust and satisfaction. This data reflects the balance struck by the elites between the need to be up-to-date with information about Israeli reality, especially when it comes to the political and economic systems, and the need to be in contact with the immediate Arab surroundings. People shift between the Israeli Hebrew stations and the authentic Arab station that most reflects their needs and aspirations. Sawt Israel in

Arabic comes only in third place with ratings of 10.6% as first choice and 11.5% as second choice, meaning that this radio station manages to win a stable percentage of listeners, but only as the third station.

Going back now to the general survey, data was also collected to elucidate patterns of listening to news programs broadcast on the radio. Here, too, important results were obtained. When people were asked about the language in which they listen to the news, 60% responded that they customarily listened in Arabic, 24.3% listened in Hebrew, and 15.5% said they did not listen to any news broadcasts. Comparing the levels of trust that the Arab public attributes to the news broadcasts by Sawt Israel in Arabic and by Radio Ashams, a clear tendency to trust the latter was observed. Among listeners, 21.8% stated that they placed greater trust in the news broadcast by Radio Ashams, and 15.6% trusted Sawt Israel in Arabic; 5.2% trusted both stations equally, and 10.2% trusted neither. Almost half (47.2%) stated that they did not know (had no opinion). That percentage was similar to the percentage of those answering that they did not listen to the radio at all (48%).

Television

During the second half of the twentieth century, television became the most widespread communications medium throughout the world, to the point where some have labeled it the "television century." The importance of examining television consumption patterns derives from the centrality of television in changing the meaning of public culture and in transforming the spaces of public deliberation and dialogue.[2] Television's penetration into daily life has changed social relationships and the face of politics, especially during elections. It has thus contributed to more than the disintegration of the family entertainment patterns that characterized the nineteenth and early twentieth centuries.[3] Television has become the principal broker in the public space, surpassing the power of many traditional mediating social institutions, including the family. It has mortally wounded the role of political parties as intermediaries placed between voters and state institutions.[4] Television has personalized politics to the point of becoming the primary arena in which candidates and ideas vie.[5] As a result, it has weakened democratic society's main representative institutions without necessarily strengthening the deliberative dimensions of democracy. Moreover, by transforming the relationship between reality and fiction into an even more complex, multidimensional phenomenon, television has escalated the force of image in all of life's spheres.[6] Finally, as a result of the sheer size of the viewing audience, television has become an object of economic competition between international conglomerates.[7] To further increase their profits, accomplished through the control of programming contents and the distribution of related forms of popular culture, conglomerates have attempted to "sell" audiences to advertisers. To these television barons, audiences have lost their subjectivity and are usually treated as commercial goods. Although the main thesis of the book does not accept such a claim, it has some truth. The commercialization of television has turned it into an important economic mechanism, besides being a cultural space in which social patterns of behavior and political relations are constructed and determined. The intermingling of reality and image on the television screen makes it into an important apparatus of socialization. Besides partially setting the political and cultural agenda of its audience, it frames their worldviews in accordance with the hegemonic economic and political interests, as recent research in this field indicates.[8]

Clearly, in a study such as this one, it is difficult to examine all of the ramifications of television's penetration into Arab society. Nevertheless, the study's results can indicate general trends in various spheres. Before describing television consumption culture in Arab society, we should note that with respect to this medium as with the other media, we again see the Arab public's consumption of a wide range of options, that is, of programs broadcast by different television channels. They consume a mix of television programs in Hebrew and in Arabic on channels originating in Israel, Arab countries, and other areas in the world broadcast via satellite.

The findings thus present a multifaceted picture. The data of the general survey shows that 81.7% of the Arab public watched television daily or almost every day. Another 7.1% watched television every few days, and 7.5% watched infrequently. Only 3.6% of the Arab society did not watch television at all. Among the last group, 41.9% indicated that they did not own a television set, and 30.2% stated that television did not interest them or that they did not have the time. When rates of television viewing were compared with rates of daily Arabic (9.3%) and Hebrew (17.4%) newspaper reading, a large difference was found in the frequency of consumption.

Among the respondents who did watch television, 54.7% did so in the company of family members, 13.9% watched alone, and 29.9% did both. Comparing these responses with what is known about viewing habits in Western societies, it appears that the penetration of television into the Arab household, despite the increasing number of channels broadcast and improvements in the standard of living, has not caused a massive increase in individual viewing, isolated from family participation. The majority of the Arab population in Israel still perceives television viewing as a joint family experience. Yet the findings indicated that 75.3% of the respondents preferred television to newspapers, radio, or the Internet as a source for news. This preference has transformed television into a fundamental socializing agent in the cultural and political arena, far and away more influential than all the other medias. This is especially true if we take into consideration the lack of alternative entertainment institutions in Arab towns and villages. These lack an established theater culture and cinemas. The number of youth clubs and cultural institutions is small, and they are limited to local initiatives, lacking almost any official state support. This reality leaves television as a very central medium of entertainment, something that explains the patterns of television viewing revealed by the data, especially the fact that entertainment channels draw the most audience attention in terms of time invested when compared with family channels and news channels.

Before delving into the Arab public's television consumption patterns in terms of distribution of viewing among the different channels, it is important to note the different types of programs of interest to Arab viewers. These preferences may greatly help us in understanding the variety of programming. To obtain this information, the interviewees were asked to rate their interest in various programming categories.

The data available from the general survey could have been anticipated, considering the fact that Arab society is a minority maintaining a complex relationship with the majority Jewish society and its institutional structures. Hence 80.7% responded that news programs most interest them, 15.7% expressed only a moderate or slight interest, and only 3.6% stated that they were totally uninterested in the news. Programs focusing on political commentary were also of interest to most Arab television viewers: 48% of the respondents stated that they were interested or very interested in such programs, 40.2% indicated that they were moderately interested or less, and only 10.7% responded that they were uninterested. Entertainment programs were also watched by a high percentage of the Arab public. Almost half of the study's participants (44.6%) responded that they were interested or very interested in televised Arabic films and series, 37.4% were moderately interested or less, and 18% were uninterested. In contrast, 62.5% of Arab television viewers were not interested in Hebrew films and series, 29.6% were moderately interested or less, and only 7.9% responded that they were positively interested.

Given its relationship to the majority society, the lack of interest in televised Hebrew films and series indicates the alienation and distance from Jewish culture felt by Arab society. As will be seen, however, these findings do not mean that Arab television viewers entirely avoid Israeli television. The viewing patterns observed indicate that the Arab public relates to Israeli television programs as a source of information required for maintaining its daily life.

The data obtained on viewing patterns also indicates that the Arab public consumes contents from the full range of Israeli and Arabic television channels available. This mix clearly indicates the Arabs' tendency to sample from both spaces, the two being perceived as complementing rather than opposing one another. The dual positioning illustrates the hybridization of the Arab public. Hybridization, a component in the identity of many minority groups, has been studied by many cultural researchers.[9] This intricate pattern of media consumption, drawing from two cultures, manifests a minority's cultural "in-betweenness," which entails taking advantage of the cultural spaces open to it in order to fulfill its social, cultural, and political needs. Arab society, too, expresses this conscious, strategic choice, one that maintains a dialectic relationship with a hybrid space and allows a group to circumvent its place in conventional time and space, by linking up to a digital world providing the cultural contents that fulfill their multiple needs.

We thus find that the Arab public watches a considerable amount of Israeli television in Hebrew. At the same time, they enjoy a lot of Arab television broadcast via satellite. Arab consumers in Israel clearly distinguish between programming areas. These distinctions express the high level of confidence and satisfaction with the contents on politics, nationality, cultural, and sociolinguistic identity provided by Arab channels. For political items, such as news addressing the Israeli-Palestinian conflict, culture, and entertainment, Arabs tend to watch channels from the Arab world. Alternatively, for contents touching on areas of everyday life—education, economics, health, and so forth—Arabs are more likely to watch Israeli television. Their objective is to obtain the greatest benefits and amounts of information available from all the options offered in digital space. Consumption of this type also enables Arab viewers to be involved in two political and cultural spaces simultaneously. Because the Arab population in Israel lives within the larger framework of Israeli society, Israeli politics and social developments are important for planning their daily lives. Simultaneously, members of Arab society in Israel view themselves as participating in regional Arab politics and culture, an identity that demands consumption of Arab television. Hence the entertainment, films, series, music programs, and talk shows viewed on Arab television speak to them. This perception of television programming is then translated into the broad distribution of viewing among numerous channels.

Due to the very low viewing of some channels, rates that might introduce bias, we were unable to include all channels within the statistical analysis. The criterion for including a television channel was a viewer rating of at least 2%. In addition, relatively few channels appear in the analysis because the respondents were asked to limit themselves to ranking only the three channels they watched most. Had the participants been allowed to indicate all the channels watched, the list obtained would have been more comprehensive but not amenable to statistical analysis. Table 7.1 therefore presents the ten channels that met the basic consumption criterion.

Table 7.1. Ten television channels ranked in popularity by Arabs in Israel

	Channel 1	Channel 2	LBC	Al-Jazeera	Rotana	MBC	Future	MBC2	Iqra'a	Al-Arabya
First choice	7.9%	11.0%	4.9%	29.6%	4.3%	10.2%	2.5%	3.2%	4.8%	0.5%
Second choice	4.8%	12.5%	4.8%	12.9%	3.6%	10.2%	4.4%	2.0%	3.1%	5.4%
Third choice	7.1%	6.1%	4.8%	8.6%	6.0%	8.0%	4.7%	1.9%	2.6%	3.9%

The findings indicated that the Arab television audience in Israel watched many channels, the most popular being Al-Jazeera, Channel 2, MBC, Channel 1, LBC, Rotana, Future, Iqra'a, Al-Arabya, and MBC2. At least 2% of the respondents ranked most of these stations in first place. The range of contents broadcast by these channels is rich, including news, family, film, sports, and religious matters. This range exhibits the pluralism characterizing Arab media consumption, on the one hand, and selectivity, on the other. Some channels originate in Israel and are broadcast in Hebrew, while others originate in the Arab world and are broadcast in Arabic. This potpourri of preferences also reflects the impact of technology on media consumption patterns and the rise of cosmopolitan popular culture. Many of the most popular channels are broadcast from places such as Qatar, Saudi Arabia, Beirut, Tel Aviv, and Jerusalem, a fact that reflects the media's globalization as well as the increasing erosion of government control over national media and cultural spaces.[10]

The high rate of viewing television channels originating outside the Israeli media space primarily stems from the Arab public's national and cultural affinity with the Arab world, which provides contents unavailable on Israeli television. Yet it is important to note that television consumption from Arab sources likewise reflects the absence of a local station that responds to this sector's programming needs in its native language. The Israeli television stations, Channel 1, Channel 2, and Channel 10, each allocate a sliver of non-primetime space to Arabic programming. These programs do not attract a large audience, and programming is not controlled by members of Arab society. One ploy used in official calculations of the time allotted to Arabic-language broadcasts is to include programs that are subtitled in Arabic within this category. As a result, only a miniscule number of programs in Arabic and produced by Arabs are broadcast.

One blatant disadvantage to this situation is that the Arab population in Israel has no possibility of influencing the programming that it consumes. This fact nurtures a certain amount of alienation between Arab consumers and the channels, but at the same time precludes any obligation to watch a given channel. For instance, Arab society has absolutely no influence on the contents that Israeli television channels broadcast to it and about it. The networks make those decisions in isolation from their Arab audience. Nor does it exert any influence on the contents of satellite broadcasts from the Arab world. Therefore, despite the high consumption of programs broadcast by Arab satellite channels, a considerable proportion of the Arab public in Israel (33.8%) stated that these channels do not represent them.

The research found that Arabs preferred Al-Jazeera over any other channel. Among the respondents, 29.6% ranked it in first place, 12.9% in second place, and 8.6% in third place. It was also found that 50.9% of all television-viewing respondents watched Al-Jazeera at varying frequencies. Channel 2, the leading Israeli channel watched by the Arab public, was ranked in first place by 11.5%, in second place by 12.5%, and in third place by 6.1%. A total of 29.4% of all television-viewing respondents reported that they watched Channel 2 at varying frequencies. These data indicate the popularity of this channel and its penetration into Arab society despite alienation from the contents and the criticism leveled against its programming. It is likewise important to note that 84.5% of Channel 2's viewers also reported that they watched Al-Jazeera. A similar finding was obtained from Channel 1 viewers, 79.5% of whom also watched Al-Jazeera. This pattern indicates a tendency to balance several sources of broadcast information. The Arab public thus watches the news broadcast by Al-Jazeera as well as the news broadcast by the Israeli channels. Consumers are thereby able to construct a more well-rounded view of the events after comparing the information obtained about regional developments, primarily regarding Israeli policies in the West Bank and Gaza Strip. The advantage provided by the opportunity to compare alternative sources of information is unavailable to Jewish society in Israel, a fact that diminishes its ability to balance the information received.

Another channel that achieved a respectable ranking by Arab viewers in Israel was MBC, formerly broadcasting from London and recently moved to Dubai: 10.2% ranked it in first place, 10.2% in second place, and 8% in third place. These rankings indicate this channel's stability within its niche. In all, 28.3% of all television viewers watch this channel at different viewing frequencies. MBC, the oldest satellite television channel received by Arabs in Israel, is a general channel, mixing news with Arab cultural and comedy programs, such as *Millionaire*, and many series in Arabic that originate in Egypt, Syria, and Saudi Arabia. The channel is conservative in style and appearance. This combination may be what helped it become the third most popular channel among Arabs in Israel. Israel's Channel 1 is the fourth most popular channel, ranked in first place by 7.9%. A total of 19.6% of all television viewers watch this channel at different viewing frequencies.

Table 7.2. Average hours Arabs in Israel
spent watching television daily

Channel 1	1.36
Channel 2	1.62
LBC	1.61
Al-Jazeera	1.50
Rotana	2.08
MBC	1.75
Future	1.31
MBC2	2.50
Iqra'a	1.18
Al-Arabya	1.48

Among the other channels that attracted a stable viewing audience was the Lebanese channel LBC, with 4.8% of viewers ranking it in one of the three leading places, and a total audience of 14.4%. LBC has thus obtained a regular viewing audience. The fifth most popular channel, ranked in first place by 4.8% of the Arab public, was the religious channel *Iqra'a,* although only 3.1% and 2.6% of the respondents ranked it second and third, respectively. The findings indicate that religious viewers prefer this channel; they did not view alternative channels, or perhaps those alternatives did not meet their needs. The music channel Rotana was ranked first by 4.3% of the viewers and third by 6%. Overall, 13.7% of all television viewers watch this channel at different frequencies, a relatively high percentage for a music channel. Rotana's increased rating in third place indicates its choice for leisure time viewing.

In order to identify differences in frequency of viewing and the time spent watching the various channels, the respondents were asked to note the average number of hours that they watched each channel daily.

This data clearly shows that the average amount of time devoted to

Table 7.3. Ten television channels ranked in popularity by Arab elites in Israel

	Channel 1	Channel 2	Channel 10	LBC	Al-Jazeera	MBC	Future	Iqra'a	Al-Arabya	Al-Manar
First choice	11.2%	12.1%	14.3%	1.3%	49.3%	3.1%	0.0%	0.0%	2.2%	1.3%
Second choice	10.3%	26.0%	10.8%	1.8%	14.3%	10.2%	0.0%	1.8%	16.2%	7.6%
Third choice	10.2%	18.1%	3.2%	3.7%	10.6%	8.0%	2.8%	5.1%	3.2%	9.7%

watching entertainment and family channels was greater than the amount of time devoted to watching news channels.

When examining the data of the selective survey, one notices that the patterns of watching television channels among the elites differs from the general public, despite the fact that the dominant channels remain almost the same.

As a general trend, one notices that the news channels—Al-Jazeera, Al-Arabya, Al-Manar, and the Israeli channels—draw more attention from the elites than from the general public. On the other hand, the main entertainment channels—Rotana Music and MBC2—do not appear to be among the most watched. Another important conclusion that could be drawn from the data is the balance between Israeli and Arab channels. The three main Israeli channels gain the attention of a high percentage of the Arab elites. This data is not surprising if we take into consideration that the Arab elites are engaged in daily contact with their Israeli environment. The data also demonstrates that the Arab news channels are given much attention by the elites. Al-Jazeera is their most watched news channel. However, unlike the data of the general survey, Al-Arabya is the main alternative to Al-Jazeera. Surprisingly, we found that the Lebanese channel Al-Manar, identified with Hezbollah, was given much attention. The family and religious channels are given less attention by the elites than by the general public. MBC, LBC, Future, and Iqra'a are not broadly watched by the Arab elites. These patterns reflect the political awareness of the elites and their attempt to be part of the regional picture, especially if we take into consideration the political and national conflicts in the region that influence the daily life of the whole of Arab society.

In order to be able to characterize the nature of the Arab public sphere concerning media contents drawn from television channels and have a deeper understanding of the communicative behavior of the Arab public, the general survey posed questions seeking to examine the relationship between certain contents and television channels. Such data is helpful in characterizing the media differentiated public sphere and in understanding dominant patterns of collective thinking and behavior. Therefore, the interviewees were asked to name the channels they viewed for certain important topics.

In comparing the viewing patterns for Israeli channels with those for Arab satellite channels, a clear division was found reflecting the duality of the media landscape and the various functions that each television sphere plays in Arab society's culture of media consumption. Thus Arab viewers who display significant interest in current events will watch news outlets on Arab satellite channels as well as news on Israeli Hebrew channels. Among the respondents, 80.7% stated that they were interested in news to a great

Table 7.4. Arab viewing patterns for topics of interest

Topics	Israeli channels	Arab satellite channels	Foreign channels	Do not watch programs on this topic	Unimportant
Israeli-Palestinian conflict	27.3%	65.4%	0.4%	3.0%	3.8%
U.S. occupation of Iraq	8.9%	80.7%	1.3%	4.1%	5.0%
Economy	45.9%	19.8%	0.8%	25.7%	7.8%
Education	51.0%	24.7%	1.1%	16.3%	6.9%
Entertainment and music	3.6%	67.5%	1.4%	20.0%	7.4%

or very great extent, and 74.2% expressed interest in political programming, although this high level of interest was manifested in varied viewing patterns.

A high percentage of Arab television viewers preferred to watch programs dealing with political issues—such as the Israel-Palestinian conflict or the American occupation of Iraq—on Arab news channels, the most outstanding of which was Al-Jazeera. Among Arabs, 65.4% preferred to watch news about the Israel-Palestinian conflict on Arab channels and 27.3% preferred to watch Israeli channels. Regarding the American occupation of Iraq, 80.7% preferred to watch Arab channels and 8.9% preferred Israeli channels. One of the reasons for this viewing pattern is the stance that the Arabic satellite channels take. They address these issues more deeply and level criticism at Israeli policies in the occupied territories and American policies in Iraq. In contrast, the Israeli channels are more sympathetic toward the two countries' policies and tend to justify whatever actions are taken by them. The Arab public therefore places little trust in the Israeli channels regarding this sphere and great trust in the Arab channels.

We obtained a similar picture with respect to cultural, entertainment, and music programs: 67.5% of Arab viewers in Israel watch such programs on Arab channels, whereas only 3.6% watch such programs on Israeli channels. The principal reasons are the identification of these viewers with the Arab world and its culture, coupled with the remoteness felt toward Jewish society and the culture that it has produced—a culture that is foreign to the Arab Middle Easterner, in general, and to local Arab society, in particular.

On subjects directly related to the conduct of daily life—for example, education and the economy—a large percentage of the Arab public watches Israeli channels. Among the respondents, 45.9% preferred to watch economic news on Israeli channels, and 19.8% preferred Arab channels; 51.0% preferred Israeli programs on education, whereas 24.7% preferred Arab programs.

Similar viewing patterns were observed in the selective elites' survey.

Whereas political, social, and cultural programs were watched mostly on Arab satellite channels, without abandoning Israeli channels completely, daily issues such as education, economics, and sports were viewed mostly on Israeli channels. The social and family programs on Arab channels gain the attention of Arab elites much more than these programs on Israeli channels. This pattern could be explained by the fact that social and family problems that characterize Arab societies in the Arab world, such as marriage, feminist issues, youth dilemmas, etc., are much closer to Arab society in Israel than these same issues in Israeli society, which is conceived to be a Western society in these matters. This should not mean, of course, that Arab society in Israel has not been influenced by developments in Israeli society. Nevertheless, Arab society in Israel views itself as part of the Arab world socially and culturally, especially once the Islamization processes began.

As has been shown, Arab media consumers in Israel enjoy a large variety of television channels. Two of the salient issues in media research pertain to the channels that the public prefers for viewing the news and how much trust they place in the news broadcast. The respondents were asked questions regarding their news program viewing pattern and their trust in the programs.

The data of the general survey shows that a very high proportion of Arab viewers are interested in the news. Of those who watched television, 80.7% stated that they were interested or very interested in news broadcasts. Only 9.1% responded that they were uninterested in the news, with another 10.2% indicating that they were only moderately interested.

Respondents were also asked to rank the three channels that they preferred or watched the most. The data demonstrates that 57% of the respondents ranked Al-Jazeera as their first choice for news programming, far beyond all the other channels. Al-Jazeera maintained its precedence in the second and third choice categories as well, with 20.7% naming it as their second choice and 14.2% as their third choice. Although Al-Arabya received few responses as a first choice (1.8%), it was a strong alternative to Al-Jazeera among viewers of televised news, with 20.7% of respondents designating it as their second choice and 17.6% as their third. Israel's Channel 2 also served as a substitute for Al-Jazeera: 17.8% indicated this channel as their first choice, 20.3% as their second choice, and 13.3% as their third. Israel's Channel 1 has lost its drawing power as a provider of news not only among the Jewish population but also among the Arab population. Of the study participants who watched television news, 11.7% stated that Channel 1 was their first choice, 10.3% their second choice, and 15.1% their third choice. Analysis of the data therefore indicates that Channel 1 represents a substitute for other channels only as a second or third choice. We can therefore conclude that Al-Jazeera is the principal provider of news to those members of Arab society who watch televised news, although a high proportion of this public watches more than one channel, while balancing between Arab satellite channels and Israeli channels.

When looking at the data drawn from the selective survey, we find some differences between the Arab elites and the general Arab public. Although Al-Jazeera is the leading channel on which the Arab elites mostly view the news (52.7% in first choice and 27.4% in second choice), a relatively high percentage of the Arab elites watch the news on the three Israeli channels: 15.5% watched Channel 1 as first choice and 8.2% as second choice. Channel 2 draws 13.2% of the Arab elites as first choice and 37% as second choice, showing that many of the viewers of Al-Jazeera choose Channel 2 as an alternative. The data regarding Channel 10 is relatively surprising, as 17.3% indicated this channel as their first choice and 11.9% as second choice, thereby choosing this channel over the most frequently viewed news channel among the Jewish public, namely, Channel 2.

As stated, the Arab public's trust in the news broadcast was a subject of great interest. Respondents were asked to compare their level of trust in the news provided by Arab satellite channels, primarily Al-Jazeera, with their level of trust in the news provided by the Israeli channels, primarily Channel 2, due to its higher preference rating among viewers of Israeli news programming. Similar to the question on trust in newspapers, a hypothetical scenario was presented. In this scenario, Al-Jazeera reported on the death of two Palestinians in the Gaza Strip from Israeli army fire. Alternatively, Channel 2 reported the same incident but claimed that the Palestinians were killed when an explosive device that they were preparing blew up. The respondents were asked to indicate which channel's report they would believe.

Given this scenario, 64.4% of the respondents said that they would believe Al-Jazeera and 4.3% would believe Channel 2. Only 12.1% responded that the trust placed in the two channels would depend on the circumstances. When looking at the data drawn from the elites' survey based on the same scenario, we found that 65.5% of the elites said that they would believe Al-Jazeera, whereas 23.6% said that they would believe Channel 2. Only 10.5% claimed that it would depend. This sizeable gap in the level of trust attributed to the news broadcasts by the two channels indicates a crisis of confidence in Israeli television on the part of Arab society in Israel, particularly regarding news reports related to the Israeli-Palestinian conflict. The Arabs in Israel, including the Arab elites, do not trust Israeli media broadcasts, since they are perceived to mirror official governmental positions, especially when it comes to Jewish-Arab relations. The Arab public and elites also believe that Israeli television promotes the government's positions by legitimizing its occupation policies in the Palestinian-occupied territories. Such attitudes seriously interfere with trust and represent factors driving viewers to alternative channels, principally Al-Jazeera, which provides comprehensive and in-depth coverage of developments in the Palestinian-occupied territories.

The Perceptions and Impact
of Arab Satellite Television

The findings on Arab society's television viewing patterns reported so far indicate a clear trend: high consumption of contents and programs broadcast by Arab satellite television. In light of this trend, the question arises as to whether and how much the Arab public believes that the contents broadcast by these channels affect the community's self-image and perceptions of its political and cultural environment. Participants in the surveys were asked to answer questions regarding the effect of satellite television on these variables. One of the questions asked related to the extent to which they believed that Arab satellite channels represent the respondents, their identity, views, and interests.

The findings show that 39.5% of the respondents of the general survey replied that the Arab satellite channels represent them, with an additional 20.5% being noncommittal (adopting the midpoint position). Among the remainder, 33.8% said they did not believe that the Arabic satellite channels represent them, whereas 6.2% did not know (had no opinion). These responses indicate that the Arab public is divided on this issue, although the majority tends to believe that satellite television does, in fact, represent them. In the elite survey, 67.2% said that the Arab satellite channels represent them, and 30.6% said that they do not represent them enough. When the elites' survey participants were asked to convey their opinion regarding the extent to which the Arab satellite television channels draw the attention of their relatives and friends, 76% responded positively. This finding shows that the dominant television sphere among the Arab population, including the elite, is the Arab sphere rather than the Israeli.

In order to better understand the Arab public's position on this issue, several statements were presented to the respondents, who were asked to rate the extent to which they agreed or disagreed with their contents. The findings indicate that the satellite television channels have a considerable impact on Arab public opinion in various areas, such as their self-awareness, political positions, and interest in cultural matters.

The data of the general survey shows that the Arabic satellite broadcasts helped maintain a sense of belonging to a great or very great extent for 40.7% of the respondents; however, 17.4% did not share this view, and 38.2% replied that they agreed with this statement only to a small or very small degree. This distribution indicates that most Arabs in Israel agree that the

Arab satellite broadcasts reinforce their sense of community with the Arab world, at least to some extent. It should be stressed that one explanation for the strong sense of belonging to the Arab world felt by many of the study's participants and evidenced in the findings precedes the onset of Arab satellite broadcasting. The availability and programming of these broadcasts can be assumed to have enhanced the existing feelings.

When looking at the data regarding this statement in the elites' survey, one finds that 22.5% felt that the Arab satellite channels strengthened and 50.5% claimed that they strongly strengthened their sense of belonging to the Arab world. This data reflects the strong impact of the satellite channels on the affiliation of the Arab elites and the Arab public with the Arab world, something that influences their self-confidence and impacts their sense of identity. Although it is premature to claim that these findings may have a strong impact on the political behavior of the Arab population in Israel, this option cannot be ruled out, especially if the Israeli discrimination policies continue.

Interviewees in the general survey were asked if they agreed that "Arab satellite broadcasts influenced my identification with problems in the Arab world." Among the respondents, 57.3% said yes. An additional 29.6% stated that they were affected by these broadcasts to a moderate or small extent. Only 9.7% replied that they did not agree with the statement at all. These findings provide support for the characterization of Arab society in Israel as a sector viewing the Arab space as an object of national, cultural, and emotional affinity. This conclusion is especially true if we take into consideration that 77.6% of the respondents in the elites' survey gave a positive answer to this statement.

The respondents in the general survey were also asked to address the effect of Arab satellite television broadcasts on their self-confidence as Arabs living in Israel. The responses were as follows: 39.5% stated that the broadcasts did reinforce their self-confidence, 32% said that the broadcasts reinforced their self-confidence to a moderate or small degree, and 25% replied that the broadcasts did not reinforce that feeling. On this issue as well, it is possible that some of the respondents had felt very self-confident as Arabs before the availability of Arab satellite broadcasts and that they therefore did not believe that attitude to have been further enhanced.

A statement addressing the influence that Arab satellite channels had on the rates of viewing Israeli television in Arabic received these responses: 43.9% affirmed that these broadcasts had an effect, with 28.4% stating that their viewing of Israeli television was affected to a moderate or small degree, while 24.3% reported no effect. A similar and even clearer picture emerged regarding the effect of these broadcasts on the rate of viewing Israeli cultural programs: 47.5% responded that the Arabic satellite broadcasts reduced their viewing of Israeli cultural programs, 25.5% said that their viewing was affected to a moderate or small degree, and 22.3% stated that the broadcasts had no effect.

When examining the selective survey regarding the influence of the contents received from the Arab satellite television channels, one can see that members of the elite consider these channels to be of central importance for their perceptions of their surrounding environment, especially for their relationship with the Arab world. The interviewees were asked to rank on a scale of 1 to 4, where 1 reflects very strong and 4 reflects very weak, the degree to which Arab satellite television contents influenced their sense of belonging to the Arab world. With an average answer of 1.423, the findings indicate that they had a very strong influence. The interviewees were also asked to rank the degree to which the Arab satellite television channels influenced their own estrangement from Israeli culture and society. The average answer of 2.11 reflects a relatively strong influence. These two measures of the impact of contents from Arab satellite television channels on the perceptions of the Arab elites are supported by other data. When asked questions about the influence of Arab satellite television channels on the relationship between Arabs in Israel and those in the Arab world, the answers (shown in table 7.5) indicate a relatively strong positive connection. Two further supports for our claim are that one answer implies that the Arab satellite channels represent the interviewee and another implies that these channels attract the attention of his or her friends and relatives. In both cases the majority of interviewees gave a clear answer reflecting strong connections between the variables. Whereas 67% agreed to the claim that Arab satellite television represents them, 76% declared that these channels manage to draw the attention of their friends and relatives.

These firm findings give the same picture we saw in the wider public, meaning that Arab satellite televisions have penetrated Arab society and become the media space in which the community feels comfortable. When

Table 7.5. Responses to questions regarding the influence of Arab satellite television on Arab in Israel

	I feel that Arab satellite television represents me	Arab satellite television fairly represents the Arabs in Israel	Arab satellite television represents Arabs in Israel as part of the Arab world	Arab satellite television channel manage to draw the attention of most of my friend and relatives
Strongly agree	10.0%	6.0%	9.0%	32.0%
Agree	57.3%	52.0%	39.1%	44.0%
Disagree to some extent	20.4%	30.7%	35.6%	14.7%
Strongly disagree	10.2%	11.1%	16.0%	8.0%
I don't know	2.2%	0.4%	0.0%	1.3%

Table 7.6. Responses to questions regarding the influence of Arab satellite television on Arab elites in Israel

	Strengthens my sense of connection to Arab culture	Strengthens my use of the Arabic language	Strengthens my relationship with Arab elites in the Arab world
Strongly strengthened	55.0%	51.6%	50.7%
Moderately strengthened	17.0%	18.0%	20.7%
Moderately weakened	1.8%	2.3%	1.4%
Strongly weakened	0.5%	0.0%	0.5%
No influence	25.2%	27.6%	25.8%
I don't know	0.0%	0.5%	0.9%

we remind ourselves that various scholars of the media have demonstrated the strong influence of media contents on setting the agenda and framing the mind of media audiences, the data provided so far is, or could be, of great political importance.

The elite survey posed another set of questions that sought to deepen our understanding of the influence that Arab satellite television channels have on the attitudes and perceptions of Arab elites in Israel. Table 7.6 presents some of the data that could be vital to understanding observations made in the introduction to this book.

The picture that can be drawn from the findings presented in table 7.6 may be summed up by saying that Arab satellite television plays an important role in strengthening the connection between the Arab elite in Israel and Arab culture and elites in the Arab world. This influence is especially important when it comes to the use of Arabic language. Some scholars of Arab society in Israel have claimed that knowledge of the Arabic language has been deteriorating among the Arab population in Israel as a result of the influence of the Hebrew language and the daily necessity of communicating in it. Furthermore, the fact that most of the Arab elite have studied at Israeli universities, where classes are taught in Hebrew, has led to a weakening of the Arabic language among the Arab elites in Israel. The data provided by table 7.6 demonstrates that the Arab satellite television channels are seen as a source of strength for the use of the Arabic language. When most of the media content is consumed in Arabic, this will have a strong impact on the use of the language, especially if we take into consideration that the basic idioms used in reference to immediate social, political, and cultural issues are thus provided on a daily basis in Arabic. This fact may lead to balancing the influence that the Israeli education system, especially the higher education institutions, has on the language use of the average Arab academic.

The total picture emerging illustrates that there are major changes taking place in the media consumption culture of Arab society in Israel. The globalization of the media has become an opportunity. Arab satellite channels provide solutions for the deficiencies in television programming previously available due to the absence of an Arab channel that was locally controlled. They have also reinforced the strong link between Arab society in Israel and events taking place in the greater Arab world. These channels have opened the surrounding Arab societies and their problems to Israel's Arab population. At the same time, they have fulfilled many of the Arab public's needs by broadcasting contents formerly inaccessible in the local media landscape. As a result, Arabic satellite television broadcasts have had a strong impact on the Arab media consumption culture, on the way leisure time is spent, and on this sector's consumption of Israel's Hebrew broadcasts. In the long run, this trend may deepen and may have growing effects on the general relationship between the Arab minority and the state of Israel, especially when we see that Arab elites in Israel demonstrate much the same patterns of media behavior and consumption as the general population. Nevertheless, when looking at the patterns of Hebrew media consumption of both the general Arab public and the elites in regard to daily issues, we notice that the Arab public and its leadership are well connected with their immediate public sphere and seek information that is at the very least necessary for their survival. Despite its negative imaging of Arabs, Israeli media is still conceived to provide valuable contents that receive the attention of Arab citizens.

The balancing between Israeli and Arab news sources among the Arab elites demonstrates the effort made by these elites to turn their structural inferiority into an opportunity, where the command of two languages and access to two separate media spaces become a source of empowerment. The Arab public is able to experience its Arab as well as Israeli context without having to pay much of a price for it. Whereas neither Arabs from the Arab world nor Israeli Jews have the wherewithal to overcome the linguistic barriers and have, as a result, no access to each other's media spaces, the Arab minority in Israel is located in between. Despite its national and cultural affiliation with the Arab world, the daily contact with Israeli media space, albeit only for instrumental reasons, has made Israeli media contents part and parcel of the Arab minority's public culture. The alienation and frustration with the under- and misrepresentation of Arabs in the Israeli media have caused major changes in Arab communicative behavior without leading to a total divorce between the two. Future developments, not only in the media field, will determine how Arabs citizens of Israel will conceive of and relate to their Israeli environment in the future.

Conclusion

The developments described and the data presented in this book lead us to several conclusions regarding strategies of communicative behavior of the Arab minority in Israel that can possibly be generalized to other national minorities in other localities in the world. First we have to remind the reader that this study has clarified the centrality of the media field as a major avenue for the study of state-minority relations, through which policies of surveillance, marginalization, and control conducted by the state can be examined and ameliorated. The examination of the media policies of the Israeli state toward its Arab minority and the counter communicative behavior of this minority has never been thoroughly studied. Therefore, this book exposes the reader to the role that the media play in state-minority relations, demonstrating that state media policies and their adoption by the Hebrew media have been one of the major sources of alienation among the Arab population of Israel vis-à-vis the Israeli state and the Hebrew culture dominant in it.

The study has demonstrated that the media policies of the Israeli state do not grant the Arab minority an open space for freedom of expression or representation but rather have aimed at determining the nature of the Arab public sphere in Israel, seeking to promote the resocialization of this community and to reshape its collective consciousness in order to serve the interests of the state. The state sought to control freedom of expression in Arab society and to penetrate the Arab collective consciousness by controlling the media available in it and infusing it with contents determined by state agencies. The freedom of expression of Arab citizens was limited, using legal, procedural, and discursive means. The study has demonstrated the centrality of the various Israeli policy components in the political, economic, demographic, social, and cultural fields that composed a sophisticated power structure, aiming to establish total dependence of the minority on state agencies.

Despite state policies and based on the study of Arab communicative behavior, one can conclude that the Arab minority, like other national minorities in other states, developed patterns of behavior well known from social movements theory, presented in the theoretical introduction, utilizing all the structural opportunities available to it in order to improve its status and strengthen its influence on its surrounding environment. This behavior demonstrates that the assumption regarding contentious politics is validated. Arab society in Israel has sought by all legal and peaceful means to overcome the control policies of the state. It has replaced its accommodative policies, which had characterized its behavior under the military government, with contentious behavior, manifested in different fields, one of which is the media. Structural opportunity, made available through the moderate liberalization in Israeli policy, especially after the occupation of the West Bank and the Gaza Strip, formed the basis for the emerging Arab elites to practice new patterns of behavior that resist state policies. The Communist Party formed the vanguard of the Arab population by utilizing its newspaper, *Al-Ittihad,* to influence the Arab public agenda and counteract the efforts made by the state to control it. *Al-Ittihad* formed an important journalistic school for many educated Arab leaders who emerged in the 1970s and later established newspapers, thereby enriching the Arab public sphere, elevating it to a counter-hegemonic space.

Furthermore, structural changes in the Israeli economy, in the late 1970s and early 1980s, encouraged Arab entrepreneurs to establish their own media institutions, mainly advertising firms and newspapers, and to strengthen the foundations of the Arab public sphere. This sphere brought to the fore issues that had been silenced by the state and not addressed by the Hebrew media. A pioneering example was the publicizing by *Al-Ittihad* of the massacre conducted by the Israeli armed forces in the village of Kufar-Qassem in October 1956. The Arabic newspapers, especially the party-affiliated ones, have contributed to the constitution of a critical collective consciousness among the entire Arab population. They set the discursive model later imitated by private newspapers, although the latter have never committed to a clear ideological line, but rather followed commercial trends that promoted their economic interests. Nevertheless, the new maneuvering spaces provided by Arab media institutions, including in the last few years Radio Ashams, challenged the Jewish public sphere and formed a solid resistance force in the face of state attempts to penetrate Arab society.

Therefore, a clear conclusion of this study is that, despite the apparent accommodative behavior that the Arab minority may have demonstrated as a result of state pressures, especially when the state sought cultural and political hegemony, it did not fully accommodate to the political and cultural reality that sought to trap it and turn it into a marginal object of historical processes. This behavior of the Arab minority was supported by the structural reality of conflict in which it found itself, caught between its nation and the Israeli state. The Israeli-Palestinian conflict has been a major source of unrest in the immediate environment of the Arab minority in Israel, especially as a result of the familial ties between this minority and the rest of the Palestinian people and the national consciousness that has been constantly rising among members of the minority.

The behavior of the Arab minority, demonstrated in the communicative field, could be generalized to minorities' behavior elsewhere. It reflects the tendency of minorities not to endanger the gains they have won based on their citizenship but to utilize their citizenship as a structure of opportunities to promote their interests. The communicative behavior of the Arab minority, as evidenced in this study, verifies that minorities adopt special patterns of contentious collective behavior that expand their ability to maneuver and resist state policies to control them and to shape their collective consciousness. Communicative behavior and media consumption patterns have been shown to be a fertile field in which to demonstrate how minorities seek to express their dissatisfaction with the policies of their state, challenge these, and strengthen their affinity with political and cultural spaces that they view as belonging to their nation, one that could be a sovereign nation in a neighboring state or a stateless nation, such as in the case of the Palestinians or the Kurds.

The study of the communicative behavior of the Arab minority in Israel has validated the claims made by the theoretical framework presented in the first chapter: that social groups can be characterized through what has been termed their "media orientation." The Arab minority has developed its own media orientation, in its own media space, in its own language. This media orientation counters state media policies. The rising number of Arabic newspapers since the early 1980s and the rise of radio stations, legal and illegal, lead to the conclusion that media institutions are tools utilized by minorities, like other social movements, to promote the interests of the minority and promote its worldview regarding issues of concern to it. As we have seen, the minority media discusses issues that are usually ignored by the majority media and, as a result, creates a counter public sphere that challenges the dominant majority public sphere or at the very least provides a public sphere in which freedom of expression and access of minority members and issues to the public agenda is not conditioned by the power structure determined by the majority.

Furthermore, the minority counter public sphere forms a cultural zone in which the use of minority language is used not only as a tool of communication but also as a countercultural space. The issue of language is central, since one of the tools used by the majority to penetrate the minority culture is language. The influence of the Hebrew language has been growing as a result of the need for the average Arab citizen to know Hebrew if he or she wishes to participate in the Israeli job market. Furthermore, Hebrew is the teaching language in Israeli universities, where most of the Arab elite have received their education. These two factors have given the Hebrew language a major push in Arab society, leading to bilingualism.

The Arabic media and the constitution of a media space in Arabic have contributed to counterbalancing the rising influence of the Hebrew language in the Arab public sphere. Arab satellite television channels, received from the Arab world, formed a media space where the Arabic language is the dominant language. This new media space has provided the Arab minority in Israel with a very important way to practice its freedom of expression and receive media contents that meet its cultural needs and expectations in its own language. The media space from the Arab world has helped the Arab minority overcome the immediate and strict control policies of the state. It accelerated the process in which the Arab minority has been constituting itself as a social agent, seeking to influence the shaping of the collective imagination of its members.

Notwithstanding this process, this study leads to the conclusion that the media consumption culture of the Arab minority in Israel mirrors the duality of its presence in the complex media spaces that cross the borders of its immediate physical location. The study supports the assumption that Arab society in Israel expresses its sociocultural "in-betweenness" by taking advantage of the diverse media opportunities available among the plethora of accessible newspapers, radio stations, and television channels. The Arab public mixes consumption of Israeli media, primarily news on practical subjects, with consumption of Arab media from the wider Arab space, behavior facilitated by the development of satellite communications during the past decade.

This pattern of communicative behavior leads us to conclude that Arab society in Israel is not a trapped minority or a passive object locked in double marginality. Instead, the communicative behavior of the Arab minority indicates deliberate, rational use of available structural opportunities manifested in the complex, multilayered, and variegated nature of this behavior. Arab citizens of Israel are affected by their Israeli reality, but they cannot be viewed as trapped in it. Their communicative behavior manifests their broad cultural repertoire, encompassing at least two languages and a broad expanse of contents and images. This reality leads us to draw the conclusion of a "double consciousness," which characterizes the Arab minority in Israel.

This does not mean that Arab society in Israel relates in similar ways to its Israeliness and to its bond with its Arab environment in the Arab world. Evidence from this research demonstrates claims made in the literature presented in the theoretical introduction, showing that one must not underestimate the history and nationality of this minority, which belongs to the Palestinian people and Arab nation both culturally and religiously. This study has provided the empirical evidence that this double consciousness of the Arab minority is manifested in its emotional, mental, sentimental, and rational identification with the Palestinian people and the Arab world, while it is mostly instrumentally and rationally connected to its Israeli reality. As a result of its exclusion and alienation from being part of Israeli society and culture, this minority has developed a rational and instrumental relationship with its Israeli reality. The lack of emotional or sentimental attachment to Israeli culture is mirrored in the data regarding Israeli cultural programming. Having said that, it is important to point out that the rational and instrumental relationship with Israeli reality has significant implications for the daily behavior of members of the Arab minority.

The study of the communicative behavior of the Arab minority in Israel leads to the conclusion that, unlike some claims made by Israeli scholars on the Israelization of the Arab minority in Israel, this minority escapes Israeli cultural contents when it has an opportunity to do so. This conclusion does not clash with the findings reflecting patterns of communicative behavior showing that the minority seeks to be updated on issues that relate to its Israeli daily life. Arab citizens of Israel are aware of the various components of Israeli society and their ways of life. They are exposed to Israeli Jewish society on a daily basis. They are fully aware of their political and economic dependence on their Israeli environment, which could not be replaced by an external agent. The globalization of the media and the economy does provide some outlet for the Arab elites and for the general public, and it balances the indispensability of the Israeli environment for daily survival. This indispensability is the main source of the double consciousness.

Therefore, the globalization of the media provides for the cultural and symbolic needs of the Arab community in Israel but does not provide political and economic solutions to its problems, leading to the communicative behavior we witnessed in the data, best described by the concept of in-betweenness. The Arab minority is practically connected to its immediate Israeli reality and culturally to the broader Arab world. This in-betweenness is a major source of strength. Arabs citizens of Israel are the only social group in the Middle East that has a foot on both edges of the Israel-Arab divide. They understand both sides and are able to communicate with each of them and potentially between them. The media behavior of this community demonstrates that it is unwilling to abandon either of these two spheres.

On the contrary, Arab citizens of Israel rationally chose to be connected to both spheres and utilize this double location to promote their ability to achieve their goals. They have an internal view of the debates and deliberations that take place in the Israeli public sphere. Despite the fact that they are not adequately represented there and despite the fact that they have only a marginal influence on it, their ability to understand it and be aware of its details becomes a very strong cultural capital and a major source of inspiration. As a result we find many Arab-Israeli intellectuals and political leaders interviewed on Arab satellite television channels, explaining Israeli political, economic, and cultural reality to an Arab audience from the Arab world. This opportunity enables these representatives from the Arab minority in Israel to bring its voice and express its needs to an Arab audience, establishing new bridges between this minority and the rest of the Arab world.

Furthermore, Arab media consumers in Israel have located themselves in the cultural space of the Arab world, even though these consumers have no influence on the contents broadcast by the Arab media and are not adequately represented by them. The considerable amount of time spent daily in consumption of media contents broadcast from the Arab world enables the Arab public to overcome the physical obstacles that separate it from Arab society in other countries. Television consumption patterns signify the collapse of borders, which symbolize the state's sovereignty, and intensify the potential for cultural cohesion among members of Arab society. The study's findings thus support the theory arguing that the traditional concept of state sovereignty, in the form known to us for the last four hundred years, is undergoing transformation as a result of globalization processes, something that was mentioned in the theoretical introduction and that needs more elaboration than could be done in this context.

These findings are especially significant because the state of Israel, despite its objection to defining its geopolitical boundaries, has exerted considerable effort to control the political and cultural awareness of its citizens. In everything concerning Arab society in Israel, Israel has acted energetically to utilize its ideological mechanisms to inculcate the dominant Jewish worldview among this minority's members. After it succeeded in controlling the Arab economy and political system, the state attempted to discipline Arab society by colonizing the Arab mind. One of the obvious expressions of these efforts is the image of the "Israeli Arab." In order to accomplish this aim, media broadcasts in Arabic, as well as in Hebrew, were utilized.

However, as the research has demonstrated, these efforts were not very successful. Arab society in Israel has culturally and politically crossed the borders of the official Israeli state. Arab society has thus put itself in a unique space, integrating the Israeli and Arab landscapes, while utilizing the contents of its choice from both. The process, culminating in Arab society's "in-betweenness," demonstrates not only the weakness of the Israeli state in the face of global processes but also the potential for excluded minorities to overcome or bypass state mechanisms to reach beyond and connect with more authentic cultural spaces.

The process we have observed gains added dimensions when we focus on the disappointment and alienation that the Arab public feels vis-à-vis the Israeli media and its cultural contents, despite the fact that consumption of Hebrew media continues to no small degree. As long as they have no possibility of participating in the Israeli public sphere, they will confront only stereotypes that cannot be overcome from the Israeli side for lack of interest, understanding, and, of course, language access. Thus alienation from the Israeli media has contributed to the alienation from Israeli Jewish society in general. Although one cannot draw conclusions about future developments from the data, the theories of media influence support the claim that if this alienation continues, it will certainly contribute to the growing tension between the Jewish majority and the Arab minority; one manifestation of such tensions could be the outburst of clashes between Arabs and Jews in different localities in Israel, such as the October 2008 events in Akka (Acre). These clashes are caused by the long estrangement between the Arab minority and the Jewish majority, especially in the last decade. This estrangement has tangible and symbolic sources. As some of the media studies quoted in the theoretical chapter claimed, one source of symbolic alienation and estrangement is the media. Therefore, one of the important conclusions of this study is that the media has a major responsibility for social relations in society, especially in conflict situations. The Israeli media has so far played a negative role in Jewish-Arab relations in Israel. It contributed to the alienation of the Arab population by the mere fact of submitting to the discourses of the official policies of the state adopted toward the Arab minority. Despite slight changes and some attempts to accommodate the Arab population in mainstream Israeli media, the Arab population is still very marginal and very negatively presented. As some studies have demonstrated, this population is still presented as an enemy and a direct security threat. As long as this is the frame by which the Arab minority is captured, one cannot help but feel that this is a self-fulfilling prophecy.

Arab society in Israel consumes Arab media contents from the Arab world and shares some aspects of the regional Arab public sphere, while being almost completely excluded from the Israeli public sphere. This contributes to the alienation between Arab society, the Jewish majority, and the Israeli state. The marginal role of Arabs in the Israeli public sphere and their misrepresentation in Israeli media encourage them to seek alternatives that meet their expectations, at least partially. One can conclude that since the Arab public consumes various media contents, including political news that exposes Arab citizens to political, social, and cultural trends in the Arab world, over time these contents will have an increasing impact on the positions and attitudes of Arab citizens of Israel. This influence of the media does not necessarily have to lead to conflict. But in a conflictual situation, where the tension between the state, the minority, and its national and cultural environment is quite high, the media could form a fruitful ground either for furthering suspicion and mistrust or for transforming them into partnership and mutual regard.

The study has demonstrated that the barriers placed by the state of Israel for the purpose of separating Arab society within from the Arab world outside have gradually collapsed. Unique relationships are therefore being constructed that rely in great part on consumption of the media. The rising attention devoted by satellite television channels to the Arab community in Israel and the time given to its leaders will contribute to intensifying this process, leading to closing the gaps between Arabs in Israel and Arabs in the Arab world, something that can be seen in the rise of Arab consciousness among the Arabs in Israel. Although this phenomenon cannot be explained solely by the media factor, neither can one ignore its centrality. This process could have been viewed as a major source of hope. The Arab minority could have become a bridge for peace between Israel and the Arab world. Unfortunately, this study has demonstrated that this is not the case. The exclusion of the Arab minority from the Israeli public sphere and the negative role played by the Israeli Hebrew media, which ignores the Arab public almost completely and when it refers to it usually presents it in stereotypical terms, contributes very much to the "immigration" of the Arab public to the Arab public sphere in the Arab world. Many Arab intellectuals and leaders in Israel have given up on the attempt to draw the attention of Israeli journalists and media people to their issues and to what they have to say. Major efforts are made, on the other hand, to integrate into the media space provided by the Arab satellite television channels, which have solid representatives from the Arab community that cover the Israeli scene and divert attention to the Arab population inside it. The satellite television channels and their use of modern technology have intensified tendencies that seek to make the Arab community in Israel part of the Arab world and thereby release it from the immediate control of the Israeli state.

Notwithstanding these conclusions, this study has demonstrated that Arab society in Israel is interested in receiving both political news broadcasts on radio and television in Israel and political news broadcasts on television but originating in the Arab world. One important implication of this study is that the unique situation of Arab society in Israel contributes to its increased consumption of news. However, there appears to be greater interest in television news than in print news; witness the higher rate of television viewing in comparison with newspaper reading. As the numbers collected show, the percentage of daily newspaper readers does not reach one-fifth the rate of daily television viewers. Within the sphere of print media, it was found that the party-affiliated Arabic newspapers enjoy greater trust than do the commercial newspapers, even though consumption of commercial newspapers is higher than is consumption of party newspapers.

Another clear conclusion derived from the study is that the various commercial newspapers do not attract a defined and loyal readership. This conclusion stems from the finding that newspaper readers are not content to read only one newspaper; they prefer to read two or more. One conclusion to be derived from this trend is that the commercial newspapers do not meet the minimal demands of their readers for news, which forces them to seek additional sources. In addition, the character of Arab commercial newspapers and how they deliver news does not encourage daily Arab newspaper reading. These factors may also explain the Arab public's moderate satisfaction with the Arab commercial press. They may likewise explain why readers of these newspapers rank sections containing news as fourth in their reading agenda, whereas television viewers rank news broadcasts as first in their viewing agenda.

Another important finding is that media consumption patterns among members of Arab society in Israel do not always reveal a clear association between the level of trust in a specific media provider and the level of its consumption. In today's electronic world, media consumers "uplink" to accessible contents that correspond to their needs, irrespective of the criticisms they level against those same media providers. The criticism that a large proportion of the Arab public expressed toward the Israeli media did not induce this public to abandon Israeli media but, rather, to selectively and critically consume its contents. Moreover, it is important to note that the media consuming public is not always aware of the gap between its level of satisfaction and the quantity of media consumed. Thus, despite dissatisfaction with certain sources, such as Arab commercial newspapers, consumption remains relatively high.

To conclude, one could say that Arab media audiences view television program from the Arab world more than those from Israeli channels. This tendency manifests the power of globalization and technology as well as the collapse of state control over the media. The globalization of the media has changed the meaning of state sovereignty and is leading to what has been called by some scholars a "global citizenship." The patterns of communicative behavior of the Arab minority reflected in this study are similar to patterns of behavior known from elsewhere in the world. The Hungarians in the Czech Republic, Romania, and Slovakia, the Russians in the Baltic States, and the Latino communities in the southern United States are all showing similar patterns of behavior. Marginalization of these communities from mainstream media has led them to seek alternatives, the most natural being the media spaces provided by what they see as their kin nation. In cases where the kin nation is in conflict with their state, the media could become a strong catalyzer for pushing the minority to take sides. Despite the fact that the study of the Arab minority demonstrated that minorities are self-protective, choosing to be in-between, this pattern of behavior could prove to be fragile in conflictual situations. Therefore, media policies are a central field to watch, not only to understand patterns of cultural collective behavior but also to contribute to the study of avoiding or at least easing social and political conflicts.

Notes

Introduction

1. Hanna Adoni, Dan Caspi, and Akiba A. Cohen, *Media, Minorities, and Hybrid Identities: The Arab and Russian Communities in Israel* (Cresskill, N.J.: Hampton Press, 2006).

2. Nadim N. Rouhana, *Palestinian Citizens in an Ethnic Jewish State* (New Haven.: Yale University Press, 1997).

3. Michael Keating and John McGarry, *Minority Nationalism and the Changing International Order* (Oxford: Oxford University Press, 2001); Richard A. Keiser and Katherine Underwood, eds., *Minority Politics at the Millennium* (New York: Garland, 2000).

4. Donald R. Browne, *Ethnic Minorities, Electronic Media, and the Public Sphere: A Comparative Approach* (Cresskill, N.J.: Hampton, 2005); Jürgen Habermas, *The Structural Transformation of the Public Sphere* (Cambridge: Polity Press, 1992); Craig Calhoun, ed., *Habermas and the Public Sphere* (Cambridge: MIT Press, 1994).

5. Shirley Biagi and Marilyn Kern-Foxworth, *Facing Difference: Race, Gender, and Mass Media* (Thousand Oaks, Calif.: Pine Forge Press, 1997); Simon Cottle, ed., *Ethnic Minorities and the Media: Changing Cultural Boundaries* (Philadelphia: Open University Press, 2000); Donald R. Browne, *Electronic Media and Indigenous Peoples: A Voice of Our Own?* (Ames: Iowa State University Press, 1996); Larry Gross, "Minorities, Majorities, and the Media," in Tamar Liebes and James Curran, eds., *Media, Ritual, and Identity* (London: Routledge, 1998), 87–102.

6. Bernard Rubin, *Small Voices and Great Trumpets: Minorities and the Media* (New York: Praeger, 1980).

7. Clint C. Wilson II and Félix Gutiérrez, *Race, Multiculturalism, and the Media: From Mass to Class Communication* (Thousand Oaks, Calif.: Sage, 1995); Christine Ogan, *Communication and Identity in the Diaspora: Turkish Migrants in Amsterdam and Their Use of Media* (Lanham, Md.: Lexington Books, 2001); Dale F. Eickelman and Jon W. Anderson, eds., *New Media in the Muslim World: The Emerging Public Sphere* (Bloomington: Indiana University Press, 2003); Paul Spoonley and Walter Hirsh, eds., *Between the Lines: Racism and the New Zealand Media* (Auckland: Heinemann Reed, 1990).

8. Karen Ross with Peter Playdon, eds., *Black Marks: Minority Ethnic Audiences and Media* (Aldershot and Burlington: Ashgate, 2001).

9. For a general critical treatment of the public sphere, see Nancy Fraser, *Unruly Practices: Power, Discourse, and Gender in Contemporary Social Theory* (Minneapolis: University of Minnesota Press, 1993); Nancy Fraser, "Rethinking the Public Sphere: A Contribution to the Critique of Actually Existing Democracy," in Bernard Robbins, ed., *The Phantom Public Sphere* (Minneapolis: University of Minnesota Press, 1993).

10. For a general examination of the Israeli public sphere that ignored the Arab minority, see Yehuda Ben Meir and Dafna Shaked, *The People Speak: Israeli Public Opinion on National Security, 2005–2007* (Tel-Aviv: Institute for National Security Studies, 2007).

11. Gadi Wolfsfeld, *Media and Political Conflict: News from the Middle East* (Cambridge: Cambridge University Press, 1997); Marda Dunsky, *Pens and Swords: How the American Mainstream Media Report the Israeli-Palestinian Conflict* (New York: Columbia University Press, 2008); Stephen Marmura, *Hegemony in the Digital Age: The Arab/Israeli Conflict Online* (Lanham, Md.: Lexington Books, 2008).

12. Karim H. Karim, ed., *The Media of Diaspora* (London: Routledge, 2003).

13. Amy Gutmann and Dennis Thompson, *Why Deliberative Democracy?* (Princeton: Princeton University Press, 2004); Jon Elster, ed., *Deliberative Democracy* (Cambridge: Cambridge University Press, 1998); James Bohman and William Rehg, eds., *Deliberative Democracy: Essays on Reason and Politics* (Cambridge: MIT Press, 1997).

14. Jacob Shamir and Michal Shamir, *The Anatomy of Public Opinion* (Ann Arbor: University of Michigan Press, 2000).

15. Slavko Splichal, *Public Opinion: Developments and Controversies in the Twentieth Century* (Lanham, Md.: Rowman and Littlefield, 1999).

16. Elizabeth Bird, *The Audience in Everyday Life: Living in a Media World* (New York: Routledge, 2003); James G. Webster, Patricia F. Phalen, and Lawrence W. Lichty, *Ratings Analysis: The Theory and Practice of Audience Research* (Mahwah, N.J.: Lawrence Erlbaum Associates, 2006); Sandra J. Ball-Rokeach and Muriel G. Cantor, eds., *Media, Audience, and Social Structure* (Newbury Park, Calif.: Sage, 1986).

17. Dan Caspi, *Tmonot Barush: Dia'at Kahal vi-Demokratia* (Pictures in Our Head: Public Opinion and Democracy) (Tel Aviv: Open University, 2001); Tamar Liebes, *Reporting the Arab-Israeli Conflict: How Hegemony Works* (London: Routledge, 1997).

18. Glenn Firebaugh, *Seven Rules for Social Research* (Princeton: Princeton University Press, 2008).

19. George Gallup and Saul Forbes Rae, *The Pulse of Democracy: The Public-Opinion Poll and How It Works* (New York: Simon and Schuster, 1940); Russell Dalton, *Citizen Politics* (New York: Chatham House, 2002); Terry Nichols Clark and Michael Rempel, eds., *Citizen Politics in Post-Industrial Societies* (Boulder, Colo.: Westview Press, 1997).

20. Dina Goren, *Tikshoret We-Mitzeut* (Media and Reality) (Jerusalem: Keter, 1993); Gabi Weiman, "The Coverage of Election Surveys in Israeli Newspapers," *State, Government, and International Relations* 19/20 [Heb.] (1982): 132–43.

21. Joseph Lampel, Jamal Shamsie, and Theresa K. Lant, eds., *The Business of Culture: Strategic Perspectives on Entertainment and Media* (Mahwah, N.J.: Lawrence Erlbaum Associates, 2006).

22. Susan Herbst, *Reading Public Opinion: Political Actors View the Democratic Process* (Chicago: University of Chicago Press, 1998).

23. Yariv Tsfati, "Why Do People Trust Media Pre-Election Polls? Evidence from the Israeli 1996 Elections," *International Journal of Public Opinion Research* 13, no. 4 (2001): 433–41.

24. Camille Fuchs, "Skarim Telefonim Bi-Ma'rekhet Bhirot: Al Metodologia, Hataya vi-Hashpa'a" (Telephone Surveys in Elections—On Methodology, Deviation, and Impact), in Camille Fuchs and Shaul Bar-Lev, eds., *Imit Wa-Seker* (Truth and Survey) (Tel Aviv: Hakibbutz Hameuchad and Haifa University, 1998), 61–74.

1. Media Space, Political Control, and Cultural Resistance

1. Brian McNair, *An Introduction to Political Communication,* 4th ed. (New York: Routledge, 2007); Hanno Hardt, *Interactions: Critical Studies in Communication, Media, and Journalism* (Lanham, Md.: Rowman and Littlefield, 1998).

2. Stephanie Greco Larson, "The Civil Rights Movement and the Mass Media," in Larson, *Media and Minorities: The Politics of Race in News and Entertainment* (Lanham, Md.: Rowman and Littlefield, 2006).

3. Jan Servaes and Rico Lie, eds., *Media and Politics in Transition: Cultural Identity in the Age of Globalization* (Leuven: Acco, 1997); Tamar Liebes and James Curran, ed., *Media, Ritual, and Identity* (London: Routledge, 1998); Mirca Madianou, *Mediating the Nation: News, Audiences, and the Politics of Identity* (London: UCL Press, 2005); Suzan Olzak and Elizabeth West, "Ethnic Conflict and the Rise and Fall of Ethnic Newspapers," *American Sociological Review* 56, no. 4 (1991): 458–74.

4. Stuart Hall, "The Whites of Their Eyes: Racist Ideologies and the Media," in George Bridges and Rosalind Brunt, eds., *Silver Linings: Some Strategies for the Eighties* (London: Lawrence and Wishart, 1981), 28–52; Ogan, *Communication and Identity in the Diaspora;* Herman Wasserman and Sean Jacobs, *Shifting Selves: Post-Apartheid Essays on Mass Media, Culture, and Identity* (Cape Town: Kwela, 2003); Abebe Zegeye and Richard L. Harris, eds., *Media, Identity, and the Public Sphere in Post-Apartheid South Africa* (Leiden: Brill, 2003).

5. Diana I. Rios and Stanley O. Gaines Jr., "Latino Media Use for Cultural Maintenance," *Journalism and Mass Communication Quarterly* 75, no. 4 (1998): 746–61.

6. Teun van Dijk, *Racism and the Press* (London: Routledge, 1991); John Twitchin, ed., *The Black and White Media Book: Handbook for the Study of Racism and Television* (Stokes-on-Trent: Trentham Books, 1988); Ella Shohat and Robert Stam, *Unthinking Eurocentrism: Multiculturalism and the Media* (London: Routledge, 1994); Augie Fleras and Jean Lock Kunz, *Media and Minorities: Representing Diversity in a Multicultural Canada* (Toronto: Thompson Educational, 2001); Anura Goonasekera and Youichi Ito, eds., *Mass Media and Cultural Identity: Ethnic Reporting in Asia* (Sterling, Va.: Pluto Press, 1999).

7. Philip Schlesinger, *Media, State, and Nation: Political Violence and Collective Identities* (London: Sage, 1991); Phillip Drummond, Richard Paterson, and Janet Willis, eds., *National Identity and Europe: The Television Revolution* (London: British Film Institute,

1993); Teun van Dijk, *Communicating Racism: Ethnic Prejudice in Thought and Talk* (Newbury Park, Calif.: Sage, 1987); Claire Frachton and Marion Vargaftig, eds., *European Television: Immigrants and Ethnic Minorities* (London: John Libbey, 1995).

8. Ella Shohat, *Israeli Cinema: East/West and the Politics of Representation* (Austin: University of Texas Press, 1989).

9. Eli Avraham, *Behind Media Marginality: Coverage of Social Groups and Places in the Israeli Press* (Lanham, Md.: Lexington Books, 2003).

10. Denis McQuail, *Audience Analysis* (Thousand Oaks, Calif.: Sage, 1997); Valery Nightingale, *Studying Audience: The Shock of the Real* (London: Routledge, 1996); Shaun Moores, *Interpreting Audiences: The Ethnography of Media Consumption* (London: Sage, 1993); David Morley, *Television, Audience, and Cultural Studies* (London: Routledge, 1992).

11. James Curran and David Morley, *Media and Cultural Theory* (New York: Routledge, 2006); Pippa Norris, *A Virtuous Circle: Political Communication in Postindustrial Societies* (Cambridge: Cambridge University Press, 2000).

12. Denis McQuail, *Mass Communication Theory*, 5th ed. (London: Sage, 2004).

13. John Thompson, *The Media and Modernity: A Social Theory of the Media* (Cambridge: Polity Press, 1995).

14. Benedict Anderson, *Imagined Communities: Reflections on the Origins and Spread of Nationalism* (London: Verso, 1991); Brian McNair, *The Sociology of Journalism* (London: Arnold, 1998); L. J. Shrum, "Media Consumption and Perceptions of Reality: Effects and Underlying Processes," in Jennings Bryant and Dolf Zillmann, eds., *Media Effects: Advances in Theory and Research* (Mahwah, N.J.: Lawrence Erlbaum, 2002), 69–95.

15. Timothy E. Cook, *Governing with the News: The News Media as a Political Institution* (Chicago: University of Chicago Press, 1998).

16. Morley, *Television, Audience, and Cultural Studies.*

17. Stuart Hall and David Morley, *The "Nationwide" Audience: Structure and Decoding* (London: BFI, 1986).

18. On the political economy of the media, see Philip Gaunt, *Choosing the News: The Profit Factor in News Selection* (New York: Greenwood Press, 1990); Neil T. Gavin, ed., *The Economy, Media, and Public Knowledge* (London: Leicester University Press, 1998); Robert W. McChesney, *The Political Economy of Media: Enduring Issues, Emerging Dilemmas* (New York: Monthly Review Press, 2008).

19. Edwin Baker, *Media Concentration and Democracy: Why Ownership Matters* (Cambridge: Cambridge University Press, 2007).

20. Ben Bagdikian, *The New Media Monopoly* (Boston: Beacon Press, 2004); Robert McChesney, *Rich Media, Poor Democracy: Communication Politics in Dubious Times* (Urbana: University of Illinois Press, 1999); Ronald Rice, ed., *Media Ownership: Research and Regulation* (Cresskill, N.J.: Hampton Press, 2008).

21. Denis McQuail, *Media Performance: Mass Communication and the Public Interest* (London: Sage, 1992); Colin MacCabe and Olivia Stewart, eds., *The BBC and Public Service Broadcasting* (Manchester: Manchester University Press, 1986); James Ledbetter, *Made Possible By . . . : The Death of Public Broadcasting in the United States* (New York: Verso, 1997).

22. McQuail, *Mass Communication Theory.*

23. Charles Husband, ed., *A Richer Vision: The Development of Ethnic Minority Media in Western Democracies* (Paris: Unesco, 1994); Mike Cormack and Niamh Hourigan, eds., *Minority Language Media: Concepts, Critiques, and Case Studies* (Buffalo: Multilingual Matters, 2007).

24. Stephen Harold Riggins, ed., *Ethnic Minority Media: An International Perspective* (London: Sage, 1992); Elizabeth Poole, *Reporting Islam: Media Representations of British Muslims* (London: I. B. Tauris, 2002).

25. Isabelle Rigoni, "Challenging Notions and Practices: The Muslim Media in Britain and France," *Journal of Ethnic and Migration Studies* 31, no. 3 (2005): 563–80.

26. Mike Cormack, "Minority Language Media in Western Europe: Preliminary Considerations," *European Journal of Communications* 13, no. 1 (1998): 33–52.

27. Ned Thomas, "The Mercator Media Forum," *Mercator Media Forum* 1 (1995): 2–11.

28. Cormack, "Minority Language Media in Western Europe."

29. Tom Moring and Charles Husband, "The Contribution of Swedish-Language Media in Finland to Linguistic Vitality," *International Journal of the Sociology of Language* 187/188 (2007): 75–101; Valerian Hrala, "Minority Media in Slovakia: A Good Example?" www.eumap.org/journal/features/2003/october/minmediaslovakia (accessed April 24, 2009).

30. Nick Couldry, Sonia Livingston, and Tim Markham, *Media Consumption and Public Engagement: Beyond the Presumption of Attention* (New York: Palgrave Macmillan, 2007); Moores, *Interpreting Audiences;* Diana Mutz, "The Future of Political Communication Research: Reflections on the Occasion of Steve Chaffee's Retirement from Stanford University," *Political Communication* 18, no. 2 (2001): 231–36.

31. Jennings Bryant and Dolf Zillmann, eds., *Media Effects: Advances in Theory and Research* (Mahwah, N.J.: Lawrence Erlbaum, 2002).

32. Nightingale, *Studying Audiences.*

33. Ross and Playdon, *Black Marks;* Diana Rios and A. N. Mohamed, eds., *Brown and Black Communication: Latino and African American Conflict and Convergence in Mass Media* (Westport, Conn.: Praeger, 2003).

34. Olzak and West, "Ethnic Conflict and the Rise and Fall of Ethnic Newspapers."

35. Herbert Marcuse, *One-Dimensional Man* (Boston: Beacon Press, 1964); Noam Chomsky, *Media Control: The Spectacular Achievements of Propaganda* (New York: Seven Stories Press, 2002); Raymond Williams, *Television: Technology and Cultural Form* (London: Routledge, 1990); Todd Gitlin, *The Whole World Is Watching: The Mass Media in the Making and Unmaking of the New Left* (Berkeley: University of California Press, 1980).

36. Stuart Hall, "The Rediscovery of Ideology: The Return of the Repressed in Media Studies," in Michael Gurevitch et al., eds., *Culture, Society, and the Media* (London: Methuen, 1982), 56–90.

37. McQuail, *Audience Analysis.*

38. Webster, Phalen, and Lichty, *Ratings Analysis.*

39. Jay Blumler and Denis McQuail, *Television in Politics: Its Uses and Influence* (London: Faber and Faber, 1968).

40. Minelle Mahtani, "Representing Minorities: Canadian Media and Minority Identities," *Canadian Ethnic Studies* 33, no. 3 (2001): 99–133.

41. Charles Tilly and Sidney Tarrow, *Contentious Politics* (Boulder, Colo.: Paradigm, 2007); Doug McAdam, Sidney Tarrow, and Charles Tilly, *Dynamics of Contention* (Cambridge: Cambridge University Press, 2001); Sidney Tarrow, *Power in Movement: Social Movements and Contentious Politics* (Cambridge: Cambridge University Press, 1998).

42. McQuail, *Audience Analysis*.

43. Lennart Weibull, "Structural Factors in Gratifications Research," in Karl Eric Rosengren, Philip Palmgreen and Lawrence A. Wenner, eds., *Media Gratifications Research: Current Perspectives* (Beverly Hills, Calif.: Sage, 1985), 123–47.

44. Paul Lazarsfeld and Elihu Katz, *Personal Influence: The Part Played by People in the Flow of Mass Communication* (Glencoe, Ill.: Free Press, 1955).

45. Elihu Katz, Jay Blumler, and Michael Gurevitch, "Utilization of the Mass Media by the Individual," in Blumler and Katz, eds., *The Uses of Mass Communication* (Beverly Hills: Sage, 1974), 19–32.

46. Austin. S. Babrow, "Theory and Method in Research on Audience Motives," *Journal of Broadcasting and Electronic Media* 32, no. 4 (1988): 471–87.

47. Ian Lustick, "Israel as a Non-Arab State: The Political Implications of Mass Immigration of Non-Jews," *Middle East Journal* 53, no. 3 (1999): 417–33.

48. Rios and Gaines, "Latino Media Use for Cultural Maintenance."

49. Linda Holtzman, *Media Messages: What Film, Television, and Popular Music Teach Us about Race, Class, Gender, and Sexual Orientation* (Armonk, N.Y.: M. E. Sharpe, 2000).

50. L. B. Becker, G. M. Kosicki, and F. Jones, "Racial Differences in Evaluation of the Mass Media," *Journalism Quarterly* 69, no. 1 (1992): 124–34; Frachton and Vargaftig, *European Television*.

51. Marie Gillespie, *Television, Ethnicity, and Cultural Change* (London: Routledge and Kegan Paul, 1995).

52. Rema Hammami and Salim Tamari, "Anatomy of Another Rebellion," *Middle East Report* 217 (2000).

53. Azmi Bishara, "Reflections on October 2000: A Landmark in Jewish-Arab Relations in Israel," *Journal of Palestine Studies* 30, no. 3 (2001); Jamal, "Strategies of Struggle."

54. Dan Rabinowitz, As'ad Ghanem, and Oren Yiftachel, eds., *After the Rift: Emergency Report on Government Policy towards the Arabs in Israel* (2000). Report submitted to Prime Minister Ehud Barak by an interuniversity team of researchers; Daniel Dor, *Intifada Hits the Headlines: How the Israeli Press Misreported the Outbreak of the Second Palestinian Uprising* (Bloomington: Indiana University Press, 2004).

55. Dan Shiftan, "Zihotam Ha-Hadasha Shil Havri Ha-Knesset Ha-A'ravim" (The New Identity of the Arab Knesset Members), *Tkhelet* 13 (2002): 23–49; Elie Rekhess, "Tahlikhe Shinuy Politim-Leumiyem Bekerev Ha-Aravim Bi-Yisrael Ki-reka'a Li-Iroe'e October 2000" (Political and National Processes of Change amongst the Arabs of Israel as Forerunners to the October 2000 Events), in Sarah Ozacky-Lazar and As'ad Ghanem, eds., *Adoyot Or: 7 Havot Da'at Miktzoiyot Sh-Hugshu Li-Va'adat Or* (The Or Commission Testimonies: Seven Professional Reports That Were Presented to the Or Commission) (Tel Aviv: Keter, 2003); Amnon Rubinstein, *Israeli Arabs and Jews: Dispelling the Myths, Narrowing the Gaps* (New York: American Jewish Committee, Dorothy and Julius Koppelman Institute on American Jewish-Israeli Relations, 2003).

56. Ari Shavit, "Survival of the Fittest: Interview with Benny Morris," *Haaretz*

Magazine, 8 January 2004; Barak Seener, "The Threat from Israel's Arab Population," *In Focus* 2, no. 1 (2008).

57. The "Future Vision," published in December 2006 by the Committee of the Heads of Arab Local Councils, the "Democratic Constitution," published in March 2007 by Adalah, and the "Haifa Declaration," published in May 2007 by Mada Al-Carmel, the Arab Center for Applied Social Research.

58. *Fasl Al-Maqal,* 30 March 2007, 2.

59. Amal Jamal, "The Political Ethos of the Palestinian Citizens of Israel: Critical Reading in the Future Vision Documents," *Israel Studies Forum* 23, no. 2 (2008): 3–28.

60. Anthony Smith, *The Ethnic Revival in the Modern World* (Cambridge: Cambridge University Press, 1981); Anderson, *Imagined Communities;* Michael Hanagan and Charles Tilly, eds., *Extending Citizenship: Reconfiguring States* (Lanham, Md.: Rowman and Littlefield, 1999).

61. David Laitin, "National Revivals and Violence," *Archives Européennes de Sociologie* 36, no. 1 (1995): 3–43.

62. Zygmunt Bauman, *Globalization: The Human Consequences* (New York: Columbia University Press, 1998); Alan Carling, ed., *Globalization and Identity: Development and Integration in a Changing World* (New York: I. B. Tauris, 2006).

63. Michael Traber, ed., *Globalization, Mass Media, and Indian Cultural Values* (Delhi: ISPCK, 2003); Hopeton Dunn, ed., *Globalization, Communications, and Caribbean Identity* (New York: St. Martin's Press, 1995).

64. Rogers Brubaker, *Nationalism Reframed: Nationhood and the National Question in the New Europe* (Cambridge: Cambridge University Press, 1996), 5.

65. Paul Havemann, ed., *Indigenous Peoples' Rights in Australia, Canada, and New Zealand* (Oxford: Oxford University Press, 1999); Michael Keating, *Nations against the State: The New Politics of Nationalism in Quebec, Catalonia, and Scotland* (London: Macmillan, 1996); John McGarry, Brendan O'Leary, and Richard Simeon, "Integration or Accommodation? The Enduring Debate in Conflict Regulation," in Sujit Choudhry, ed., *Constitutional Design for Divided Societies: Integration or Accommodation?* (Oxford: Oxford University Press, 2008), 41–88.

66. Will Kymlicka, "The Internationalization of Minority Rights," *International Journal of Constitutional Law* 6, no. 1 (2008): 1–32.

67. Amal Jamal, "Strategies of Minority Struggle for Equality in Ethnic States: Arab Politics in Israel," *Citizenship Studies* 11, no. 3 (2007): 263–82.

68. Sammy Smooha and Priit Jarve, *The Fate of Ethnic Democracy in Post-Communist Europe* (Budapest: LGI Books, 2005).

69. Partha Chatterjee, *The Nation and Its Fragments: Colonial and Postcolonial Histories* (Princeton: Princeton University Press, 1993).

70. Keating and McGarry, *Minority Nationalism;* David Laitin, "National Revivals and Violence," *Archives Européennes de Sociologie* 36, no. 1 (1995): 3–43; William Connor, "Beyond Reason," *Ethnic and Racial Studies* 16, no. 3 (1993): 373–89.

71. Rogers Brubaker and David Laitin, "Ethnic and Nationalist Violence," *Annual Review of Sociology* 24 (1998): 423–52; Peter Waldmann, *Ethnischer Radikalismus: Ursachen und Folgen gewaltsamer Minderheitskonflikte am Beispiel des Baskenlandes, Nordirlands, und Quebecs* (Opladen: Westdeutscher Verlag, 1989).

72. Farimah Daftary and Stefan Troebst, eds., *Radical Ethnic Movements in Contemporary Europe* (New York: Berghahn Books, 2003).

73. Waldmann, *Ethnischer Radikalismus* (1989).

74. Allen Buchanan, *Secession: The Morality of Political Divorce from Fort Sumter to Lithuania and Quebec* (Boulder: Westview Press, 1991); Smith, *The Ethnic Revival.*

75. Barbara Hobson, *Recognition Struggles and Social Movements: Contested Identities, Agency, and Power* (Cambridge: Cambridge University Press, 2003); Daftary and Troebst, *Radical Ethnic Movements;* Hanagan and Tilly, *Extending Citizenship.*

76. Majid Al-Haj, "The Impact of the Intifada on Arabs in Israel: The Case of the Double Periphery," in Akiba A. Cohen and Gadi Wolfsfeld, eds., *Framing the Intifada: Media and People* (Norwood, N.J.: Ablex, 1993), 64–75; Ramzi Suleiman, "Minority Self-Categorization: The Case of the Palestinians in Israel," *Peace and Conflict: Journal of Peace Psychology* 8, no. 1 (2002): 31–46.

77. Dan Rabinowitz, "The Palestinian Citizens of Israel, the Concept of Trapped Minority, and the Discourse of Transnationalism in Anthropology," *Ethnic and Racial Studies* 24, no. 1 (2001): 64–85.

78. Jamal, "Strategies of Minority Struggle."

79. Karl Deutsch, *Nationalism and Social Communication: An Inquiry into the Foundations of Nationality* (Cambridge: MIT Press, 1966); Habermas, *Structural Transformation.*

80. Edward S. Herman and Noam Chomsky, *Manufacturing Consent: The Political Economy of the Mass Media,* 2nd ed. (New York: Pantheon Books, 2002).

81. Calhoun, *Habermas and the Public Sphere.*

82. Habermas, *Structural Transformation,* 17.

83. Ibid., 99.

84. W. E. B. Du Bois, *The Souls of Black Folk: Essays and Sketches* (New York: Barnes and Noble, 2003), 9.

85. Homi Bhabha, *The Location of Culture* (London: Routledge, 1994).

86. Rico Lie, *Spaces of Intercultural Communication: An Interdisciplinary Introduction to Communication, Culture, and Globalizing/Localizing Identities* (Cresskill, N.J.: Hampton Press, 2003).

2. The Indigenous Arab Minority in the Israeli State

1. Ilan Pappe, *The Ethnic Cleansing of Palestine* (Oxford: Oneworld, 2006); Nur Masalha, *Imperial Israel and the Palestinians: The Politics of Expansion* (Sterling, Va.: Pluto Press, 2000); Nur Masalha, *The Politics of Denial: Israel and the Palestinian Refugee Problem* (Sterling, Va.: Pluto Press, 2003); Salman H. Abu-Sitta, *Atlas of Palestine, 1948* (London: Palestine Land Society, 2004) .

2. Benny Morris, *The Birth of the Palestinian Refugee Problem, 1947–1949* (Cambridge: Cambridge University Press, 1987).

3. Tamir Goren, "Separate or Mixed Municipalities? Attitudes of Jewish Yishuv Leadership to the Mixed Municipality during the British Mandate: The Case of Haifa," *Israel Studies* 9, no. 1 (2004): 101–24.

4. Daniel Monterescu and Dan Rabinowitz, *Mixed Towns, Trapped Communities:*

Historical Narratives, Spatial Dynamics, Gender Relations, and Cultural Encounters in Palestinian-Israeli Towns (Burlington, Va.: Ashgate, 2007).

5. Oren Yiftachel and Haim Yacobi, "Urban Ethnocracy: Ethnicization and the Production of Space in an Israeli 'Mixed City,'" *Environment and Planning D: Society and Space 21* (2003): 673–93.

6. Rouhana, *Palestinian Citizens;* Elia Zureik, *The Palestinians in Israel: A Study in Internal Colonialism* (London: Routledge and Kegan Paul, 1979); Sabri Jiryis, *The Arabs in Israel* (New York: Monthly Review Press, 1976).

7. Ian Lustick, *Arabs in the Jewish State: Israel's Control of a National Minority* (Austin: University of Texas Press, 1980).

8. Benny Morris, *1948 and After: Israel and the Palestinians* (Oxford: Clarendon Press, 1994).

9. Sarah Ozacky-Lazar, "Ha-Mimshal Ha-Tzva'i Ki-Manganon Li-Shleta Ba-Izarhim Ha-Aravim: Ha-Asur Ha-Rishon, 1948–1958" (The Military Government as a Mechanism of Controlling Arab Citizens: The First Decade, 1948–1958), *Ha-Mizrah Ha-Hadash* 33 (2002): 103–32; Yair Bauml, "Ha-Mimshal Ha-Tzva'i vi-Bitolo, 1958–1968 (The Military Government and Its Termination: 1958–1968), *Ha-Mizrah Ha-Hadash* 33 (2002): 133–56.

10. Dan Horowitz and Moshe Lissak, *Trouble in Utopia: The Overburdened Polity of Israel* (Albany: State University of New York Press, 1989).

11. Sarah Ozacky-Lazar, "Security and Israel's Arab Minority," in Danny Bar-Tal, Dan Jacobson, and Aharon Klieman, eds., *Security Concerns: Insights from the Israeli Experience* (Stamford, Conn.: JAI, 1998), 347–69; Sarah Ozacky-Lazar, *Ikrit vi-Bira'm: Ha-Sipor Ha-Maleh* (Ikrit and Bir'am: The Full Story) (Givat Haviva: Institute for Peace Research, 1993); Hillel Cohen, *Aravim Toveem: Ha-Modiein Ha-Yisraeli vi-Aravim Bi-Yisrael* (Good Arabs: The Israeli Intelligence and Arabs in Israel) (Jerusalem: Keter, 2006).

12. Uri Ben-Eliezer, *The Making of Israeli Militarism* (Bloomington: Indiana University Press, 1998).

13. Nur Masalha, *Expulsion of the Palestinians: The Concept of "Transfer" in Zionist Political Thought, 1882–1948* (Washington: Institute for Palestine Studies, 1992); Nur Masalha, *A Land without People: Israel and the Palestinians* (London: Faber and Faber, 1997); Nafez Nazzal, *The Palestinian Exodus from Galilee, 1948* (Beirut: Institute for Palestine Studies, 1978).

14. Morris, *1948 and After;* Pappe, *The Ethnic Cleansing of Palestine.*

15. Walid Khalidi, *All That Remains: The Palestinian Villages Occupied and Depopulated by Israel in 1948* (Washington, D.C.: Institute for Palestine Studies, 1992); Majid Al-Haj, "Adjustment Patterns of the Arab Internal Refugees in Israel" *Internal Migration* 24 (September 1986).

16. Amal Jamal, "The Palestinian IDPs in Israel and the Predicament of Return: Between Imagining the 'Impossible' and Enabling the 'Imaginative,'" in Ann Lesch and Ian Lustick, eds., *Exile and Return: Predicaments of Palestinians and Jews* (Philadelphia: University of Pennsylvania Press, 2005), 133–60.

17. Muhammad Abu Al-Hayja, "Ayn Hawd and the 'Unrecognized Villages,'" *Journal of Palestine Studies* 31, no. 1 (2001): 39–49.

18. Al-Haj, "Adjustment Patterns," 654.

19. Joseph Schechtman, *The Arab Refugee Problem* (New York: Philosophical Library, 1952); Don Peretz, *Israel and the Palestinian Arabs* (Washington D.C..: Middle East Institute, 1958).

20. Sammy Smooha, *The Orientation and Politicization of the Arab Minority in Israel,* rev. ed. (Haifa: University of Haifa, Jewish-Arab Center, Institute of Middle Eastern Studies, 1984), 79.

21. Hillel Cohen, *Hanukhahim Nifkadim: Ha-Plitim Ha-Falastinim me-1948* (The Present Absentees: The Palestinian Refugees in Israel since 1948) (Jerusalem: Institute for Israeli Arab Studies, 2000).

22. Imad Jaradat, *The Public Campaign for the Defense of the Palestinian Refugee Rights in the Historical Palestine* (Bethlehem: Badil Resource Center, 2000).

23. Yitzhak Oded, "Land Losses among Israel's Arab Villages," *New Outlook* 7, no. 7 (1964): 19–25; Masalha, *The Politics of Denial.*

24. Ronit Barzily and Mustafa Kabha, *Plitim Bi-Artzam: Plitim Pnimyeem Bi-Midinat Yisrael, 1948–1996* (Refugees in Their Homeland: Internal Refugees in the State of Israel, 1948–1996) (Givat Haviva: Institute for Peace Research, 1996); Dahoud Bader, *El-Ghabsiya: Tabka fi Al-Kalb* (El-Ghabsiya: Remains Ever in the Heart) (special publication of the Association for the Defense of the Rights of the Displaced Persons in Israel, May 2002).

25. Emanuel Mrakovski, the first Israeli military governor of the Triangle area, spoke of 4,000, whereas Goel Lavitski spoke of deporting 8,500 refugees after the Triangle was transferred to Israel. IDF Archives, 841/72/721 and 843/72/721, respectively. Cited also in H. Cohen, *Present Absentees,* 40.

26. In his speech for the Hirtzelya Conference, the treasury minister in the Sharon government, Benjamin Netanyahu, declared that Israel's demographic problem is not with the Palestinians in the West Bank and Gaza, who are supposed to have self-determination, but rather with Arab citizens of the state of Israel. Available at http://news.walla.co.il/?w=//479922 (accessed April 27, 2009).

27. Arnon Sofer and Yisrael E. Bystrov, "Demografia, 2004–2020: Li- or Tokhnit Ha-Hitnatkut" (Israeli Demography, 2004–2020: In Light of the Process of Disengagement) (Haifa: Chair of Geostrategy, 2005).

28. Oren Yiftachel, *Ethnocracy: Land and Identity Politics in Israel/Palestine* (Philadelphia: University of Pennsylvania Press, 2006); Eyal Ben-Ari and Yoram Bilu, eds., *Grasping Land: Space and Place in Contemporary Israeli Discourse and Experience* (Albany: State University of New York Press, 1997).

29. Thabet Abu Ras, "The Impact of Local and Regional Planning on Arab Towns in the 'Little' Triangle Area, Israel," in Aygen Erdentug and Freek Colombijn, eds., *Urban Ethnic Encounters: The Spatial Consequences* (London: Routledge, 2002), 61–80.

30. Nabih Bashir, *Tahweed Al-Makan: Al-Majles Al-Iklimi Misgav fi Al-Galil* (Judaizing the Place: Misgav Regional Council in the Galilee) (Haifa: Mada Al-Carmel, 2004).

31. Oren Yiftachel, "The Internal Frontier: Territorial Control and Ethnic Relations in Israel," *Regional Studies* 30, no. 4 (1996): 493–508.

32. Sandy Kedar and Oren Yiftachel, "Land Regime and Social Relations in Israel," in Hernando de Soto and Francis Cheneval, eds., *Realizing Property Rights* (Zurich: Ruffer and Rub, 2006); Sandy Kedar and Geremy Forman, "From Arab Lands to 'Israel Lands':

The Legal Dispossession of the Palestinians Displaced by Israel in the Wake of 1948," *Environment and Planning D: Society and Space* 22, no. 6 (2004): 809–30.

33. Oren Yiftachel, "Binoi Oma vi Halokat Hamirhav Bietnokratia Hayisraelet: Karka-oot vi Pi'arim Idatyem" (Nation-Building and National Land: Social and Legal Dimensions), *Iyoni Ha-Mishpat* 21, no. 3 (1998): 637–64.

34. On 2 March 2003, the state destroyed 18 houses in Kfar Kassem. Another 150 houses were defined by the authorities as illegal and destined for destruction. See the report of the Arab Institute for Human Rights at www.arabhra.org/pressre1030305.htm. See also *Al-Ittihad*, 9 March 2003; *Al-Ahali*, 10 March 2003; *Assennara*, 7 March 2003; *Al-Akhbar*, 7 March 2003; *Fasl Al-Maqal*, 7 March 2003.

35. Rassem Khmaisi, *Mitikhnon Magbil Litikhnon Maftiyah Bayishovim Haa'ravim Biyisrael* (From Limiting Design to Developing Design in the Arab Towns in Israel) (Jerusalem: Floersheimer Institute for Policy Studies, 1993).

36. *Haaretz*, 28 November, 2006.

37. Aref Abu-Rabia, "The Bedouin Refugees in the Negev," *Refuge* 14, no. 6 (1994).

38. The website of the Association of Unrecognized Villages speaks of fifty-eight villages, nine of which are in the north and the rest in the Negev desert. See www.assoc40 .org. (accessed April 24, 2009). The first planning laws were passed by the Knesset in the 1960s. On the unrecognized villages, see interview with the head of the Committee of Forty in Abu Al-Hayja, "'Ayn Hawd and the 'Unrecognized Villages.'"

39. See Master Plan for Housing, Development and Preservation (Tama 35), which was confirmed in the National Council for Planning and Housing in November 2005, at www.mmi.gov.il/iturtabot/tochmitararzi.asp (accessed April 24, 2009).

40. One example was the persecution of the leaders of the nationalist Al-Ard movement in the 1950s and 1960s and the banning of the movement in 1965.

41. The 1984 attempt to prevent the Progressive List for Peace (PLP), seen as the continuation of Al-Ard, failed and even led to a new law (Article 7 in the Basic Law, Knesset) that made illegal any attempt to challenge the assertion that Israel is the state of the Jewish people. See Yoav Peled, "Ethnic Democracy and the Legal Construction of Citizenship: Arab Citizen of the Jewish State," *American Political Science Review* 86, no. 2 (1992): 432–43. An attempt in 2003 by several Zionist parties, supported by the state attorney general, to prevent certain Arab leaders and parties from running for the Knesset was blocked by the Israeli High Court. High Court Verdict, *Central Elections Committee v. MK Ahmad Tibi and MK Azmi Bishara*, 11280/02 47(4), 1, p. 22.

42. On policies toward Arab leaders, see Amal Jamal, "Arab Leadership in Israel: Ascendance and Fragmentation," *Journal of Palestine Studies* 35, no. 2 (2006): 1–17.

43. Shiftan, "Zihotam Ha-Hadasha Shil Havri Ha-Knesset Ha-A'ravim."

44. Anat First, "Are They Still the Enemy? The Representation of Arabs in the Israeli News," Tudor Parfitt and Yulia Egorova, eds., *Jews, Muslims, and Mass Media: Mediating the "Other"* (New York: RoutledgeCurzon, 2005), 190–213.

45. Zureik, *The Palestinians in Israel*.

46. Noah Lewin-Epstein, Majid Al-Haj, and Moshe Semyonov, *Ha-Aravim Be-Shuk Ha-Avoda Ha-Yisraeli* (The Arabs in Israel in the Labor Market) (Jerusalem: Floersheimer Institute for Policy Studies, 1994).

47. The economic goals of the military government were never clearly enunciated,

especially relating to the economic dimensions of land confiscation and the blocking of Arab working force from competing freely in the job market as a result of the regimen of movement permits. For more details on the mechanisms of the military governments, see Ozacky-Lazar, "Ha-Mimshal Ha-Tzva'i Ki-Manganon Li-Shleta Ba-Izarhim Ha-Aravim.

48. H. Cohen, *Aravim Toveem.*

49. Noah Lewin-Epstein and Moshe Semyonov, *The Arab Minority in Israel's Economy* (Boulder: Westview, 1993).

50. Evidence of this gap in between income levels can be found in the reports produced by the National Insurance Institute of Israel, available at www.btl.gov.il/English%20Homepage/Publications (accessed April 24, 2009) and by Adva: Information on Equality and Social Justice in Israel available at www.adva.org (accessed April 24, 2009).

51. Adva Institute, *Moa'sakim Lifi Mishlah Yad, Yabishit Lida, Kvotsat Okhlosia vi-Mean* (Employment According to Trade, Continent of Origin, Group Affiliation, and Gender), 1999. Accessed at www.adva.org/ivrit/pearim/occupation-continents.htm (accessed April 24, 2009).

52. Ali Haider, *The Equality Index of Jewish and Arab Citizens in Israel* (Haifa: Sikkuy, 2008).

53. Ibid.; Amin Fares, *Taktsiv Hamdina Li Shnat 2002 vi Hilka Shil Haokhlosia Haa'ravit* (The State's Budget for the Year 2002 and the Share of the Arab Population). (Haifa: Mosawa Center, 2002).

54. The report of "Shiluv," integration plan (Haifa: Sikkuy Center, 2000).

55. Jack Bendleck, *"Mimotsaa" Skhar vi Hakhnasa Lifi Yishov vi Lifi Mishtanin Kalkaliyem Shonim, 1999–2000* (Average Wages and Incomes According to Settlement and Different Economic Variables, 1999–2000) (Jerusalem: National Insurance Institute, 2002).

56. Shlomo Swirski and Etty Konor-Attias, *Israel: A Social Report, 2005* (Tel Aviv: Adva Center, 2006).

57. Pierre Bourdieu and Jean-Claude Passeron, *Reproduction in Education, Society, and Culture* (London: Sage, 1990); Louis Althusser, *Lenin and Philosophy, and Other Essays* (New York: Monthly Review Press, 1972), 127–77.

58. Ilan Saban, "Ha-Zkhoiot Hakibotsiot Shil Hamioot Ha-Aravi-Falastini: Ha-Yish Ha-Ain vi-Tkhom Ha-Tabo" (Group Rights of the Arab-Palestinian Minority: Present, Absent, and Taboo), *Iyoni Ha-Mishpat* 26, no. 1 (2002): 241–319.

59. Khaled Abu-Asbah, *Ma-Arekhet Ha-Hinukh Ha-Aravit Bi-Yisrael* (Arab Education System in Israel), in Shlomo Hasson and Khaled Abu-Asbah, eds., *Yehudim vi-Aravim Bi-Yisrael Be-Mitzeot Mishtana* (Jews and Arabs in Israel Facing a Changing Reality) (Jerusalem: The Floersheimer Institute for Policy Studies, 2004), 81–97.

60. Khaled Abu Asbah, *Maa'rikhit Hahinookh Haa'ravi Biyisrael: Matsav Kaiyam vi-Halofot Irgoniyot Ifshariyot* (The Arab Education System in Israel: Current Conditions and Possible Organizational Alternatives) (Givat Haviva: Institute for Peace Research, 1997).

61. Victor Lavi, *Hivdilem Bimashabem vi Bihisigem Bahinukh Haa'ravi Biyisrael* (Differences in Resources and Achievements in the Arab Education in Israel) (Jerusalem: Floersheimer Institute for Policy Studies, 1997).

62. See www.nrg.com, 31 August 2005, 31 August 2006.

63. Khaled Abu-Asbah, *Ha-hinukh Ha-Aravi Bi-Yisrael: Dilemot Shel Mi-Out Liumi* (Arab Education in Israel: Dilemmas of a National Minority) (Jerusalem: Floersheimer Institute for Policy Studies, 2007); Majid Al-Haj, *Education, Empowerment, and Control: The Case of the Arabs in Israel* (Albany: State University of New York Press, 1995).

64. Sami Mari, *Arab Education in Israel* (Syracuse: Syracuse University Press, 1978).

65. Abu-Asbah, *Ha-hinukh Ha-Aravi Bi-Yisrael*; Al-Haj, *Education, Empowerment, and Control*.

66. Amal Jamal, *Mo'agam Al-Muwatana Lil-Madares Al-Arabiya fi Israel* (Citizenship Lexicon for Arab Schools in Israel) (Jerusalem: Gilo Center for Civic Education and Democracy, 2005).

3. Israeli Media Policies toward the Arab Minority

1. Udi Lebel, ed., *Bitahon vi-Tekshoret: Denamika shel Yahasim* (Security and Media: The Dynamics of a Relationship) (Sdeh Boker: Ben Gurion University Press, 2005); Erwin Frenkel, *The Press and Politics in Israel: The Jerusalem Post from 1932 to the Present* (Westport, Conn.: Greenwood Press, 1994); Daniel Dor, *The Suppression of Guilt: The Israeli Media and the Occupation of the West Bank* (Ann Arbor, Mich.: Pluto Press, 2005).

2. Dan Caspi and Yehiel Limor, *The In/Outsiders: The Media in Israel* (Cresskill, N.J.: Hampton Press, 1999); Liebes, *Reporting the Arab-Israeli Conflict*; Akiba Cohen and Gadi Wolfsfeld, *Framing the Intifada: People and Media* (Norwood, N.J.: Ablex, 1993).

3. Dan Rabinowitz, "Nostalgia Mizrahit: Kitzad Hafkhu Ha-Falastinim Le-Arviye Yisrael" (Oriental Nostalgia: How the Palestinians Were Transformed into "Israeli Arabs"), *Tioria vi-Bekoret* (Theory and Criticism) 4 (1993): 141–51.

4. Amal Jamal, "Aal Tala'ot Hazman Ha-Mogza'a" (On the Troubles of Racialized Time), in Yehouda Shenhav and Yossi Yonah, eds., *Gazanut Bi-Yisrael* (Racism in Israel) (Jerusalem: Van Leer and Hakibbutz Hameuchad, 2008), 348–80.

5. Pappe, *The Ethnic Cleansing of Palestine*; Baruch Kimmerling and Joel Migdal, *The Palestinian People: A History* (Cambridge: Harvard University Press, 2003); Rashid Khalidi, *Palestinian Identity: The Construction of Modern National Consciousness* (New York: Columbia University Press, 1997); Lustick, *Arabs in the Jewish State*; Jiryis, *The Arabs in Israel*; Habib Kahwaji, *Al-'Arab fi Dhal al-Ihtalal al-Israili min 1948* (The Arabs in the Shadow of the Israeli Occupation since 1948) (Beirut: PLO Research Center, 1972); Peretz, *Israel and the Palestinian Arabs*.

6. Mustafa Kabha, *Itunut Bi-Ayen Ha-Sa'ara: Ha-Itunut Ha-Falastinit Ki-Makhsher Le-Itzuv Da'at Kahal, 1929–1939* (Journalism in the Eye of the Storm: Palestinian Journalism as a Tool for Shaping Public Opinion, 1929–1939) (Jerusalem: Yad Yitzhak Ben Zvi, 2004); Ami Ayalon, *Reading Palestine: Printing and Literacy, 1900–1948* (Austin: University of Texas Press, 2004); Gershon Shafir and Yoav Peled, *Being Israeli: The Dynamics of Multiple Citizenship* (Cambridge: Cambridge University Press, 2002).

7. Khalidi, *Palestinian Identity*; Ayalon, *Reading Palestine*.

8. Mustafa Kabha, *Ha-Itunut Ha-Aravit Bi-Yisrael, 1948–2006: Ki-Makhsher Li-Itzuv Zihut Hadasha* (The Arab Press in Israel, 1948–2006: A Vehicle of Shaping a New

Identity) (Tel Aviv: Haim Hertzog Institute for Communication, Society, and Politics, 2006).

9. There were many attempts to close *Al-Ittihad,* some of which were temporarily successful. For an examination of the treatment of *Al-Ittihad* as well as other dissentient publications in Israel, see Moshe Negbi, *Hofesh Ha-Itunut Bi-Yisrael: Arakheem Bri'e Ha-Mishpat* (The Freedom of the Press in Israel: Values in Light of the Law (Jerusalem: Jerusalem Institute for Israel Research, 1995).

10. H. Cohen, *Aravim Toveem,* 55–84.

11. Dread of expulsion was exacerbated by the announcements made by governmental officials and the military governors in Arab areas.

12. On the refugees in Arab countries, see Laleh Khalili, "Commemorating Contested Lands," in Lesch and Lustick, eds., *Exile and Return,* 19–40; on the fate of refugees that remained in Israel, see Jiryis, *Arabs in Israel* (1979); Lustick, *Arabs in the Jewish State* (1980).

13. The Palestinian author Emile Habibi reflected the fears of those Palestinians who remained in his masterwork, *Al-Mutashael: Al-Waqae'a Al-Gharebah fi Ikhtifa'a Said Abi Al-Nahs Al-Mutashael* (The Optimist: The Strange Events in the Disappearance of Said Abu Al-Nahs) (Haifa: Arabisk, 1974).

14. Masalha, *The Politics of Denial.*

15. Ben Gurion consulted with people in his close circle on whether it would be practical to convert all the remaining Palestinians to Judaism. See Pappe, *The Ethnic Cleansing.*

16. David Day, *Conquest: How Societies Overwhelm Others* (Oxford: Oxford University Press, 2008).

17. Jamal, "Aal Tala'ot Hazman Ha-Mogza'a"; Edward Said, *The Question of Palestine* (London: Routledge, 1980).

18. On the centrality of place in modern national thinking, see Edward Casey, *The Fate of Place: A Philosophical History* (Berkeley: University of California Press, 1998); on the relationship between imperialism and the construction of the modern subject, see Michael Hardt and Antonio Negri, *Empire* (Cambridge: Cambridge University Press, 2001).

19. Meron Benvenisti, *Sacred Landscape: Buried History of the Holy Land since 1948* (Berkeley: University of California Press, 2002).

20. Noga Kadman, *Be-Tzede Haderkh vi-Bisholee Hatoda'a: Dhikat Hakfarim Ha'aravim Shi-Hitrokno bi-1948 Mi-Hasieh Ha-Yisraeli* (On the Roadsides and the Margins of Consciousness: The Suppression of Arab Villages Evacuated in 1948 from Israeli Discourse) (Tel Aviv: November Books, 2008).

21. Moshe Yegar, *Li-Toldoteha shel Ma'arekhet Hahasbarat Hahutz shel Yisraelit* (On the History of the Israeli Foreign Propaganda Policy) (Tel Aviv: Lahav, 1986).

22. Interview with Shmuel Tolidano, who was the prime minister's advisor on Arab affairs in the years 1957 to 1968. Cited in Odelya Natan, MA thesis, Tel Aviv University, 2008.

23. Sabri Jiryis, "Domination by the Law," *Journal of Palestine Studies* 11, no. 1 (1981): 67–92; David Kretzmer, *The Legal Status of the Arabs in Israel* (Boulder: Westview Press, 1990).

24. Yehouda Shenhav, *The Arab Jews: Postcolonial Reading of Nationalism, Religion, and Ethnicity* (Stanford, Calif.: Stanford University Press, 2006).

25. Pnina Motzafi-Haller, "Intelektualem Mizrahiem 1946–1951: Zihut Itnit vi-Migbaloteha" (Mizrahi Intellectuals, 1946–1951: Ethnic Identity and Its Limits), in Hannan Hever, Yehouda Shenhav, and Pnina Motzafi-Haller, eds., *Mizrahim Bi-Yisrael: Iyun Bikorti Mihudash* (Mizrahim in Israel: A Critical Observation in Israel's Ethnicity) (Jerusalem: Van Leer and Hakibbutz Hameuchad, 2002), 152–90; "A Mizrahi Call for a More Democratic Israel," *Tikkun: A Bimonthly Jewish Critique of Politics, Culture, and Society* 13, no. 2 (1998): 50–52.

26. Mustafa Kahba, "Mizrahi Jews in the Arabic Press, 1948–1967," *Iyonim* 17 (2006): 445–61.

27. State Archives, file 3551/10.

28. It is amazing that no serious study of the role that Oriental Jews played in the Israeli control and surveillance policies has ever been done. In the recently published literature on Oriental Jews in Israel, they are usually presented as victims of Zionism. See Ella Shohat, *Taboo Memories: Diasporic Voices* (Durham, N.C.: Duke University Press, 2006); Sami Shalom Shitrit, *Mizrahi Ha-Ma'vak Ha-Mizrahi Bi-Yisrael: Ben Dikuy Li-Shihror, Ben Hi-Zdaht Li-Altenativa, 1948–2003* (Struggle in Israel: Between Suppression and Liberation, between Identification and Alternative, 1948–2003) (Tel Aviv: Am Oved, 2004).

29. See conclusions of editorial meeting of *Al-Yom* newspaper from 8 November 1964, State Archives, file 3551/6.

30. Interview with Samir Darweesh, author of the column, on the phone on 21 September 2008.

31. Personal interview with a prominent Arab journalist who was close to *Al-Yom* at the time, 2 October 2008.

32. Niccolo Machiavelli, *The Prince: Letter to Francesco Vettori* (Roma: Libreria del Littorio, 1930).

33. See letter from Yossef Aliyahu to Haim Plechter from Union of Construction Workers in the Histadrut from 27 December 1964, State Archives, file 3551/10.

34. Letter from the manager of the newspaper, Aliyahu Agasi, to the pedagogic secretary at the Hebrew University, dated 5 October 1964, State Archives, file 3551/10.

35. Letter, dated 20 October 1964, State Archives, file 3551/10.

36. Letter, dated 10 October 1964, State Archives, file 3551/10.

37. See letter of intentions written by Samuel Bar-Haim regarding the issuing of a newspaper in Arabic to the Arab public in Israel, 18 September 1958, State Archives, file G-5498/12.

38. State Archives, file GL-17084.

39. State Archives, file GL-17033/6.

40. See meeting with Anwar Nusseibeh, a minister in the Jordanian government before occupation, documented in a letter sent by the editor, Yitzhak Bar-Moshe, to members of the committee on 19 May 1969, State Archives, file GL-17033/6.

41. See discussion of the directors of the newspaper on 19 October 1971 and on 23 March 1972, State Archives, file 17084/13.

42. See document summing up the agreement reached in the meeting of the newspaper directors on 19 October 1971, State Archives, file 17084/13.

43. Toledano, State Archives, file G-304/63.

44. On the financial difficulties of *Al-Anbaʾa,* see State Archives, file GL-17084/13.

45. Sammy Smooha, *Arabs and Jews in Israel* (Boulder, Colo.: Westview Press, 1989).

46. Azmi Bishara, *Al-Arab fi Israel: Ruʾoya min-Al-Dakhel* (The Arabs in Israel: A View from Within) (Ramallah: Muwatin. 2003).

47. H. Cohen, *Aravim Toveem.*

48. Ilana Kaufman, *Arab National Communism in the Jewish State* (Gainesville: University Press of Florida, 1997); Elie Rekhess, *Ha-Miuot Ha-Aravi Bi-Yisrael: Ben Komunism Li-Liumiot Aravit, 1965–1991* (The Arab Minority in Israel: Between Communism and Arab Nationalism, 1965–1991) (Tel Aviv: Hakibbutz Hameuchad, 1993), 64–65.

49. On 16 January 1950, Tawfik Toubi asked in the Knesset "why the government is excluding the Arab citizens from the rule of army service, despite the fact that many of them showed willingness to fulfill their duty expecting to win all their rights? No doubt that this is one of the aspects of the racial discrimination in governmental policy, which stands in opposition to all efforts to win the loyalty of the Arab masses." See the *Knesset Chronicals.*

50. Amal Jamal, "The Ambiguities of Minority Patriotism: Love for Homeland versus State among Palestinian Citizens of Israel," *Nationalism and Ethnic Politics* 10, no. 3 (2004): 433–71.

51. Kaufman, *Arab National Communism.*

52. Aharon Layish, "Social and Political Changes in Arab Society in Israel," in Michael Curtis, Jack Neyer, C. Waxman, and A. Pollack, eds., *The Palestinians: People, History, and Politics* (New Brunswick: Transaction Books, 1975); Jacob Landau, *The Arab Minority in Israel: Political Aspects, 1967–1991* (Oxford: Clarendon Press, 1993).

53. Jamal, "Arab Leadership in Israel."

54. Atallah Manzur, "Ha-Itunut Ha-Aravit Bi-Zisrael" (Arab Press in Israel), *Kesher* 7 (1990): 71–77.

55. Jacob Landau, *The Arabs in Israel: A Political Study* (London: Oxford University Press, 1969), 92–107.

56. It is interesting to note that the program used the song "Jaib Le Salam" of Fairuz, one of the most adored Arab national singers from Lebanon, as its opening and closing song.

57. Personal interview on 21 September 2008 with a prominent Arab citizen who worked at that radio station for a long time and wished to remain anonymous.

58. See the IBA website at www.iba.co.il (accessed April 24, 2009).

59. Amal Jamal, "Abstention as Participation: The Paradoxes of Arab Politics in Israel," in Asher Arian and Michal Shamir, eds., *The Elections in Israel, 2001* (Jerusalem: Israeli Institute for Democracy, 2002), 57–100; Asʾad Ghanem, *The Palestinian-Arab Minority in Israel, 1948–2000* (New York: State University of New York Press, 2001).

60. Azmi Bishara, "Aʾal Shieilat Ha-Miut Ha-Falstini Bi-Yisrael" (On the Question of the Palestinian Minority in Israel), *Tioria vi-Bekoret* (Theory and Criticism) 3 (1993): 7–20.

61. The poem appeared in books for teaching the Arabic language in Arab schools that are not in use anymore. See the book *Al-Sanabil,* produced by the Israeli Ministry of Education.

62. Bishara, "A'al Shieilat Ha-Miut Ha-Falstini Bi-Yisrael."

63. Kaufman, *Arab National Communism.*

64. Tawfik Toubi, speech, in *The 13th Congress of the Israeli Communist Party* (Tel Aviv-Jaffa: The Central Committee of the Israeli Communist Party, 1957), 78.

65. The meaning of the Israeliness that the Communist Party propagated was different from the Israeliness model promoted by the dominant Ashkenazi secular elite of the labor movement that was in power in Israel between 1948 and 1977. The Communists imagined a new model based on civic equality and class brotherhood far removed from narrow nationalist affiliation. On the meaning of Israeliness in Israeli society, see Baruch Kimmerling, *The Invention and Decline of Israeliness: State, Society, and the Military* (Berkeley: University of California Press, 2001).

66. Emile Habibi, speech, in *The 13th Congress of the Israeli Communist Party* (Tel Aviv-Jaffa: Central Committee of the Israeli Communist Party, 1957), 97.

67. Ibid., 96.

68. Ibid., 93.

69. Kaufman, *Arab National Communism;* Rekhess, *Ha-Miuot Ha-Aravi Bi-Yisrael.*

70. Yisrael Vashitz, "In Exchange for the Lives of Israeli Arabs." *New East,* no. 4 (1950): 257–64; Dunia Habib-Nahas, *The Israeli Communist Party* (London: Croom Helm, 1976).

71. Tawfiq Zayyad, "The Fate of the Arabs in Israel," *Journal of Palestine Studies* 10, no. 1 (1976): 92–103.

72. Emile Tuma, "Palestinian Arabs and Israeli Jews," *Journal of Palestine Studies* 10, no. 2 (1977): 5.

73. Zayyad, "The Fate of the Arabs in Israel," 95.

4. Arabic Media Space in the Jewish State

1. Lustick, *Arabs in the Jewish State.*

2. Jamal, "Strategies of Minority Struggle."

3. No studies have been conducted on the press consumption culture and the effect of the Communist Party publications during the first decades of Israel's existence. For a general overview of this subject, see Kahwaji, *Al-'Arab fi Dhal al-Ihtalal al-Israili min 1948.*

4. Ghassan Kanafani, *Al-Adab Al-Filastini Al-Muqawem That al-Ihtilal, 1948–1968* (Palestinian Resistance Literature under Occupation, 1948–1968) (Beirut: Arab Research Institute, 1968).

5. On the closing of *Kol Ha-Am* and on *Israeli Supreme Court 73/53 Kol Ha-Am Company vs. Minister of Interior,* see Negbi, *Hofesh Ha-Itunut Bi-Yisrael.*

6. H. Cohen, *Aravim Toveem;* Lustick, *Arabs in the Jewish State.*

7. Kahwaji, *Al-'Arab fi Dhal al-Ihtalal al-Israili min 1948.*

8. Jiryis, *The Arabs in Israel;* Landau, *The Arabs in Israel.*

9. Rouhana, *Palestinian Citizens.*

10. Mari, *Arab Education in Israel.*

11. Salim Fattal, *Be-Simtaut Bagdad* (In the Alleys of Bagdad) (Jerusalem: Carmel, 2003).

12. Jamal, *Journalism and Media in Israel*, 97–121.

13. Landau, *The Arab Minority in Israel*.

14. Personal interview with Awad Abdel Fatah, the editor of the weekly at the time, 4 October 2008.

15. Jamal, "Arab Leadership in Israel."

16. Jamal, *Al-Sahafa Wa-Al-I'lam fi Israel*, 178.

17. Zuhair Andrawus, "Tnu lanu Tilivisia Aravit" (Give Us an Arab Television), *Ha'ayeen Ha-Shvie'et* (The Seventh Eye) 25 (2000): 48.

5. Arabic Print Media and the New Culture of Newspaper Reading

1. Kasisomayajula Viswanath and Pamela Arora, "Ethnic Media in the United States: An Essay on Their Role in Integration, Assimilation, and Social Control," *Mass Communication and Society* 2, no. 1 (2000): 39–56.

2. The newspaper *Al-Fajr al-Jadeed* began publication in August 2004 and was relatively new when the survey was conducted in December 2004 and January 2005.

3. Philip Meyer, *The Vanishing Newspaper: Saving Journalism in the Information Age* (Columbia: University of Missouri Press, 2004).

4. Muhammad Amara and Abd Al-Rahman Mar'i, *Language and Education Policy: The Arab Minority in Israel* (Dordrecht: Kluwer Academic, 2002).

5. Amal Jamal, *Al-Kiyadat al-Arabiya fi Akhbar al-Sahafa al-Arabiya al-Tijariya fi Israel* (Arab Leadership in the News of the Arab Commercial Newspapers in Israel) (Nazareth: I'lam Center, 2006); Amal Jamal and Diab Umayma, *Al-Nissa' fi Akhbar al-Sahafa al-Arabiya al-Tijariya fi Israel* (Women in the News of Arab Commercial Newspapers in Israel) (Nazareth: I'lam Center, 2006).

6. This hypothesis is confirmed by a random sample of editors and journalists I interviewed in October 2006.

7. In-depth interviews were conducted with groups of students at the Western Galilee College.

8. It is important to note that the newspaper *Kul al-Arab*, which was found to rank first among readers in the Arab community, launched a public relations campaign using the data of the research to increase its advertisement business.

9. It is important to note that some of the weekly newspapers are distributed only locally; hence the percentage of their readers is much smaller than that of regional newspapers. Moreover, the fact that the comparative analysis was done nationally further emphasizes the differences between national and local newspaper consumers. However, because the research was not aimed at ranking newspapers themselves but at assessing the effect of media consumption as reflected in public opinion, the analyses throughout were conducted on the national level.

10. This last rate is influenced by the fact that the survey is selective and it was easier to reach people from the southern faction of the Islamic movement than from the northern wing, the natural readers of a different Islamist newspaper, *Sawt al-Haq wal-Hurriya*.

11. Convenience sampling of a number of gas stations owned by Arabs in Galilee indicated that each station distributes six to seven hundred free copies of commercial newspapers every week (*Kul al-Arab, Assennara,* and *Panorama*). When taking into account

the number of gas stations, which is around forty, this figure can add up to thousands of copies of each newspaper, which in turn increases its readership and explains the fact that people read more than one newspaper.

12. Yariv Tsafti and Joseph N. Cappella recently found that, although the Israeli public has a low level of confidence in the Israeli media, particularly in the written press, a relatively high percentage of that same public reads the newspapers. Tsfati and Cappella, "Why Do People Watch News They Do Not Trust? The Need for Cognition as a Moderator in the Association between News Media Skepticism and Exposure," *Media Psychology* 7 (2005): 251–71.

13. The interviews were conducted with students of the Western Galilee Academic College.

14. Jamal, *Al-Kiyadat al-Arabiya.*

15. As regards the ambivalent responses to the questions on Arab leadership, the demolition of homes, etc., one has to note that there is reluctance in Arab society to answer questions of a political nature due to the fear of repercussions. There is a general sense of suspicion toward questions that reveal a person's political inclinations should they fall outside of the dominant political narrative in Israel. This derives from the triumph of successive Israeli regimes in quashing dissent using everything from psychological pressures (threats against one's livelihood, family, etc.) to the more overt use of physical violence (e.g., October 2000). The historical context of the military government and its impact on the generation that lived through it might be worth mentioning here.

16. Gross, "Minorities, Majorities, and the Media."

17. Rios and Gaines, "Latino Media Use for Cultural Maintenance."

18. Yehiel Limor and Rafi Mann, *Ituna'ut: Isuf Mia'a, Ktiva Ve-Aricha* (Journalism: Collecting Information, Writing, and Editing) (Tel Aviv: Open University, 1997).

6. Resisting Cultural Imperialism

1. Anat First and Eli Avraham, *Yitzug Ha-Okhlusia Ha-Aravit Ba-Tikshoret Ha-Ivrit: Hashava'a ben Skor Yom Ha-Adama Ha-Rishon 1976 lben Sikor Iroe'e Intifadat Al-Aqsa 2000* (The Representation of the Arab Population in the Hebrew Media: Comparing the Coverage of Land Day 1976 and the Coverage of Al-Aqsa Intifada 2000) (Tel Aviv: Tami Steinmetz Center, 2004).

2. Gadi Wolfsfeld, Eli Avraham, and Issam Aburayya, "When Prophesy Always Fails: Israeli Press Coverage of the Arab Minority's Land Day Protests," *Political Communication* 17 (2000): 115–31.

3. Kanafani, *Al-Adab Al-Filastini Al-Muqawem That al-Ihtilal;* Jamal, "The Ambiguities of Minority Patriotism"; Habib Boulos, *Lu'obat Al-Ieham Wal-Waqea': Maqalat fi Al-Fan Al-Masrahi* (Illusion and Reality: Essays on Arab Palestinian Theater) (Nazareth: Al-Midan Theater, 2000).

4. Jamal, "Strategies of Minority Struggle."

5. Tsfati and Cappella, "Why Do People Watch News They Do Not Trust?"

6. Jamal, "Arab Leadership in Israel."

7. Oren Yiftachel, "The Internal Frontier: Territorial Control and Ethnic Relations in Israel," *Regional Studies* 30, no. 4 (1996): 493–508.

8. Wolfsfeld, Avraham, and Aburayya, "When Prophesy Always Fails."

9. Daniel Dor, *Intifada Hits the Headlines*.

10. First and Avraham, *Yitzug Ha-Okhlusia Ha-Aravit Ba-Tikshoret Ha-Ivrit*.

11. Dor, *The Suppression of Guilt*.

12. John Stuart Mill, *On Liberty* (New Haven: Yale University Press, 2003).

13. Wolfsfeld, *Media and Political Conflict*.

7. Electronic Media and the Strategy of In-Betweenness

1. On the gaps, see the report commissioned by the Israeli Knesset that examines the crisis in the official Broadcasting Authority. This report shows that in 2001 the budget devoted to the Arabic television channel (17,467,000 NIS) is 4% of the budget devoted to the Hebrew channel (378,296,000 NIS), despite the fact that the Arab population is almost 20% of the population. For more details, see www.knesset.gov.il/mmm/data/docs/m00538.rtf (accessed April 24, 2009).

2. John Fisk, *Television Culture* (London: Routledge, 1987); Neil Postman, *Amusing Ourselves to Death: Public Discourse in the Age of Show Business* (New York: Penguin Books, 1986); Horace Newcomb, ed., *Television: The Critical View* (New York: Oxford University Press, 2007).

3. Pierre Bourdieu, *On Television* (New York: New Press, 1998).

4. Jay G. Blumler and Dennis Kavanagh, "The Third Age of Political Communication: Influence and Features," *Political Communication* 16, no. 3 (1999): 209–30.

5. Yoram Peri, *Telepopulism: Media and Politics in Israel* (Stanford: Stanford University Press, 2004).

6. Jacques Lacan, *Television* (Paris: Seuil, 1974); Roland Barth, *Image, Music, Text* (New York: Hill and Wang, 1977).

7. Ben Bagdikian, *The Media Monopoly*, 5th ed. (Boston: Beacon Press, 1997).

8. Todd Gitlin, *Media Unlimited: How the Torrent of Images and Sounds Overwhelms Our Lives* (New York: Henry Holt, 2002).

9. Homi Bhabha, *The Location of Culture* (London: Routledge, 1994); Bill Ashcroft, Gareth Griffiths, and Helen Tiffin, eds., *The Empire Writes Back: Theory and Practice in Post-Colonial Literatures*, 2nd ed. (London: Routledge, 2002).

10. Monroe Price, *Media and Sovereignty: The Global Information Revolution and Its Challenges to State Power* (Cambridge: MIT Press, 2002).

Bibliography

Books

Aburayya, Issam, Eli Avraham, and Gadi Wolfsfeld. *The Arab Population in the Hebrew Press: Media and Socio-political De-legitimization* [Heb.]. Ra'anana: Research Center for Arab Society in Israel, 1998.

Abu-Sitta, Salman H. *Atlas of Palestine, 1948.* London: Palestine Land Society, 2004.

Adoni, Hanna, Dan Caspi, and Akiba A. Cohen. *Media, Minorities, and Hybrid Identities: The Arab and Russian Communities in Israel.* Cresskill, N.J.: Hampton Press, 2006.

Al-Haj, Majid. *Education, Empowerment, and Control: The Case of the Arabs in Israel.* Albany: State University of New York Press, 1995.

Althusser, Louis. *Lenin and Philosophy, and Other Essays.* New York: Monthly Review Press, 1972.

Amara, Muhammad, and Adb Al-Rahman Mar'i. *Language and Education Policy: The Arab Minority in Israel.* Dordrecht: Kluwer Academic, 2002.

Anderson, Benedict. *Imagined Communities: Reflections on the Origins and Spread of Nationalism.* London: Verso, 1991.

Anderson, M. Bonnie. *News Flash: Journalism, Infotainment, and the Bottom-Line Business of Broadcast News.* San Francisco: Joseey-Bass, 2004.

Ashcroft, Bill, Gareth Griffiths, and Helen Tiffin, eds. *The Empire Writes Back: Theory and Practice in Post-Colonial Literatures.* 2nd ed. London: Routledge, 2002.

Avraham, Eli. *Behind Media Marginality: Coverage of Social Groups and Places in the Israeli Press.* Lanham, Md.: Lexington Books, 2003.

Avraham, Eli, Anat First, and Noah Elfant-Lefler. *The Absent and the Present during Peak Viewing: Cultural Diversity in Commercial Television Channel Broadcasts* [Heb.]. Jerusalem: The Second Radio and Television Authority, 2004.

Ayalon, Ami. *Reading Palestine: Printing and Literacy, 1900–1948.* Austin: University of Texas Press, 2004.

Bader, Dahoud. *El-Ghabsiya: Tabka fi Al-Kalb* [El-Ghabsiya: Remains Ever in the Heart]. Association for the Defense of the Rights of the Displaced Persons in Israel, May 2002.

Bagdikian, Ben. *The Media Monopoly*. 5th ed. Boston: Beacon Press, 1997.

———. *The New Media Monopoly*. Boston: Beacon Press, 2004.

Baker, Edwin. *Media Concentration and Democracy: Why Ownership Matters.* Cambridge: Cambridge University Press, 2007.

Ball-Rokeach, Sandra J., and Muriel G. Cantor, eds. *Media, Audience, and Social Structure.* Newbury Park, Calif.: Sage, 1986.

Barth, Roland. *Image, Music, Text.* New York: Hill and Wang, 1977.

Barzily, Ronit, and Mustafa Kabha. *Plitim Bi-Artzam: Plitim Pnimyeem Bi-Midinat Yisrael, 1948–1996* [Refugees in Their Homeland: Internal Refugees in the State of Israel, 1948–1996]. Givat Haviva: Institute for Peace Research, 1996.

Bashir, Nabih. *Tahweed Al-Makan: Al-Majles Al-Iklimi Misgav fi Al-Galil* [Judaizing the Place: Misgav Regional Council in the Galilee]. Haifa: Mada Al-Carmel, 2004.

Bauman, Zygmunt. *Globalization: The Human Consequences.* New York: Columbia University Press, 1998.

Ben-Ari, Eyal, and Yoram Bilu, eds. *Grasping Land: Space and Place in Contemporary Israeli Discourse and Experience.* Albany: State University of New York Press, 1997.

Ben-Eliezer, Uri. *The Making of Israeli Militarism.* Bloomington: Indiana University Press, 1998.

Ben Meir, Yehuda, and Dafna Shaked, *The People Speak: Israeli Public Opinion on National Security, 2005–2007.* Tel-Aviv: Institute for National Security Studies, 2007.

Bendleck, Jack. *"Mimotsaa" Skhar vi Hakhnasa Lifi Yishov vi Lifi Mishtanin Kalkaliyem Shonim, 1999–2000* [Average Wages and Incomes According to Settlement and Different Economic Variables, 1999–2000]. Jerusalem: National Insurance Institute, 2002.

Benvenisti, Meron. *Sacred Landscape: Buried History of the Holy Land since 1948.* Berkeley: University of California Press, 2002.

Bhabha, Homi. *The Location of Culture.* London: Routledge, 1994.

Biagi, Shirley, and Marilyn Kern-Foxworth. *Facing Difference: Race, Gender, and Mass Media.* Thousand Oaks, Calif.: Pine Forge Press, 1997.

Bird, Elizabeth. *The Audience in Everyday Life: Living in a Media World.* New York: Routledge, 2003.

Bishara, Azmi. *Al-Arab fi Israel: Ru'oya min-Al-Dakhel* [The Arabs in Israel: A View from Within]. Ramallah: Muwatin, 2003.

Blumler, Jay, and Denis McQuail. *Television in Politics: Its Uses and Influence.* London: Faber and Faber, 1968.

Bohman, James, and William Rehg, eds. *Deliberative Democracy: Essays on Reason and Politics.* Cambridge: MIT Press, 1997.

Boulos, Habib. *Lu'obat Al-Ieham Wal-Waqea': Maqalat fi Al-Fan Al-Masrahi* [Illusion and Reality: Essays on Arab Palestinian Theater]. Nazareth: Al-Midan Theatre, 2000.

Bourdieu, Pierre. *Language and Symbolic Power.* Cambridge: Polity Press, 1991.

———. *On Television.* New York: New Press, 1998.

Bourdieu, Pierre, and Jean-Claude Passeron. *Reproduction in Education, Society, and Culture.* London: Sage, 1990.

Browne, Donald R. *Electronic Media and Indigenous Peoples: A Voice of Our Own?* Ames: Iowa State University Press, 1996.

————. *Ethnic Minorities, Electronic Media, and the Public Sphere: A Comparative Approach.* Cresskill, N.J.: Hampton, 2005.

Brubaker, Rogers. *Nationalism Reframed: Nationhood and the National Question in the New Europe.* Cambridge: Cambridge University Press, 1996.

Bryant, Jennings, and Dolf Zillmann, eds. *Media Effects: Advances in Theory and Research.* Mahwah, N.J.: Lawrence Erlbaum, 2002.

Buchanan, Allen. *Secession: The Morality of Political Divorce from Fort Sumter to Lithuania and Quebec.* Boulder, Colo.: Westview Press, 1991.

Calhoun, Craig, ed. *Habermas and the Public Sphere.* Cambridge: MIT Press, 1994.

Carling, Alan, ed. *Globalization and Identity: Development and Integration in a Changing World.* New York: I. B. Tauris, 2006.

Casey, Edward. *The Fate of Place: A Philosophical History.* Berkeley: University of California Press, 1998.

Caspi, Dan. *Tmonot Barush: Dia'at Kahal Wi-Demokratia.* [Pictures in Our Head: Public Opinion and Democracy]. Tel Aviv: Open University, 2001.

Caspi, Dan, and Yehiel Limor. *The In/Outsiders: The Media in Israel.* Cresskill, N.J.: Hampton Press, 1999.

Chatterjee, Partha. *The Nation and Its Fragments: Colonial and Postcolonial Histories.* Princeton: Princeton University Press, 1993.

Chomsky, Noam. *Media Control: The Spectacular Achievements of Propaganda.* New York: Seven Stories Press, 2002.

Clark, Terry Nichols, and Michael Rempel, eds. *Citizen Politics in Post-Industrial Societies.* Boulder, Colo.: Westview Press, 1997.

Cohen, Akiba, and Gadi Wolfsfeld. *Framing the Intifada: People and Media.* Norwood, N.J.: Ablex, 1993.

Cohen, Hillel. *Hanukhahim Nifkadim: Ha-Plitim Ha-Falastinim me-1948* [The Present Absentees: The Palestinian Refugees in Israel since 1948]. Jerusalem: Institute for Israeli Arab Studies, 2000.

————. *Aravim Toveem: Ha-Modiein Ha-Yisraeli Wi-Aravim Bi-Yisrael* [Good Arabs: The Israeli Intelligence and Arabs in Israel]. Jerusalem: Keter, 2006.

Cook, E. Timothy. *Governing with the News: The News Media as a Political Institution.* Chicago: University of Chicago Press, 1998.

Cormack, Mike, and Niamh Hourigan, eds., *Minority Language Media: Concepts, Critiques, and Case Studies.* Buffalo: Multilingual Matters, 2007.

Cottle, Simon, ed. *Ethnic Minorities and the Media: Changing Cultural Boundaries.* Philadelphia: Open University Press, 2000.

Couldry, Nick, Sonia Livingston, and Tim Markham. *Media Consumption and Public Engagement: Beyond the Presumption of Attention.* New York: Palgrave Macmillan, 2007.

Curran, James, and David Morley, eds. *Media and Cultural Theory.* New York: Routledge, 2006.

Daftary, Farimah, and Stefan Troebst, eds. *Radical Ethnic Movements in Contemporary Europe.* New York: Berghahn Books, 2003.

Dalton, Russell. *Citizen Politics: Public Opinion and Political Parties in Advanced Industrial Democracies.* New York: Chatham House, 2002.

Day, David. *Conquest: How Societies Overwhelm Others*. Oxford: Oxford University Press, 2008.

Deutsch, Karl. *Nationalism and Social Communication: An Inquiry into the Foundations of Nationality*. Cambridge: MIT Press, 1966.

Dor, Daniel. *Intifada Hits the Headlines: How the Israeli Press Misreported the Outbreak of the Second Palestinian Intifada*. Bloomington: Indiana University Press, 2004.

———. *The Suppression of Guilt: The Israeli Media and the Occupation of the West Bank*. Ann Arbor, Mich.: Pluto Press, 2005.

Drummond, Phillip, Richard Paterson, and Janet Willis, eds. *National Identity and Europe: The Television Revolution*. London: British Film Institute, 1993.

Du Bois, W. E. B. *The Souls of Black Folk: Essays and Sketches*. New York: Barnes and Noble, 2003.

Dunn, Hopeton, ed. *Globalization, Communications, and Caribbean Identity*. New York: St. Martin's Press, 1995.

Dunsky, Marda. *Pens and Swords: How the American Mainstream Media Report the Israeli-Palestinian Conflict*. New York: Columbia University Press, 2008.

Eickelman, Dale F., and Jon W. Anderson, eds. *New Media in the Muslim World: The Emerging Public Sphere*. Bloomington: Indiana University Press, 2003.

Elster, Jon, ed. *Deliberative Democracy*. Cambridge: Cambridge University Press, 1998.

Ezrahi, Yaron, Goshen Zohar, and Leshem Shmuel. *Ba'alut Tzulevet: Shlita vi-Taharut Bishuk Ha-Tikshoret Ha-Yisraeli* [Cross Ownership: Control and Competition in the Israeli Media]. Jerusalem: Israel Democracy Institute, 2003.

Fattal, Salim. *Be-Simtaut Bagdad* [In the Alleys of Bagdad]. Jerusalem: Carmel, 2003.

Firebaugh, Glenn. *Seven Rules for Social Research*. Princeton, N.J.: Princeton University Press, 2008.

First, Anat, and Eli Avraham. *Yitzug Ha-Okhlusia Ha-Aravit Ba-Tikshoret Ha-Ivrit: Hashava'a ben Skor Yom Ha-Adama Ha-Rishon 1976 lben Sikor Iroe'e Intifadat Al-Aqsa 2000* [The Representation of the Arab Population in Hebrew Media: Comparing the Coverage of Land Day 1976 and Al-Aqsa Intifada 2000]. Tel-Aviv: Tami Steinmetz Center, 2004.

Fiske, John. *Television Culture*. London: Routledge, 1987.

Fleras, Augie, and Jean Lock Kunz. *Media and Minorities: Representing Diversity in a Multicultural Canada*. Toronto: Thompson Educational Publishing, 2001.

Frachton, Claire, and Marion Vargaftig, eds. *European Television: Immigrants and Ethnic Minorities*. London: John Libbey, 1995.

Fraser, Nancy. *Unruly Practices: Power, Discourse, and Gender in Contemporary Social Theory*. Minneapolis: University of Minnesota Press, 1993.

Frenkel, Erwin. *The Press and Politics in Israel: The Jerusalem Post from 1932 to the Present*. Westport, Conn.: Greenwood Press, 1994.

Gallup, George, and Saul Forbes Rae. *The Pulse of Democracy: The Public-Opinion Poll and How It Works*. New York: Simon and Schuster, 1940.

Gaunt, Philip. *Choosing the News: The Profit Factor in News Selection*. New York: Greenwood Press, 1990.

Gavin, Neil T., ed. *The Economy, Media, and Public Knowledge*. London: Leicester University Press, 1998.

Ghanem, As'ad. *The Palestinian-Arab Minority in Israel, 1948–2000*. New York: State University of New York Press, 2001.

Gillespie, Marie. *Television, Ethnicity, and Cultural Change*. London: Routledge and Kegan Paul, 1995.

Gitlin, Todd. *The Whole World Is Watching: Mass Media in the Making and Unmaking of the New Left*. Berkeley: University of California Press, 1980.

———. *Media Unlimited: How the Torrent of Images and Sounds Overwhelms Our Lives*. New York: Henry Holt, 2002.

Goodman, Amy, and David Goodman. *The Exception to the Rulers: Exposing Oily Politicians, War Profiteers, and the Media That Love Them*. New York: Hyperion, 2004.

Goonasekera, Anura, and Youichi Ito, eds. *Mass Media and Cultural Identity: Ethnic Reporting in Asia*. Sterling, Va.: Pluto Press, 1999.

Goren, Dina. *Tikshoret We-Mitzeut* [Media and Reality]. Jerusalem: Keter, 1993.

Gutmann, Amy, and Dennis Thompson. *Why Deliberative Democracy?* Princeton, N.J.: Princeton University Press, 2004.

Habermas, Jürgen. *The Structural Transformation of the Public Sphere: An Inquiry into a Category of Bourgeois Society*. Cambridge: Polity Press, 1992.

Habibi, Emile. *Al-Mutashael: Al-Waqae'a Al-Gharebah fi Ikhtifa'a Said Abi Al-Nahs Al-Mutashael* [The Optimist: The Strange Events in the Disappearance of Said Abu Al-Nahs]. Haifa: Arabisk, 1974.

Habib-Nahas, Dunia. *The Israeli Communist Party*. London: Croom Helm, 1976.

Haeijer, Birgitta, and Werner Anita, eds. *Cultural Cognition: New Perspectives in Audience Theory*. Goeteborg: Nordicom, 1998.

Haider, Ali. *The Equality Index of Jewish and Arab Citizens in Israel*. Haifa: Sikkuy, 2008.

Haider, Aziz. *On The Margins: The Arab Population in the Israeli Economy*. London: Hurst, 1995.

Hall, Stuart, and David Morley. *The "Nationwide" Audience: Structure and Decoding*. London: BFI, 1986.

Hanagan, Michael, Leslie Moch Page, and Wayne te Brake, eds. *Challenging Authority: The Historical Study of Contentious Politics*. Minneapolis: University of Minnesota Press, 1998.

Hanagan, Michael, and Charles Tilly, eds. *Extending Citizenship: Reconfiguring States*. Lanham, Md.: Rowman and Littlefield, 1999.

Hardt, Hanno. *Interactions: Critical Studies in Communication, Media, and Journalism*. Lanham, Md.: Rowman and Littlefield, 1998.

Hardt, Michael, and Antonio Negri. *Empire*. Cambridge: Cambridge University Press, 2001.

Havemann, Paul, ed. *Indigenous Peoples' Rights in Australia, Canada, and New Zealand*. Oxford: Oxford University Press, 1999.

Henschel, Thomas. *Ethnischer Radikalismus: Ursachen und Folgen gewaltsamer Minderheitskonflikte am Beispiel des Baskenlandes, Nordirlands, und Quebecs*. Opladen: Westdeutscher Verlag, 1989.

Herbst, Susan. *Reading Public Opinion: Political Actors View the Democratic Process*. Chicago: University of Chicago Press, 1998.

Herman, Edward S., and Noam Chomsky. *Manufacturing Consent: The Political Economy of the Mass Media.* 2nd ed. New York: Pantheon Books, 2002.

Hobson, Barbara. *Recognition Struggles and Social Movements: Contested Identities, Agency, and Power.* Cambridge: Cambridge University Press, 2003.

Holtzman, Linda. *Media Messages: What Film, Television, and Popular Music Teach Us about Race, Class, Gender, and Sexual Orientation.* Armonk, N.Y.: M. E. Sharpe, 2000.

Horowitz, Dan, and Moshe Lissak. *Trouble in Utopia: The Overburdened Polity of Israel.* Albany: State University of New York Press, 1989.

Husband, Charles, ed. *A Richer Vision: The Development of Ethnic Minority Media in Western Democracies.* Paris: Unesco, 1994.

Jamal, Amal. "The Construction of Arab Images in Israeli Television." Manuscript. I'lam Center, Nazareth.

———. *Al-Sahafa Wa-Al-I'lam fi Israel: Bayn Al-Ta'adudiya Al-Bunyawiya Wa-Haymanat Al-Khitab Al-Kawmi* [Press and Media in Israel: Between the Multiplicity of the Establishment Structure and the Hegemony of the National Discourse]. Ramallah: Madar, 2005.

———. *Mo'agam Al-Muwatana Lil-Madares Al-Arabiya fi Israel* [Citizenship Lexicon for Arab Schools in Israel]. Jerusalem: Gilo Center for Civic Education and Democracy, 2005.

———. *Al-Kiyadat al-Arabiya fi Akhbar al-Sahafa al-Arabiya al-Tijariya fi Israel* [Arab Leadership in the News of the Arab Commercial Newspapers in Israel]. Nazareth: I'lam Center, 2006.

Jamal, Amal, and Diab Umayma. *Al-Nissa' fi Akhbar al-Sahafa al-Arabiya al-Tijariya fi Israel* [Women in the News of Arab Commercial Newspapers in Israel]. Nazareth: I'lam Center, 2006.

Jameson, Frederic. *Postmodernism or the Cultural Logic of Late Capitalism.* Durham, N.C.: Duke University Press, 1991.

Jaradat, Imad. *The Public Campaign for the Defense of the Palestinian Refugee Rights in the Historical Palestine.* Bethlehem: Badil Resource Center, 2000.

Jiryis, Sabri. *The Arabs in Israel.* New York: Monthly Review Press, 1976.

Kabha, Mustafa. *Itunut Bi-Ayen Ha-Sa'ara: Ha-Itunut Ha-Falastinit Ki-Makhsher Le-Itzuv Da'at Kahal, 1929–1939* [Journalism in the Eye of the Storm: Palestinian Journalism as a Tool for Shaping Public Opinion, 1929–1939]. Jerusalem: Yad Yitzhak Ben Zvi, 2004.

———. *Ha-Itunut Ha-Aravit Bi-Yisrael, 1948–2006: Ki-Makhsher Li-Itzuv Zihut hadasha* [The Arab Press in Israel, 1948–2006: A Vehicle of Shaping a New Identity]. Tel Aviv: Haim Hertzg Institute for Communication, Society, and Politics, 2006.

Kadman, Noga. *Be-Tzede Haderkh vi-Bisholee Hatoda'a: Dhikat Hakfarim Ha'aravim Shi-Hitrokno bi-1948 Mi-Hasieh Ha-Yisraeli* [On the Roadsides and the Margins of Consciousness: The Suppression of Arab Villages Evacuated in 1948 from Israeli Discourse]. Tel Aviv: November Books, 2008.

Kahwaji, Habib. *Al-'Arab fi Dhal al-Ihtalal al-Israili min 1948* [The Arabs in the Shadow of the Israeli Occupation since 1948]. Beirut: PLO Research Center, 1972.

Kanafani, Ghassan. *Al-Adab Al-Filastini Al-Muqawem That al-Ihtilal, 1948–1968* [Pales-tinian Resistance Literature under Occupation, 1948–1968]. Beirut: Arab Research Institute, 1968.

Karim, Karim H., ed. *The Media of Diaspora*. London: Routledge, 2003.

Kaufman, Ilana. *Arab National Communism in the Jewish State*. Gainesville: University Press of Florida, 1997.

Keating, Michael. *Nations against the State: The New Politics of Nationalism in Quebec, Catalonia, and Scotland*. London: Macmillan, 1996.

Keating, Michael, and John McGarry. *Minority Nationalism and the Changing Interna-tional Order*. Oxford: Oxford University Press, 2001.

Keiser, Richard A., and Katherine Underwood, eds. *Minority Politics at the Millennium*. New York: Garland, 2000.

Kendal, Diana. *Framing Class: Media Representation of Wealth and Poverty in America*. Lanham, Md.: Rowman and Littlefield, 2005.

Khalidi, Rashid. *Palestinian Identity: The Construction of Modern National Conscious-ness*. New York: Columbia University Press, 1997.

Khalidi, Walid. *All That Remains: The Palestinian Villages Occupied and Depopulated by Israel in 1948*. Washington, D.C.: Institute for Palestine Studies, 1992.

Kimmerling, Baruch. *The Invention and Decline of Israeliness: State, Society, and the Mili-tary*. Berkeley: University of California Press, 2001.

Kimmerling, Baruch, and Joel Migdal. *The Palestinian People: A History*. Cambridge: Harvard University Press, 2003.

Kretzmer, David. *The Legal Status of the Arabs in Israel*. Boulder, Colo.: Westview Press, 1990.

Lacan, Jacques. *Television*. Paris: Seuil, 1974.

Lampel, Joseph, Jamal Shamsie, and Theresa K. Lant, eds. *The Business of Culture: Stra-tegic Perspectives on Entertainment and Media*. Mahwah, N.J.: Lawrence Erlbaum Associates, 2006.

Landau, Jacob. *The Arabs in Israel: A Political Study*. London: Oxford University Press, 1969.

———. *The Arab Minority in Israel: Political Aspects, 1967–1991*. Oxford: Clarendon Press, 1993.

Lavi, Victor. *Hivdilim Bi-Masha'abim O-Bihesegem Bi-Ma'arekhet Ha-Hinukh Ha-Ara-vit Bi-Yisrael* [Differences in Resources and Achievements in the Arab Education in Israel]. Jerusalem: Floersheimer Institute, 1997.

Layish, Aharon. "Social and Political Changes in Arab Society in Israel." In Michael Cur-tis, Jack Neyer, C. Waxman, and A. Pollack, eds., *The Palestinians: People, History, and Politics*. New Brunswick: Transaction Books, 1975.

Lazarsfeld, Paul, and Elihu Katz. *Personal Influence: The Part Played by People in the Flow of Mass Communication*. Glencoe, Ill.: Free Press, 1955.

Lebel, Udi, ed. *Bitahon Wi-Tekshoret: Denamika shel Yahasim* [Security and Media: The Dynamics of a Relationship]. Sdeh Boker: Ben Gurion University Press, 2005.

Ledbetter, James. *Made Possible By . . . : The Death of Public Broadcasting in the United States*. New York: Verso, 1997.

Lewin-Epstein, Noah, Majid Al-Haj, and Moshe Semyonov. *Ha-Aravim Be-Shuk Ha-Avoda Ha-Yisraeli* [The Arabs in Israel in the Labor Market]. Jerusalem: Floersheimer Institute, 1994.

Lewin-Epstein, Noah, and Moshe Semyonov. *The Arab Minority in Israel's Economy.* Boulder, Colo.: Westview, 1993.

Lie, Rico. *Spaces of Intercultural Communication: An Interdisciplinary Introduction to Communication, Culture, and Globalizing/Localizing Identities.* Cresskill, N.J.: Hampton Press, 2003.

Liebes, Tamar. *Reporting the Arab-Israeli Conflict: How Hegemony Works.* London: Routledge, 1997.

Liebes, Tamar, and James Curran, eds. *Media, Ritual, and Identity.* London: Routledge, 1998.

Limor, Yehiel, and Rafi Mann. *Ituna'ut: Isuf Mia'a, Ktiva Ve-Aricha* [Journalism: Collecting Information, Writing, and Editing]. Tel Aviv: Open University, 1997.

Lustick, Ian. *Arabs in the Jewish State: Israel's Control of a National Minority.* Austin: University of Texas Press, 1980.

MacCabe, Colin, and Olivia Stewart, eds. *The BBC and Public Service Broadcasting.* Manchester: Manchester University Press, 1986.

Machiavelli, Niccolo. *The Prince: Letter to Francesco Vettori.* Roma: Libreria del Littorio, 1930.

Madianou, Mirca. *Mediating the Nation: News, Audiences, and the Politics of Identity.* London: UCL Press, 2005.

Marcuse, Herbert. *One-Dimensional Man.* Boston: Beacon Press, 1964.

Mari, Sami. *Arab Education in Israel.* Syracuse: Syracuse University Press, 1978.

Marmura, Stephen. *Hegemony in the Digital Age: The Arab/Israeli Conflict Online.* Lanham, Md.: Lexington Books, 2008.

Masalha, Nur. *Expulsion of the Palestinians: The Concept of "Transfer" in Zionist Political Thought, 1882–1948.* Washington: Institute for Palestine Studies, 1992.

———. *A Land without People: Israel and the Palestinians.* London: Faber and Faber, 1997.

———. *Imperial Israel and the Palestinians: The Politics of Expansion.* London: Pluto Press, 2000.

———. *The Politics of Denial: Israel and the Palestinian Refugee Problem.* Sterling, Va.: Pluto Press, 2003.

McAdam, Doug, Sidney Tarrow, and Charles Tilly. *Dynamics of Contention.* Cambridge: Cambridge University Press, 2001.

McChesney, Robert W. *Rich Media, Poor Democracy: Communication Politics in Dubious Times.* Urbana: University of Illinois Press, 1999.

———. *The Political Economy of Media: Enduring Issues, Emerging Dilemmas.* New York: Monthly Review Press, 2008.

McNair, Brian. *The Sociology of Journalism.* London: Arnold, 1998.

———. *An Introduction to Political Communication.* 4th ed. New York: Routledge, 2007.

McQuail, Denis. *Media Performance: Mass Communication and the Public Interest.* London: Sage, 1992.

———. *Audience Analysis.* Thousand Oaks, Calif.: Sage, 1997.

———. *Mass Communication Theory.* 5th ed. London: Sage, 2004.

Meyer, Philip. *The Vanishing Newspaper: Saving Journalism in the Information Age.* Columbia: University of Missouri Press, 2004.

Mill, John Stuart. *On Liberty.* New Haven: Yale University Press, 2003.

Monterescu, Daniel, and Dan Rabinowitz. *Mixed Towns, Trapped Communities: Historical Narratives, Spatial Dynamics, Gender Relations, and Cultural Encounters in Palestinian-Israeli Towns.* Burlington, Vt.: Ashgate, 2007.

Moores, Shaun. *Interpreting Audiences: The Ethnography of Media Consumption.* London: Sage, 1993.

Morley, David. *Television, Audience, and Cultural Studies.* London: Routledge, 1992.

Morris, Benny. *The Birth of the Palestinian Refugee Problem, 1947–1949.* Cambridge: Cambridge University Press, 1987.

———. *1948 and After: Israel and the Palestinians.* Oxford: Clarendon Press, 1994.

Natan, Odelya. MA thesis, Tel Aviv University, 2008.

Nazzal, Nafez. . *The Palestinian Exodus from Galilee, 1948.* Beirut: Institute for Palestine Studies, 1978.

Negbi, Moshe. *Hofesh Ha-Itunut Bi-Yisrael: Arakheem Bri'e Ha-Mishpat* [The Freedom of the Press in Israel: Values in Light of the Law]. Jerusalem: Jerusalem Institute for Israel Research, 1995.

Newcomb, Horace, ed. *Television: The Critical View.* New York: Oxford University Press, 2007.

Nightingale, Virginia. *Studying Audiences: The Shock of the Real.* London: Routledge, 1996.

Norris, Pippa. *A Virtuous Circle: Political Communications in Postindustrial Societies.* Cambridge: Cambridge University Press, 2000.

Ogan, Christine. *Communication and Identity in the Diaspora: Turkish Migrants in Amsterdam and Their Use of Media.* Lanham, Md.: Lexington Books, 2001.

Ozacky, Sarah. *Ikrit vi-Bira'm: Ha-Sipor Ha-Maleh* [Ikrit and Bir'am: The Full Story]. Givat Haviva: Institute for Peace Research, 1993.

Pappe, Ilan. *The Ethnic Cleansing of Palestine.* Oxford: Oneworld, 2006.

Peretz, Don. *Israel and the Palestinian Arabs.* Washington, D.C.: Middle East Institute, 1958.

Peri, Yoram. *Telepopulism: Media and Politics in Israel.* Stanford: Stanford University Press, 2004.

Poole, Elizabeth. *Reporting Islam: Media Representation of British Muslims.* London: I. B. Tauris, 2002.

Postman, Neil. *Amusing Ourselves to Death: Public Discourse in the Age of Show Business.* New York: Penguin Books, 1986.

Price, Monroe. *Media and Sovereignty: The Global Information Revolution and Its Challenges to State Power.* Cambridge: MIT Press, 2002.

Rabinowitz, Dan, As'ad Ghanem, and Oren Yiftachel, eds. *After the Rift: Emergency Report on Government Policy towards the Arabs in Israel.* Submitted to Prime Minister Ehud Barak by an interuniversity team of researchers, 2000.

Rekhess, Elie. *Ha-Miuot Ha-Aravi Bi-Yisrael: Ben Komunism Li-Liumiot Aravit, 1965–1991* [The Arab Minority in Israel: Between Communism and Arab Nationalism]. Tel Aviv: Hakibbutz Hamiuchad, 1993.

Rice, Ronald, ed. *Media Ownership: Research and Regulation.* Cresskill, N.J.: Hampton Press, 2008.

Riggins, Stephen Harold, ed. *Ethnic Minority Media: An International Perspective.* London: Sage, 1992.

Rios, Diana, and A. N. Mohamed, eds. *Brown and Black Communication: Latino and African American Conflict and Convergence in Mass Media.* Westport, Conn.: Praeger, 2003.

Ross, Karen, and Virginia Nightingale. *Media and Audience: New Perspectives.* Maidenhead: Open University Press, 2003.

Ross, Karen, with Peter Playdon, eds. *Black Marks: Minority Ethnic Audiences and Media.* Aldershot and Burlington: Ashgate, 2001.

Rouhana, Nadim N. *Palestinian Citizens in an Ethnic Jewish State.* New Haven, Conn.: Yale University Press, 1997.

Rubin, Bernard. *Small Voices and Great Trumpets: Minorities and the Media.* New York: Praeger, 1980.

Rubinstein, Amnon. *Israeli Arabs and Jews: Dispelling the Myths, Narrowing the Gaps.* New York: American Jewish Committee, Dorothy and Julius Koppelman Institute on American Jewish-Israeli Relations, 2003.

Said, Edward. *The Question of Palestine.* London: Routledge, 1980.

Schechtman, Joseph. *The Arab Refugee Problem.* New York: Philosophical Library, 1952.

Schlesinger, Philip. *Media, State, and Nation: Political Violence and Collective Identities.* London: Sage, 1991.

Schuster, Thomas. *Market and the Media: Business News and Stock Market Movements.* Lanham, Md.: Lexington Books, 2006.

Servaes, Jan, and Rico Lie, eds. *Media and Politics in Transition: Cultural Identity in the Age of Globalization.* Leuven: Acco, 1997.

Shafir, Gershon, and Yoav Peled. *Being Israeli: The Dynamics of Multiple Citizenship.* Cambridge: Cambridge University Press, 2002.

Shamir, Jacob, and Michal Shamir. *The Anatomy of Public Opinion.* Ann Arbor: University of Michigan Press, 2000.

Shenhav, Yehouda. *The Arab Jews: Postcolonial Reading of Nationalism, Religion, and Ethnicity.* Stanford, Calif.: Stanford University Press, 2006.

Shitrit, Sami Shalom. *Mizrahi Ha-Ma'vak Ha-Mizrahi Bi-Yisrael: Ben Dikuy Li-Shihror, Ben Hi-Zdaht Li-Altenativa, 1948–2003* [Struggle in Israel: Between Suppression and Liberation, between Identification and Alternative, 1948–2003]. Tel Aviv: Am Oved, 2004.

Shohat, Ella. *Israeli Cinema: East/West and the Politics of Representation.* Austin: University of Texas Press, 1989.

———. *Taboo Memories: Diasporic Voices.* Durham, N.C.: Duke University Press, 2006.

Shohat, Ella, and Robert Stam. *Unthinking Eurocentrism: Multiculturalism and the Media.* London: Routledge, 1994.

Smith, Anthony. *The Ethnic Revival in the Modern World.* Cambridge: Cambridge University Press, 1981.

Smooha, Sammy. *The Orientation and Politicization of the Arab Minority in Israel.* Rev. ed. Haifa: University of Haifa, Jewish-Arab Center, Institute of Middle Eastern Studies, 1984.

———. *Arabs and Jews in Israel*. Boulder, Colo.: Westview Press, 1989.

Smooha, Sammy, and Priit Jarve. *The Fate of Ethnic Democracy in Post-Communist Europe*. Budapest: LGI Books, 2005.

Splichal, Slavko. *Public Opinion: Developments and Controversies in the Twentieth Century*. Lanham, Md.: Rowman and Littlefield, 1999.

Spoonley, Paul, and Walter Hirsh, eds. *Between the Lines: Racism and the New Zealand Media*. Auckland: Heinemann Reed, 1990.

Swirski, Shlomo, and Etty Konor-Attias. *Israel: A Social Report, 2005*. Tel Aviv: Adva Center, 2006.

Tarrow, Sidney. *Power in Movement: Social Movements and Contentious Politics*. Cambridge: Cambridge University Press, 1998.

The 13th Congress of the Israeli Communist Party. Tel Aviv-Jaffa: Central Committee of the Israeli Communist Party, 1957.

Thompson, John. *The Media and Modernity: A Social Theory of the Media*. Cambridge: Polity Press, 1995.

Tilly, Charles, and Sidney Tarrow. *Contentious Politics*. Boulder, Colo.: Paradigm, 2007.

Traber, Michael, ed. *Globalization, Mass Media, and Indian Cultural Values*. Delhi: ISPCK, 2003.

Twitchin, John, ed. *The Black and White Media Book: Handbook for the Study of Racism and Television*. Stokes-on-Trent: Trentham Books, 1988.

van Dijk, Teun A. *Communicating Racism: Ethnic Prejudice in Thought and Talk*. Newbury Park, Calif.: Sage, 1987.

———. *Racism and the Press*. London: Routledge, 1991.

Waldmann, Peter. *Ethnischer Radikalismus: Ursachen und Folgen gewaltsamer Minderheitskonflikte am Beispiel des Baskenlandes, Nordirlands, und Quebecs*. Opladen: Westdeutscher Verlag, 1989.

Walker, Richard W., and Herrmann J. Douglas, eds. *Cognitive Technology: Essays on the Transformation of Thought and Society*. Jefferson, N.C.: McFarland, 2005.

Wasserman, Herman, and Sean Jacobs. *Shifting Selves: Post-Apartheid Essays on Mass Media, Culture, and Identity*. Cape Town: Kwela, 2003.

Webster, James G., Patricia F. Phalen, and Lawrence W. Lichty. *Ratings Analysis: The Theory and Practice of Audience Research*. Mahwah, N.J.: Lawrence Erlbaum Associates, 2006.

Williams, Raymond. *Television: Technology and Cultural Form*. London: Routledge, 1990.

Wilson, Clint C., II, and Félix Gutiérrez. *Race, Multiculturalism, and the Media: From Mass to Class Communication*. Thousand Oaks, Calif.: Sage, 1995.

Wolf, J. P. Mark. *Abstracting Reality: Art, Communication, and Cognition in the Digital Age*. Lanham, Md.: University Press of America, 2000.

Wolfsfeld, Gadi. *Media and Political Conflict: News from the Middle East*. Cambridge: Cambridge University Press, 1997.

Yegar, Moshe. *Li-Toldoteha shel Ma'arekhet Hahasbarat Hahutz shel Yisraelit* [On the History of the Israeli Foreign Propaganda Policy]. Tel Aviv: Lahav, 1986.

Yiftachel, Oren. *Ethnocracy: Land and Identity Politics in Israel/Palestine*. Philadelphia: University of Pennsylvania Press, 2006.

Zegeye, Abebe, and Richard L. Harris, eds. *Media, Identity, and the Public Sphere in Post-Apartheid South Africa*. Leiden: Brill, 2003.

Zureik, Elia. *The Palestinians in Israel: A Study in Internal Colonialism*. London: Routledge and Kegan Paul, 1979.

Articles

Abu Al-Hayja, Muhammad. "'Ayn Hawd and the 'Unrecognized Villages.'" *Journal of Palestine Studies* 31, no. 1 (2001): 39–49.

Abu-Asbah, Khaled. *Maa'rikhit Hahinookh Haa'ravi Biyisrael: Matsav Kaiyam vi-Halofot Irgoniyot Ifshariyot* [The Arab Education System in Israel: Current Conditions and Possible Organizational Alternatives]. Givat Haviva: Institute for Peace Research, 1997.

———. *Ma-Arekhet Ha-Hinukh Ha-Aravit Bi-Yisrael* [The Arab Education System in Israel]. In Shlomo Hasson and Khaled Abu-Asbah, eds., *Yehudim Wi-Aravim Bi-Yisrael Be-Mitzeot Mishtana* [Jews and Arabs in Israel Facing a Changing Reality], 81–97. Jerusalem: Floersheimer Institute for Policy Studies, 2004.

———. *Ha-hinukh Ha-Aravi Bi-Yisrael: Dilemot Shel Mi-Out Liumi* [Arab Education in Israel: Dilemmas of a National Minority]. Jerusalem: Floersheimer Institute, 2007.

Abu-Rabia, Aref. "The Bedouin Refugees in the Negev." *Refuge* 14, no. 6 (1994).

Abu Ras, Thabet. "The Impact of Local and Regional Planning on Arab Towns in the 'Little' Triangle Area, Israel." In Aygen Erdentug and Freek Colombijn, eds., *Urban Ethnic Encounters: The Spatial Consequences*, 61–80. London: Routledge, 2002.

Al-Haj, Majid. "Adjustment Patterns of the Arab Internal Refugees in Israel." *Internal Migration* 24 (September 1986).

———. "The Impact of the Intifada on Arabs in Israel: The Case of the Double Periphery." In Akiba A. Cohen and Gadi Wolfsfeld, eds., *Framing the Intifada: Media and People*, 64–75. Norwood, N.J.: Ablex, 1993.

———. *Hakhanat Tokhniot Limodem Bimaa'rikhit Hahinokh Haa'ravi: Tmorot vi Hamlatzot* [Preparing Curriculums for the Arab Education System: Alternatives and Recommendations]. Jerusalem: Floersheimer Institute for Policy Studies, 1994.

———. "Zihut We-Orietatzia Politit bkerev Ha-Aravim Bi-Yisrael" [Identity and Political Orientation among the Arabs in Israel]. *Medina Mimshal ve-Yahasim Benle'umiyyim* [State, Government, and International Relations] 41/42 (1997): 103–22.

Andrawus, Zuhair. "Tnu Lano Televisia Aravit" [Give Us an Arab Television]. *Ha'ayeen Ha-Shvie'et* [The Seventh Eye] 25 (2000): 48.

Babrow, Austin S. "Theory and Method in Research on Audience Motives." *Journal of Broadcasting and Electronic Media* 32, no. 4 (1988): 471–87.

Bauml, Yair. "Ha-Mimshal Ha-Tzva'i vi-Bitolo, 1958–1968" [The Military Government and Its Termination, 1958–1968]. *Ha-Mizrah Ha-Hadash* 33 (2002): 133–56.

Becker L. B., G. M. Kosicki, and F. Jones. "Racial Differences in Evaluation of the Mass Media." *Journalism Quarterly* 69, no. 1 (1992): 124–34.

Bishara, Azmi. "A'al Shieilat Ha-Miut Ha-Falstini Bi-Yisrael" [On the Question of the Palestinian Minority in Israel]. *Tioria vi-Bekoret* [Theory and Criticism], no. 3 (1993): 7–20.

———. "Ha-Aravi Ha-Yisraeli: Iyunim Be-Seiyah Politi Shasua" [The Arab Israeli:

Observations on a Fractured Political Discourse]. In Pinhas Ginnosaur and Avi Bar-ali, eds., *Tzionut: Pulmos ben Zmaneno* [Zionism: A Polemic of Our Time], 312–39. Sade Boker: Ben-Gurion Legacy Center, 1996.

———. "Reflections on October 2000: A Landmark in Jewish-Arab Relations in Israel," *Journal of Palestine Studies* 30, no. 3 (2001).

Blumler, G. Jay, and Dennis Kavanagh. "The Third Age of Political Communication: Influence and Features." *Political Communication* 16, no. 3 (1999): 209–30.

Brubaker, Rogers, and David Laitin. "Ethnic and Nationalist Violence." *Annual Review of Sociology* 24 (1998): 423–52.

Connor, William. "Beyond Reason." *Ethnic and Racial Studies* 16, no. 3 (1993): 373–89.

Cormack, Mike. "Minority Language Media in Western Europe: Preliminary Consider-ations." *European Journal of Communications* 13, no. 1 (1998): 33–52.

D'Angelo, Paul. "News Framing as a Multiparadigmatic Research Program: A Response to Entman." *Journal of Communication* 52, no. 4 (2002): 870–88.

Fares, Amin. *Taktsiv Hamdina Li Shnat 2002 vi Hilka Shil Haokhlosia Haa'ravit* [The State's Budget for the Year of 2002 and the Share of the Arab Population]. Haifa: Mosawa Center, 2002.

First, Anat. "Who Is the Enemy? The Portrayal of Arabs in Israeli Television News." *Gazette* 60, no. 3 (1998): 239–51.

———. "Are They Still the Enemy? The Representation of Arabs in the Israeli News." In Tudor Parfitt and Yulia Egorova, eds., *Jews, Muslims, and Mass Media: Mediating the "Other,"* 190–213. New York: RoutledgeCurzon, 2005.

Fiske, John. "Postmodernism and Television." In James Curran and Michael Gurevitch, eds., *Mass Media and Society,* 55–67. London: Edward Arnold, 1991.

Fraser, Nancy. "Rethinking the Public Sphere: A Contribution to the Critique of Actu-ally Existing Democracy." In Bernard Robbins, ed., *The Phantom Public Sphere.* Min-neapolis: University of Minnesota Press, 1993.

Fuchs, Camille. "Skarim Telefonim Bi-Ma'rekhet Bhirot: Al Metodologia, Hataya vi-Hashpa'a" [Telephone Surveys in Elections—On Methodology, Deviation, and Impact]. In Camille Fuchs and Shaul Bar-Lev, eds., *Imit Wa-Seker* [Truth and Sur-vey], 61–74. Tel Aviv: Hakibbutz Hameuchad and Haifa University, 1998.

Gamson, William, David Croteau, William Hoynes, and Theodore Sasson. "Media Images and the Social Construction of Reality." *Annual Review of Sociology* 18 (1992): 373–93.

Goren, Tamir. "Separate or Mixed Municipalities? Attitudes of Jewish Yishuv Leader-ship to the Mixed Municipality during the British Mandate: The Case of Haifa." *Israel Studies* 9, no. 1 (2004): 101–24.

Gross, Larry. "Minorities, Majorities, and the Media." In Tamar Liebes and James Cur-ran, eds., *Media, Ritual, and Identity,* 87–102. London: Routledge, 1998.

Hall, Stuart. "The Whites of Their Eyes: Racist Ideologies and the Media." In G. Bridges and R. Brunt, eds., *Silver Linings: Some Strategies for the Eighties,* 28–52. London: Lawrence and Wishart, 1981.

———. "The Rediscovery of Ideology: The Return of the Repressed in Media Studies." In Michael Gurevitch et al., eds., *Culture, Society, and the Media,* 56–90. London: Methuen, 1982.

———. "Cultural Studies: Two Paradigms." In Richard Collins, James Curran, Nicholas Granham, Paddy Scannell, Philip Schlesinger, and Collin Sparks, eds., *Media, Culture, and Society: A Critical Reader,* 33–48. London: Sage, 1986.

———. "Encoding/Decoding." In Simon During, ed., *The Cultural Studies Reader,* 90–103. New York: Routledge, 2001.

Hammami, Rema, and Salim Tamari. "Anatomy of Another Rebellion," *Middle East Report* 217 (2000).

———. "The Second Uprising: End or New Beginning." *Journal of Palestine Studies* 30, no. 2 (2001): 5–25.

Hareven, Aluf, and As'ad Ghanem, eds. "Imdut Politiyut shel Aravim klape Memshelet Yisrael, 1992–1996" [Political Stands of Arabs toward the Israeli Government, 1992–1996]. In Alyf Hareven, ed., *Mabat Li-Ahur O-Mabat Kadima: Ha-Umanam Izrahu Mlea' Wi-Shava* [One Look Back and One Forward: Is It Really Equal and Full Citizenship?], 57–58. Jerusalem: Sikkuy, 1996.

Jamal, Amal. "Abstention as Participation: The Paradoxes of Arab Politics in Israel. In Asher Arian and Michal Shamir, eds., *The Elections in Israel, 2001,* 57–100. Jerusalem: Israeli Institute for Democracy, 2002.

———. "The Ambiguities of Minority Patriotism: Love for Homeland versus State among Palestinian Citizens of Israel." *Nationalism and Ethnic Politics* 10, no. 3 (2004): 433–71.

———. "Citizenship as Opposition: Another Look at Arab Politics in Israel." In Nimer Sultany, ed., *Israel and the Palestinian Minority: The Third Annual Political Monitoring Report,* 163–73. Haifa: Mada al-Carmel, 2005.

———. "The Palestinian IDPs in Israel and the Predicament of Return: Between Imagining the 'Impossible' and Enabling the 'Imaginative.'" In Ann Lesch and Ian Lustick, eds., *Exile and Return: Predicaments of Palestinians and Jews,* 133–60. Philadelphia: University of Pennsylvania Press, 2005.

———. "Arab Leadership in Israel: Ascendance and Fragmentation." *Journal of Palestine Studies* 35, no. 2 (2006): 1–17.

———. "Nationalizing States and the Constitution of 'Hollow Citizenship': Israel and Its Palestinian Citizens." *Ethnopolitics* 6, no. 4 (2007): 471–93.

———. "Strategies of Minority Struggle for Equality in Ethnic States: Arab Politics in Israel." *Citizenship Studies* 11, no. 3 (2007): 263–82.

———. "Aal Tala'ot Hazman Ha-Mogza'a" [On the Troubles of Racialized Time]. In Yehouda Shenhav and Yossi Yonah, eds., *Gazanut Bi-Yisrael* [Racism in Israel], 348–80. Jerusalem: Van Leer and Hakibbutz Hameuchad, 2008.

———. "The Political Ethos of the Palestinian Citizens of Israel: Critical Reading in the Future Vision Documents." *Israel Studies Forum* 23, no. 2 (2008): 3–28.

Jiryis, Sabri. "Domination by the Law." *Journal of Palestine Studies* 11, no. 1 (1981): 67–92.

Kabha, Mustafa. "Mizrahi Jews in the Arabic Press, 1948–1967." *Iyonim* 17 (2006): 445–61.

Katz, Elihu, Jay Blumler, and Michael Gurevitch. "Utilization of the Mass Media by the Individual." In Jay Blumler and Elihu Katz, eds., *The Uses of Mass Communication,* 19–32. Beverly Hills: Sage, 1974.

Khalili, Laleh. "Commemorating Contested Lands." In Ann Lesch and Ian Lustick, eds.,

Exile and Return: Predicaments of Palestinians and Jews, 19–40. Philadelphia: University of Pennsylvania Press, 2005.

Khmaisi, Rassem. *Mitikhnon Magbil Litikhnon Maftiyah Bayishovim Haa'ravim Biyisrael* [From Limiting Design to Developing Design in the Arab Towns in Israel]. Jerusalem: Floersheimer Institute for Policy Studies, 1993.

Kedar, Sandy, and Oren Yiftachel. "Land Regime and Social Relations in Israel." In Hernando de Soto and Francis Cheneval, eds., *Realizing Property Rights.* Zurich: Ruffer and Rub, 2006.

Kedar, Sandy, and Geremy Forman. "From Arab Lands to 'Israel Lands': The Legal Dispossession of the Palestinians Displaced by Israel in the Wake of 1948." *Environment and Planning D: Society and Space* 22, no. 6 (2004): 809–30.

Kymlicka, Will. "The Internationalization of Minority Rights." *International Journal of Constitutional Law* 6, no. 1 (2008): 1–32.

Laitin, David. "National Revivals and Violence." *Archives Européennes de Sociologie* 36, no. 1 (1995): 3–43.

Larson, Stephanie Greco. "The Civil Rights Movement and the Mass Media." In her *Media and Minorities: The Politics of Race in News and Entertainment.* Lanham: Rowman and Littlefield, 2006.

Lavi, Victor. *Hivdilem Bimashabem vi Bihisigem Bahinukh Haa'ravi Biyisrael* [Differences in Resources and Achievements in the Arab Education in Israel]. Jerusalem: Floersheimer Institute for Policy Studies, 1997.

Lustick, Ian. "Israel as a Non-Arab State: The Political Implications of Mass Immigration of Non-Jews." *Middle East Journal* 53, no. 3 (1999): 417–33.

Mahtani, Minelle. "Representing Minorities: Canadian Media and Minority Identities." *Canadian Ethnic Studies* 33, no. 3 (2001): 99–133.

Manzur, Atallah. "Ha-Itunut Ha-Aravit Bi-Zisrael" [Arab Press in Israel]. *Kesher* 7 (1990): 71–77.

Masalha, Nur. "Debate on the 1948 Exodus." *Journal of Palestine Studies* 21, no. 1 (Autumn 1991): 90–97.

Mazzoleni, Gianpietro, and Winfried Schulz. "'Mediatization' of Politics: A Challenge to Democracy." *Political Communication* 16, no. 3 (1999): 247–61.

McGarry, John, Brendan O'Leary, and Richard Simeon, "Integration or Accommodation? The Enduring Debate in Conflict Regulation." In Sujit Choudhry, ed., *Constitutional Design for Divided Societies: Integration or Accommodation,* 41–88. Oxford: Oxford University Press, 2008.

"A Mizrahi Call for a More Democratic Israel." *Tikkun: A Bimonthly Jewish Critique of Politics, Culture, and Society* 13, no. 2 (1998): 50–52.

Moring, Tom, and Charles Husband. "The Contribution of Swedish-Language Media in Finland to Linguistic Vitality." *International Journal of the Sociology of Language* 187/188 (2007): 75–101.

Motzafi-Haller, Pnina. "Intelektualem Mizrahiem, 1946–1951: Zihut Itnit Wi-Migbaloteha" [Mizrahi Intellectuals, 1946–1951: Ethnic Identity and Its Limits]. In Hannan Hever, Yehouda Shenhav, and Pnina Motzafi-Haller, eds., *Mizrahim Bi-Yisrael: Iyun Bikorti Mihudash* [Mizrahim in Israel: A Critical Observation in Israel's Ethnicity], 152–90. Jerusalem: Van Leer and Hakibbutz Hameuchad, 2002.

Mutz, Diana. "The Future of Political Communication Research: Reflections on the Occasion of Steve Chaffee's Retirement from Stanford University." *Political Communication* 18, no. 2 (2001): 231–36.

Oded, Yitzhak. "Land Losses among Israel's Arab Villages." *New Outlook* 7, no. 7 (1964): 19–25.

Olzak, Susan, and Elizabeth West. "Ethnic Conflict and the Rise and Fall of Ethnic Newspapers." *American Sociological Review* 56, no. 4 (1991): 458–74.

Ozacky-Lazar, Sarah. "Security and Israel's Arab Minority." In Danny Bar-Tal, Dan Jacobson, and Aharon Klieman, eds., *Security Concerns: Insights from the Israeli Experience,* 347–69. Stamford, Conn: JAI, 1998.

———. "Ha-Mimshal Ha-Tzva'i Ki-Manganon Li-Shleta Ba-Izarhim Ha-Aravim: Ha-Asur Ha-Rishon, 1948–1958" [The Military Government as a Mechanism of Controlling Arab Citizens: The First Decade, 1948–1958]. *Ha-Mizrah Ha-Hadash* 33 (2002): 103–32.

Patterson, G. Thomas. "Political Roles of the Journalist." In Doris Graber, Denis McQuail, and Pippa Norris, eds., *The Politics of News and the News of Politics,* 17–31. Washington, D.C.: CQ Press, 1998.

Peled, Yoav. "Ethnic Democracy and the Legal Construction of Citizenship: Arab Citizen of the Jewish State." *American Political Science Review* 86, no. 2 (1992): 432–43.

Rabinowitz, Dan. "Nostalgia Mizrahit: Kitzad Hafkhu Ha-Falastinim Le-Arviye Yisrael" [Oriental Nostalgia: How the Palestinians Were Transformed into "Israeli Arabs"]. *Tioria vi-Bekoret* [Theory and Criticism] 4 (1993): 141–51.

———. "The Palestinian Citizens of Israel, the Concept of Trapped Minority, and the Discourse of Transnationalism in Anthropology." *Ethnic and Racial Studies* 24, no. 1 (2001): 64–85.

Rekhess, Elie. "Tahlikhe Shinuy Politim-Leumiyem Bekerev Ha-Aravim Bi-Yisrael Kireka'a Li-Iroe'e October 2000" [Political and National Processes of Change amongst the Arabs of Israel as Forerunners to the October 2000 Events]. In Sarah Ozacky-Lazar and As'ad Ghanem, eds., *Adoyot Or: 7 Havot Da'at Miktzoiyot Sh-Hugshu Li-Va'adat Or* [The Or Commission Testimonies: Seven Professional Reports That Were Presented to the Or Commission]. Tel Aviv: Keter, 2003.

Rigoni, Isabelle. "Challenging Notions and Practices: The Muslim Media in Britain and France." *Journal of Ethnic and Migration Studies* 31, no. 3 (2005): 563–80.

Rios, Diana I., and Stanley O. Gaines Jr. "Latino Media Use for Cultural Maintenance." *Journalism and Mass Communication Quarterly* 75, no. 4 (1998): 746–61.

Saban, Ilan. "Ha-Zkhoiot Hakibotsiot Shil Hamioot Ha-Aravi-Falastini: Ha-Yish Ha-Ain Vi-Tkhom Ha-Tabo" [Group Rights of the Arab-Palestinian Minority: Present, Absent, and Taboo]. *Iyoni Ha-Mishpat* 26, no. 1 (2002): 241–319.

Seener, Barak. "The Threat from Israel's Arab Population." *In Focus* 2, no. 1 (2008).

Shavit, Ari. "Survival of the Fittest: Interview with Benny Morris." *Haaretz Magazine,* 8 January 2004.

Shiftan, Dan. "Zihotam Ha-Hadasha Shil Havri Ha-Knesset Ha-A'ravim" [The New Identity of the Arab Knesset Members]. *Tkhelet* 13 (2002): 23–49.

Shiluv. Integration plan. Haifa: Sikkuy Center, 2000.

Shrum, L. J. "Media Consumption and Perceptions of Reality: Effects and Underlying Processes." In Jennings Bryant and Dolf Zillmann, eds., *Media Effects: Advances in Theory and Research,* 69–95. Mahwah, N.J.: Lawrence Erlbaum, 2002.

Sofer, Arnon, and Yisrael E. Bystrov. "Demografia, 2004–2020: Li- or Tokhnit Ha-Hit-natkut" [Israeli Demography, 2004–2020: In Light of the Process of Disengagement]. Haifa: Chair of Geostrategy, 2005.

Suleiman, Ramzi. "Minority Self-Categorization: The Case of the Palestinians in Israel." *Peace and Conflict: Journal of Peace Psychology* 8, no. 1 (2002): 31–46.

Thomas, Ned. "The Mercator Media Forum." *Mercator Media Forum* 1 (1995): 2–11.

Tsfati, Yariv. "Why Do People Trust Media Pre-Election Polls? Evidence from the Israeli 1996 Elections." *International Journal of Public Opinion Research* 13, no. 4 (2001): 433–41.

Tsfati, Yariv, and Joseph N. Cappella. "Why Do People Watch News They Do Not Trust? The Need for Cognition as a Moderator in the Association between News Media Skepticism and Exposure." *Media Psychology* 7 (2005): 251–71.

Tuma, Emile. "Palestinian Arabs and Israeli Jews." *Journal of Palestine Studies* 10, no. 2 (1977): 5.

Vashitz, Yisrael. "In Exchange for the Lives of Israeli Arabs." *New East,* no. 4 (1950): 257–64.

Viswanath, Kasisomayajula, and Pamela Arora. "Ethnic Media in the United States: An Essay on Their Role in Integration, Assimilation, and Social Control." *Mass Communication and Society* 2, no. 1 (2000): 39–56.

Weibull, Lennart. "Structural Factors in Gratifications Research." In Karl Eric Rosengren, Philip Palmgreen, and Lawrence A. Wenner, eds., *Media Gratifications Research: Current Perspectives,* 123–47. Beverly Hills, Calif.: Sage, 1985.

Weiman, Gabi. "The Coverage of Election Surveys in Israeli Newspapers." In *State, Government, and International Relations* 19/20 [Heb.] (1982): 132–43.

Wolfsfeld, Gadi, Eli Avraham, and Issam Aburayya. "When Prophesy Always Fails: Israeli Press Coverage of the Arab Minority's Land Day Protests." *Political Communication* 17 (2000): 115–31.

Yiftachel, Oren. "The Internal Frontier: Territorial Control and Ethnic Relations in Israel." *Regional Studies* 30, no. 4 (1996): 493–508.

———. "Binoi Oma vi Halokat Hamirhav Bietnokratia Hayisraelet: Karkaoot vi Pi'arim Idatyem" [Nation-Building and National Land: Social and Legal Dimensions]. *Iyunei Mishpat* 21, no. 3 (1998): 637–64.

Yiftachel, Oren, and Haim Yacobi. "Urban Ethnocracy: Ethnicization and the Production of Space in an Israeli 'Mixed City.'" *Environment and Planning D: Society and Space* 21 (2003): 673–93.

Yitzhak, Oded. "Land Losses among Israel's Arab Villages." *New Outlook* 7, no. 7 (September 1964): 19–25.

Zayyad, Tawfiq. "The Fate of the Arabs in Israel." *Journal of Palestine Studies* 10, no. 1 (1976): 92–103.

Zelizer, Barbie. "Journalists as Interpretive Communities." In Donald Berkowitz, ed., *Social Meaning of News,* 401–19. London: Sage, 1997.

Reports and Documents

Governmental Archives, Jerusalem. Files G 304/63, G 5498/12, GL 17084/13, GL 17084, 3551/6, 3551/10.

Or, Theodor, Shimun Shamir, and Hashem Khatib. Wa'adat Hakira Mamlakhtit Le-Biror Ha-Hitnagshoyot ben Kohot Ha-Bitahun lben Izrahim Yisraelim Bi-October 2000 [Or Commission Report]. Jerusalem: Ministry of Justice, 2005.

Index

AMAL JAMAL is Senior Lecturer and Chair of the Department of Political Science at Tel Aviv University. He is the author of *The Palestinian National Movement: Politics of Contention, 1967–2005* (Indiana University Press, 2005) and *Media Politics and Democracy in Palestine: Political Culture, Pluralism, and the Palestinian Authority.*

Milton Keynes UK
Ingram Content Group UK Ltd.
UKHW022218310823
427851UK00007B/431

9 780253 221414